Two Part Harmony

Patrick M. MORLEY

THOMAS NELSON PUBLISHERS
Nashville • Atlanta • London • Vancouver

Published in Nashville, Tennessee, by Thomas Nelson, Inc., Publishers, and distributed in Canada by Word Communications, Ltd., Richmond, British Columbia, and in the United Kingdom by Word (UK), Ltd., Milton Keynes, England.

Unless otherwise noted, Scripture quotations are taken from the HOLY BIBLE, NEW INTERNATIONAL VERSION ®. Copyright © 1973, 1978, 1984 by International Bible Society. Used by permission of Zondervan Bible Publishing House. All rights reserved.

The "NIV" and "New International Version" trademarks are registered in the United States Patent and Trademark Office by International Bible Society. Use of either trademark requires the permission of International Bible Society.

Scripture quotations noted KJV are from The Holy Bible, KING JAMES VERSION.

Scripture quotations noted TLB are from *The Living Bible* (Wheaton, Illinois: Tyndale House Publishers, 1971) and are used by permission.

Scripture quotations noted NASB are from THE NEW AMERICAN STANDARD BIBLE, Copyright © 1960, 1962, 1963, 1968, 1971, 1972, 1973, 1975, 1977 by The Lockman Foundation and are used by permission.

Library of Congress Cataloging-in-Publication Data

Morley, Patrick M.
    Two-Part Harmony / Patrick M. Morley.
      p. cm.
    Includes bibliographical references.
    ISBN 0-7852-8062-6 (hc)
    1. Married people—Prayer-books and devotions—English. 2. Marriage—Religious aspects—Christianity. I. Title.
BV4596.M3M67   1994
242'.644—dc20   94-4984
                                                                              CIP

Printed in the United States of America
1 2 3 4 5 6 7 — 00 99 98 97 96 95 94

To Jen and John

_I dream that one day
you and your mate will
take up this book.
Marriage is tough work.
To enjoy the intimacy and
pleasure God intends for
married couples
we must be vulnerable and
honest with each other._

Other books by Patrick M. Morley

The Man in the Mirror
Getting to Know the Man in the Mirror
Walking with Christ in the Details of Life
The Rest of Your Life

If you are interested in having Patrick Morley
speak to your group or would like more information about his ministry, please call:

1–800–9AWAKEN

Contents

Foreword   *viii*

Introduction   *ix*

Part One: Deepening Our Relationship With Each Other

Laughing at Life   2

The Meaning of Rings   4

The Emotional Bank Account   6

Sharing Household Chores   8

Pray for Each Other   10

Pray with Each Other   12

The Need to Feel Wanted   14

In Sickness and in Health   16

In Plenty and in Want   18

In Joy and in Sorrow   20

The Good and Bad of Marriage   22

Walls   24

Something I've Always Wanted
   to Share   26

Frustration with Life   28

Values or Christ?   30

Robbed of the Blessing   32

Ten Ways to Bless Each Other   34

Love Always Perseveres   36

In Summary   38

Part Two: The Delicate Art of Communication

Differences in Communication   40

Bridges   42

Two Tools to Tear Down Walls   44

Frankness   46

The Fear of Criticism   48

The Fear of Criticism, Part 2   50

The Fear of Receiving Advice   52

Listen for and Express Feelings   54

Deep Listening: The Ultimate
   Deposit   56

The Power of Words   58

The Ministry of Words   60

Let the Little Ones Go   62

Don't Let the Sun Go Down on
   Your Anger   64

Ten Principles for Resolving
   Conflicts   66

Practical Ideas to Resolve
   Conflict   68

In Summary   70

Part Three: Understanding Each Other

Understanding Each Other 72
His Greatest Need 74
Her Greatest Need 76
Toward Greater Intimacy 78
His Principal Activity 80
Understanding His Pressure 82
Her Principal Activity 84
Understanding Her Fear 86
The Prudent Wife 88
His Duty to Love 90
Husbands: Anointed Spiritual
    Leaders 92
The Nature of Submission 94
To Respect Her 96
The Overarching Goal:
    Oneness 98
His Needs, Her Needs 100
Emotional Versus Physical
    Love 102
How to Achieve Oneness 104
The Radical Effect of the Fall 106
Introvert or Extrovert? 108
In Summary 110

Part Four: What Pulls Us Apart

The Need to Be Significant
    Misplaced 112
Deep Frustrations 114
"There Is a Big Wall Here" 116
Sexual Union 118
The Bridges of Madison County 120
Spiritual Leadership 122
Spiritual Leadership: Another
    Angle 124
Overcoming Bitterness 126
What Anger Does 128
The Need to Be Right 130
Power Struggles 132
Fights and Quarrels 134
Comfort Zone/Pressure Zone 136
Unrealistic Expectations 138
Taciturn and Loquacious 140
A Critical Spirit 142
The Making of a Mistress 144
In Summary 146

Part Five: Staying Together

Sharing Those Moments 148
Love Is What Love Does 150
Love Is Patient 152
Becoming Best Friends 154
Intentionally Hurting Each Other 156
To Pray for One Another 158
Divorce 168
A Lack of Common Interests 170
Balancing Needs for Social
    Interaction 172
Big Things and Little Things 174
Making Vacations Count 176

Overdrawn and Unaware 160
Making Deposits at the Change
    of Life 162
The Anatomy of a Withdrawal 164
Making Your Mate Your Top
    Priority 166

Special Instructions Just for
    Him 178
Special Instructions Just for
    Her 180
In Summary 182

Part Six: Our Children

Worthy of Our Children 184
The Value of the Dinner Table 186
Family Devotions 188
Woody Allen Parenting 190
Showing Self-control with
    Our Kids 192
Providing Structure 194
Praying for Our Children 196

Leading Our Children to Faith 198
Spending Time with Our Kids 200
Encouraging Daily Devotions 202
On Dragging Children to
    Church 204
Children Need Something They
    Can Do Well 206
In Summary 208

Part Seven: Our Future Together

Love Is Not Selfish 210
Showing Mutual Respect 212
Living by Priorities 214
Financial Pressure 216
Debt Is Dumb 218
Making Major Decisions:
    A Perspective 220
Discerning God's Will 222
Making Major Decisions:
    A Process 224
Building Marriage Around the
    Bible 226

Connected to the Church 228
Finding a Christ-centered
    Church 230
Planning for Premature
    Death 232
Providing for Retirement 234
Providing for Retirement—
    Part 2 236
One Person Who Really
    Cares 238
In Summary 240

Notes 243

Foreword

I am excited for you as you begin this book!

My husband, Pat, presents the core ideas of what it takes to have a growing marriage. I think you'll find the format makes all of the information highly accessible and extremely practical.

What I like most about the book, though, and what I think you will like too, is that it's real. It's authentic. I know, because I was there! The lessons Pat shares in this book, we learned together.

As we all know, marriage can be both lots of fun and at the same time, very frustrating. Our marriage has had its share of ups and downs, and we are still "in process." Yet, I have seen God produce huge changes in our relationship as we have both surrendered our wills to Him and worked at the principles contained in *Two-Part Harmony*.

We have learned to be more open and vulnerable with each other. We have learned to communicate on a deeper level. We understand each other today in ways I never dreamed possible. It has been wonderfully rewarding.

I sincerely hope you enjoy talking over the issues presented. They provide tremendous opportunities to work through topics that couples don't often discuss together openly. I honestly believe this book will stimulate your marriage to a new, higher level and will draw you closer than ever before.

Patsy Morley
Orlando, Florida

Introduction

A good marriage should be like great music—passionate, harmonious, colorful. Spouses all want the same thing—a marriage filled with excitement and closeness. We marry because we want to make beautiful music with the mate we love.

Many marriages, of course, sound more like screeching tires on dry pavement. What happens? How do all those shared hopes and dreams get bogged down? Are we to believe that after the initial romance, marriage is simply a downhill proposition? Is the best we can hope for some sort of negotiated truce? I would have thought so until a few years ago when I began to discover the principles presented in *Two-Part Harmony*.

My wife Patsy and I have wrestled with, tested, and personally applied every principle you are about to learn—not perfectly, and still not completely. Yet these ideas have transformed our life together into a tremendous friendship, partnership, and adventure. By learning to open up to each other, build trust, and become more vulnerable we have deepened our communication. As a result, we now have a marriage without barriers, secrets, or regrets. We have disagreements nearly every day, but we have learned how to deal with life together constructively and to achieve harmony.

Men, sometimes marriage is a process of give and take in which the wife gives and the husband takes! Too many of us are chasing our rainbows, forgetting the vows and pledges we made. Relationships create responsibilities, and we've started to let some of those go. We haven't been talking to our wives, who are often desperate for some of our time and interaction on issues in the home. Time and regular communication are everything to a relationship. It is time to give time to whom time is due.

Women, do you long for a more intimate relationship with your husband? Do you wish you felt more connected to him emotionally and spiritually? Here again, we have problems. Women, too, are busier than ever, and the less time we spend together, the less clear-cut communication we have, the greater emotional and spiritual distance between us. The end of a long day often ends up in chaos, not harmony.

We don't take enough time to talk deeply about the gut-level issues shaping the quality of our life together. When will we take time to build each other up? When will we open up to each other? This book will help surface many of the things you should be saying to each other, but aren't. It may also help deal with things that have been said to no one's benefit.

HOW TO BENEFIT FROM THIS BOOK

I suggest you do two or three chapters a week, but the format is completely flexible. If you want to do a chapter every day or go more slowly, that's fine. Each devotional is designed to be a conversation starter, so choose a time when you can spend twenty to thirty minutes together. Write it on your calendar like any other important appointment.

Most readers will want to start at the beginning and work through the book in sequence. The book does build on itself from section to section, but feel free to go to any section or particular chapter if you feel a special need in that area.

From time to time you may experience some stress or conflict in a particular chapter, but it can lead to a healthy resolution. I know that becoming more transparent and vulnerable can be scary, but remember, your marriage will glean greater warmth, depth, and feelings of love as a result. If one chapter zings too much, though, skip it! You can always come back to it later. The goal is to build up your union, not tear you apart. Above all, be sensitive and tender with each other.

To get the overall "feel" of the book, one or both spouses may want to read or skim the whole book before beginning the devotionals as a couple.

For various reasons, some readers will not be able to read this book with their spouse. Anyone—married, single, divorced, separated—can read it for great benefit. I particularly encourage engaged couples to work through this book together.

I've made a great deal of effort to understand and be sensitive to the needs of men and women. Some chapters focus more on one or the other, but I have tried hard to balance things out overall. Please forgive me where my own limitations and blind spots got in the way.

My strong desire is that your marriage will be counted as one of those that works the way it's supposed to. May God bless you richly and deeply as you build a marriage that blends you and your mate together in two-part harmony.

LAUGHING AT LIFE

A cheerful heart is good medicine.
PROVERBS 17:22

*D*uring the early 1980s I attended a resident executive education program at the Harvard Business School. Lonely for Patsy, my wife, I asked her to fly to Boston for a weekend.

We painted the town. The highlight for us both was an evening at the Boston Pops with John Williams conducting. The atmosphere was electric as the audience sipped wine, munched on chips, ate sandwiches, and waited for the concert to begin. I had reserved fabulous seats right in the middle of the floor about ten rows from the stage. Perfect!

The seating hostess led us to our seats. The waitress came. We ordered our sandwiches and coffee. We chatted with the two ladies seated at our table. Patsy looked radiant in a beautiful silk skirt and blouse. A few minutes before the concert was to begin we both decided to make one last pit stop.

As Patsy and I stood, her slippery silk skirt slid across her slippery silk slip and landed down around her ankles. Patsy's horrified eyes grew into giant saucers. Stunned to a crimson red, I managed to blurt out, "What in the world is going on?"

Patsy grabbed up her skirt and we bolted out of there! Once in the hall, tears of laughter began to stream down our cheeks. She had forgotten that she had loosened the button on her tight skirt during our meal.

Too embarrassed to return to our seats, we sneaked into the balcony. The slightly irritated family seated next to us never could understand what we found so humorous about a Pops performance. And we sure didn't tell them!

God has given couples no greater gift than the ability to laugh at life together. The joy of sharing humorous secrets and private jokes breathes energy into a marriage.

Some of these tales bear repeating. I cannot begin to tell you how much mileage we have had from our Boston Pops story with our kids, our parents, and our friends. It always produces raucous howling.

Yet, as much as others enjoy this story, no one will ever enjoy this treasured experience as we do. We were there! And no one can ever take this adventure away from us.

Even our faux pas and embarrassments can make a merry heart. If we don't let our pride get in the way and go with the flow, every experience can be a source of growing more deeply in love with one another.

DISCUSSION

Both answer: What has been your most humorous moment together as a couple? How does that shared experience bond you more deeply together? What are some other humorous experiences you have shared?

APPLICATION

Let the humor in your life become family folklore. Share a humorous experience with your children, parents, and close friends at the next opportune moment. What other humorous experiences can you share? Don't hesitate to tell them over and over again. Who knows—you may create a legend!

PRAYER

Either: Heavenly Father, thank You from the bottom of our hearts for the precious gift of humor. Thank You for the laughter you have allowed to grace our marriage. May we always treasure our most humorous experiences. May they be a blessing both to us and to our family. Most of all, we thank You for giving us to each other. Amen.

The Meaning of Rings

So they are no longer two, but one. Therefore what God has joined together, let man not separate.

MATTHEW 19:6

*R*ecently I was standing in line at a jewelry store behind a middle-aged woman. The jeweler retrieved her order and with finicky precision placed the tightly wrapped package on the black-felt counter pad. As he pulled back the wrapping she gasped in obvious delight. After twenty-five years of marriage, she had decided to have her wedding rings reset with a new design. I goggled at them myself. The rings gleamed in the carefully refracted lights of the jeweler's studio.

What is your favorite part of a wedding ceremony? Is it the processional? The giving of the bride? The reading of the Scriptures? Saying the "I do's"? The exchange of vows? The pronouncement of "husband and wife"? Is it when the bride and groom kiss? My personal favorite is the ring exchange:

> "This ring I give you, as a symbol and pledge of my constant and abiding love."

symbol *n.* Something representing something else by association, especially a material object representing something abstract.
pledge *n.* A solemn promise to do or not do something.

Every part of the wedding ceremony has a purpose. The ring exchange tangibly symbolizes the vows we make. The next day, rings provide the only visible evidence that a wedding ever took place. The ring says to the watching world that this person has taken a vow:

> *"I, (name), take you, (name), to be my wedded (wife/husband), and I do promise and covenant, before God and these witnesses, to be your loving and faithful (wife/husband), in sickness and in health, in plenty and in want, in joy and in sorrow, as long as we both shall live."*

The ring exchange also symbolizes that a pledge has been made:

> *"Will you have (name) to be your wedded (wife/husband) to live with (her/him) after God's commandments in the holy state of marriage, and will you love, honor, and cherish (her/him) so long as you both shall live?"*

Some people use rings for decoration. Some use rings to communicate status. Others to show wealth. Wedding rings, however, speak of commitment. When a husband or wife wears a wedding ring, he or she tells the world, "I am committed to a person. I have given my life to this person. This person has pledged to love, honor, and cherish me for the rest of our lives together. This person has taken a vow to be faithful and I, in return, have also vowed to be loving and faithful. It is a pledge. It is a vow. And this ring is a symbol of love and affection both given and received."

Do you remember the vows, pledges, and professions you made on your wedding day? Today's devotional is a good reminder. In the hubbub of car pools, fast-paced jobs, and mortgage payments, it's easy to become distracted from the vows we made. A ring is a good reminder.

DISCUSSION

Both answer: Which part of your wedding ceremony was your favorite? Why? How do rings demonstrate commitment?

APPLICATION

Take each other's hands and, if you can find them, exchange the vows and pledges you made on your wedding day. If you can't put your hands on your original vows, use those above.

PRAYER

Each pray: Lord Jesus, I thank You for the commitment my life partner has made to me. I renew my pledge of commitment to my mate. Thank You for the privilege of being married to the very person You sovereignly wanted for me. May we glorify You in our marriage. Amen.

THE EMOTIONAL BANK ACCOUNT

Above all, love each other deeply, because love covers over a multitude of sins.

1 PETER 4:8

*F*ifteen years ago I first heard what is to me the single most revolutionary concept for healthy human relationships. The leader of a parenting class told us that every person has an *emotional tank* that needs to be continuously filled.

Many have given thought and shape to this simple yet profoundly helpful idea. In his book *His Needs, Her Needs*, Willard Harley, Jr., dubs it a *love bank*. Ross Campbell, in his book *How to Really Love Your Child,* refers to it as an *emotional tank*. In *The Seven Habits of Highly Effective People*, author Stephen Covey names it the *emotional bank account.* Some may want to call it an *emotional bank*. Personally, I like Covey's term because it is so graphic. Every person has an emotional bank account—like a savings or checking account—into which others make deposits and withdrawals.

When the balance in both spouses' emotional bank accounts is high, the marriage will not be overdrawn when either the husband or wife makes that inevitable withdrawal through selfishness or insensitivity. When the balance in the account is low, however, each infraction is magnified because there are no reserves of trust and admiration against which to make withdrawals. Worst of all, if we are already overdrawn and living on borrowed capital, each additional withdrawal pushes our marriage ever closer to bankruptcy.

We make deposits into each other's emotional bank accounts by meeting our partner's needs for deep listening, support, communication, intimacy, time together, and kindness. For example, when the husband wakes his wife with a lingering hug, a cup of coffee, and the newspaper, makes the bed, takes out the garbage, folds his and her clothes, drives the children to school, and calls her parents, he makes deposits into her emotional bank account. When the wife surprises her husband with a new John Grisham novel, welcomes him home with a kiss, asks him about the big project at work, prepares a favorite meal, holds off wanting to discuss Junior's report card until he's unwound, and orders him to the family room to watch Saturday's big game, she makes deposits into his emotional bank account.

One secret of a marriage made of two-part harmony is to fill each other's emotional bank account to overflowing, to make so many deposits that a vast reserve of trust, love, caring, affection, and intimacy shows up on the balance sheet. Then assets will far exceed liabilities. The net worth of the marriage will exceed both of your expectations. You will have made each other wealthy in love, abundant in intimacy, and overflowing in trust.

We make withdrawals from each other's emotional bank accounts by failing to make our marriage partner our top priority after the Lord. We make withdrawals when we fail to meet our partner's needs for sexual fulfillment, companionship, deep listening, cooperation around the home, and encouragement. When the husband scoffs at his wife's concerns and worries, explodes in anger over life's little irritations, spends all of his emotional energy on work, and says negative things about her habits, appearance, or moods, he makes withdrawals from her emotional bank account.

When the wife rebuffs the romantic advances of her husband, refuses to participate in any of his interests and hobbies, neglects her personal appearance and emotional well-being, and shows dissatisfaction with the family's economic status even though he works diligently, she makes withdrawals from his emotional bank account.

Whether you prefer emotional tank, love bank, emotional bank, or emotional bank account, no idea I've encountered has more potential to bring the walls that separate us tumbling down. The emotional bank account is *the big idea*. Thinking about how to make deposits and avoid withdrawals can be a powerful tool to help maximize your marriage.

DISCUSSION

Both answer: How would you describe the balance in your emotional bank account: overflowing? half full? near empty? Why do you feel this way? Each answer: Are you surprised by your spouse's answer? Why?

APPLICATION

Begin to think in terms of each other's emotional bank account. Get comfortable with the term. Consider your actions and words as deposits or withdrawals. *Everything* you do is either a deposit or a withdrawal.

PRAYER

Either partner: Heavenly Father, sometimes we make so many withdrawals from each other's emotional bank accounts that our relationship is overdrawn. Lord, help us to make deposits into each other of love, caring, faith, patience, trust, help, time, deep listening, and companionship. Give us, we pray, the desire and time to heal each other's wounds and build up our account balances to overflowing. Amen.

SHARING HOUSEHOLD CHORES

But the wisdom that comes from heaven is first of all pure; then peace-loving,
considerate, submissive, full of mercy and good fruit, impartial and sincere.
JAMES 3:17

*I*t was a crisp, sunny Sunday. After a cheerful ride home from church each member of the Morley family followed tradition and made his or her own lunch. After lunch, Patsy asked me for the umpteenth time, "When are you going to hang up the two pictures my sisters gave me for my birthday?" The pictures had been awaiting hanging since October 24th (it was now mid-January). However, I had been busy, very busy, and I did not appreciate the subtle intimation that I was neglecting my responsibilities around the house.

"Do you have any idea of how busy I have been these last few months?" I asked calmly. "I have to weigh all of my responsibilities and then do the things I think are most important. I will hang your pictures, but I just have not had the time to even think about it."

Then Patsy said (rather insensitively, I thought), "Aren't you the one who is always teaching everybody that they need to live by priorities? Hanging up those two pictures is a family priority. Now when are you going to have time?"

I could not believe my ears. She was not about to back down, not to mention that she was using my own message against me. *Everybody wants a piece of me,* I thought. *Life's not fair. I don't have to take this!*

"Two stinking pictures," I said in self-pity. "I can't believe you would do this to me over two stinking pictures!"

At that precise moment, I was holding a ceramic mug in my hand (I was making a cup of coffee). I could feel the indignation swelling within. As I glared at the mug in my hand, I heard two little voices in my mind that I'm fairly confident were not from the Lord. One voice urged me, *Smash the mug onto the counter so hard that it bursts into a hundred thousand little pieces!* The other voice said, *No, slam it on the counter just hard enough to make your point, but not so hard that it explodes.*

The two voices still competing with one another, I reared back and slammed the mug on the counter. Nothing happened. *Do it again,* came the voices. I cocked my arm and cracked the counter once again. Nothing. At this Patsy erupted in tears.

Meanwhile my teenaged daughter overheard the entire exchange. She charged me, shook her head, and said, "I can't believe you would talk to your wife like that."

8

Things pretty much went downhill from there, and it took about two hours to patch things up. As a peace offering, I not only hung the two pictures, but saw to a half dozen other chores that needed tending as well.

Balancing priorities is hard and, sadly, we often become blinded to the needs of those closest to us. Yes, I had been busy with important activities. But was I so busy that I needed to wait three months before spending five minutes to hang some pictures? That was insensitive, wrong, and certainly didn't exhibit "the wisdom that comes from heaven."

On one hand, husbands need their wives to understand the anxiety caused by household "fix-it" chores. Some men really enjoy this work around the house, but these men should not be held up as the standard against which all husbands are measured. Wives need to be realistic about their husbands' capabilities. Personally, I have trouble getting the lid off the peanut butter jar.

On the other hand, men have a responsibility to show discernment in the arenas in which they live. A consuming career is no excuse for shortchanging the family chores, or any family priority for that matter.

Husbands need to balance their work priorities so their family's needs are met. If simple chores are left undone it may also be that more important matters, like time spent with the children, are being left undone too.

DISCUSSION

Both: What are the areas of your home life that are out of balance right now? To what extent are work or other outside priorities causing your family life to be out of balance?

APPLICATION

Wife: Make a list of chores and other things you would like the husband to do for the family and leave it at an agreed-upon location, like next to the coffeepot. Then give him the freedom to get it done anytime within the next month. Husband: Commit to complete any chores or other requests within a week or two.

PRAYER

Either, as appropriate: Lord, I confess that I often stumble over the little things. I can see how not taking care of chores would cause a wall to go up. Help me to be more attentive to the chores my mate would have me do. Amen.

PRAY FOR EACH OTHER

Therefore confess your sins to each other and pray for each other so that you may be healed. The prayer of a righteous man is powerful and effective.
JAMES 5:16

*D*wight L. Moody is my greatest posthumous hero. No other biography has ever gripped my own life more than his. I think he was the greatest lay preacher who ever lived. I admire him to no end and have used him as a model for my own speaking.

One day I was telling Patsy how pleased I was with the progress I was making in my public speaking. She reminded me that she had been praying about that every day for over two years.

"You have?" I asked in surprise.

"Yes, don't you remember? A long time ago you asked me to pray for you—that you would become a preacher like Dwight L. Moody."

Wow! That's right! I knew I had been praying that way but, candidly, I had forgotten that I had asked Patsy to pray that way for me too.

I cannot begin to tell you what this did for our relationship. This impressed me that I had in Patsy a friend like no other. This persuaded me that this person was truly committed to me. This gave me a new understanding of the term *faithful*.

Nothing our spouse can do for us can touch us so deeply as faithfully praying for us day after day—long after the normal person would have moved on to something new.

Praying for our mate is another way of saying "I love you." It is an expression of loyalty to our partner.

When we pray for each other we draw on the power of God to bring healing to our partner and lead him or her to wholeness. We say by our prayers that we are committed to bless and be a blessing to our mate.

When we pray for each other our Father in heaven hears our prayers and, when in accordance with His will, He answers them. Our prayers help unlock the rich treasures of God's kingdom for our spouse.

When we pray for each other the attitude of our own heart becomes softer and more forgiving toward our mate. It is impossible to earnestly pray for someone and be filled with hatred for them at the same time. If we will start to pray, even if angry, the Lord will give us peace. As you pray for your partner you will find yourself letting go of your animosities, your reservations, your pettiness, and your insistence upon having your own way.

When we pray for each other we deepen our love for our partner. To pray for our mate is to open us up to our mate. The more we pray, the more receptive we become to him/her. We begin to see more of Christ in their lives. We begin to accept their weaknesses without so much condemnation. We begin to see that we are not as smart, wise, and spiritual as we may have thought.

When we pray for each other we deepen our partner's love for us. Through a spiritual operation our loving and gracious Father sews our hearts more closely together. Our heart is bonded to our partner when we know he/she is bringing petitions for us before the throne of God's grace.

Pray for your spouse every day. You may be the only person in the entire world willing to pray for your mate on a regular basis. Occasionally affirm your husband or wife by letting him/her know you are praying. Ask how he/she would like you to pray specifically. Finally, be faithful over the long haul. Imagine the surprise when your partner finds out, as I did, the wonderful thing that has happened as an answer to your prayers.

DISCUSSION

Both answer: Have you been praying for your mate on a regular basis? Why or why not? Has the failure to pray been a blind spot in your marriage? What would be one benefit to your marriage if you faithfully prayed for each other on a daily basis?

APPLICATION

For the next thirty days, pray for your mate every day. Ask your spouse to share the two or three requests he/she would most like to see answered during the next thirty days. Write these down and put the prayer requests where you will see them every day. Tape them to the mirror, dashboard, or refrigerator. If the requests are deeply personal, keep them from public view. Mark your calendar and in thirty days tell each other how you have prayed and see what God has done.

PRAYER

Either or both: Lord Jesus, thank You for the prayers that my mate has lifted up to You on my behalf. Help me to be more faithful to pray for the life mate You have given to me. Amen.

PRAY WITH EACH OTHER

Do not be anxious about anything, but in everything, by prayer and petition, with thanksgiving, present your requests to God. And the peace of God, which transcends all understanding, will guard your hearts and your minds in Christ Jesus.

PHILIPPIANS 4:6–7

*W*e were running late. I hate to be late. A dear couple was hosting a luncheon so we could introduce our ministry to their friends, and we were not going to arrive on time. A cauldron of anxious feelings swirled around inside of me as my wife and I drove along the expressway toward the restaurant. I was not feeling very spiritual. I knew that I was walking in the flesh.

The problem with walking in the flesh is that while we don't like it, we like the idea of humbling ourselves and admitting it even less.

I debated back and forth about what to do. I knew I shouldn't go into this luncheon in the flesh, but neither did I want to admit I was feeling rebellious. Finally, I told Patsy what was happening and asked her if we could pray together.

"Good idea," she said.

"Lord," I began, "You have said that we don't need to be anxious for anything, but that in everything with prayer and supplication we can make our requests known to You, and Your peace which transcends all understanding will keep our hearts and minds in Christ Jesus. I ask that You forgive me of my sins, take away my anxiety, fill me with Your Spirit, and give me Your peace."

Patsy continued. "Lord, I agree with Pat, and ask You to answer this prayer in Jesus' name. Amen."

Instantly, the shroud of gloom lifted. I noticed what a beautiful day it was outside. Billowy clouds that looked like giant cotton balls filled a clear, blue sky. The Lord had set me free from behind the locked doors of my stubbornness.

I must tell you that it took every ounce of strength in me to ask Patsy to pray. Why is that? Satan likes nothing more than to keep us separated from each other's problems. Satan knows that when two are gathered in Jesus' name there is extraordinary power. Satan knows that a couple cannot achieve their fullest potential together if they do not pray with one another. The full array of God's power is released in each other's lives when we humble ourselves and pray.

It is easier to pray *for* each other than it is to pray *with* each other. To pray with each other is a brave step toward intimacy. If you find it difficult, you are not alone. To share our prayers to the Almighty God with another person is to let him or her view the most personal aspects of our life.

DISCUSSION

Both answer: What are the benefits to your relationship of praying together? Rate your prayer life together: Are you satisfied with the amount of time you spend together in prayer?

APPLICATION

Take a few moments right now and pray together. If this is all new to you, be satisfied to get a single sentence or two out. Try it again over the next several days and see what kind of progress you can make. If you simply cannot do it, then pray silently together. If you already pray together regularly, ask the Lord to keep you faithful to praying together.

PRAYER

Both: Lord God, thank You for the gift of prayer that allows us to ask You for help in times of need, and to praise and adore You. Help us to set times together to pray. May we achieve a degree of intimacy that can only come to those who pray together. Amen.

THE NEED TO FEEL WANTED

My command is this: Love each other as I have loved you.
JOHN 15:12

I have a terrible confession to make. Before we married, I told Patsy that if she ever got fat I would divorce her. Can you believe that? Oh sure, I said it in a kidding tone of voice, but we both knew I felt strongly about the subject. In truth, *I knew* I would never divorce Patsy. The problem was that *she didn't* know how I really felt. Once the statement was made, it was the truth to Patsy until I made a retraction. But instead of retracting, I half-jokingly repeated my threat over several years. I thought I was a real comedian. It wasn't funny. I was being a real jerk.

This became a huge wall between us. What Patsy wanted more than anything was for me to tell her that I accepted her as a person without conditions. She accused me of conditional love. She was right, of course, but I still wanted her to know that I didn't want my wife to be overweight. The truth is, the issue really wasn't whether Patsy was fat or not. What I cared about was me. I didn't want someone to think Pat Morley's wife was fat. Completely self-centered.

For years Patsy never felt fully wanted. I allowed her to dangle emotionally because of the weight issue. I loved her conditionally. She never felt a full, complete sense of security in our marriage.

One day the Lord convicted me of my sin and I repented. I had a change of heart and mind. I told Patsy that I loved her and wanted her no matter what. Frankly, she didn't believe me the first time I said this. It took a number of years of demonstrating that I really wanted her and accepted her for who she was before she began to sense and feel that I was sincere.

You and I have a powerful need to feel wanted. Each of us longs to be significant in the life of another person. We yearn for a sense of being valuable to our mate for who we are, with no strings attached. This is the heart of intimacy.

When we feel unwanted we pretend it doesn't matter, but it does. When feelings of not being wanted creep into marriage, the pain of rejection is so deep that it threatens to shatter the core of our identity and being. We feel unimportant, rejected, useless.

Wanting to be wanted in marriage is linked to the need for acceptance. We long to have one person in the world who knows us as we are, for who we are, who understands us completely and, in spite of it all, accepts us unconditionally. When we put conditions on the acceptance of our mate—like weight control—we say to our mates, "I only want you if. . . ." What our mates must hear is, "I want you regardless—in joy and in sorrow, in plenty and in want, in sickness and in health, for better or for worse."

If your mate feels unwanted, you have sinned. The feelings may be vague and not well articulated. But if the feeling of being unwanted is there, it must be dealt with. No pain is deeper than not feeling fully wanted by the most important person in your life.

DISCUSSION

Both answer: Do you feel fully wanted by your mate? (If yes, thank your spouse and the Lord. If not, can you articulate your feelings? Give it a try!) Spouse, listen and reflect on what you hear without giving a quick reply.

APPLICATION

If you can see that you have sinned against your mate by making your acceptance conditional, confess it to the Lord and repent (a change of heart, a turning from self). Ask your mate for forgiveness and begin to accept her/him without conditions or reservations.

PRAYER

Either or both, as appropriate: Heavenly Father, I can see how my mate would not feel fully wanted by me. This causes me deep sorrow for the grief I have caused my mate. Lord, I repent of my sin and ask You to allow me to love her/him with Your love, unconditionally, without reservations. Strengthen me to fulfill this commitment. Amen.

IN SICKNESS AND IN HEALTH

Even though I walk
through the valley of the shadow of death,
I will fear no evil,
for you are with me;
your rod and your staff,
they comfort me.

PSALM 23:4

*L*ast year my wife's sister, Nancy, made an appointment for her annual checkup. Ever efficient, Nancy went in for a routine mammogram before her appointment. Her doctor called a few days later and said, "Before you see me I want you to visit with a surgeon." It was a hard blow.

The surgeon reviewed her previous mammograms and recommended a biopsy, which was performed two days later. Usually the labs can tell if a malignancy exists the next day, but in her case they had to send it away, which added a week. The wait was excruciating. Unknown to her husband, Hal, Nancy asked the surgeon to call him with the results rather than her.

The following week the surgeon phoned Hal at his office and told him his wife's breast showed cancer. At that moment Hal's whole world collapsed. A frightening feeling that he could lose his wife swept over him. It had not been that long ago that he had lost his mother to cancer, and his father had recently passed away. He had to leave his office to get hold of himself. He had to be alone, to think, to talk to God.

That evening Nancy and Hal had made plans to go to dinner with friends. Hal knew the timing was not right, so he held the grim news inside. The next morning Hal and Nancy put their two daughters in the car pool for school. When the house finally felt quiet, Hal said, "Honey, I need to talk to you."

Nancy literally started shaking all over.

Hal continued tenderly, "The doctor called me yesterday. We need to have surgery. They did find some cancer." It was hard. They sat down together and both sobbed for fifteen minutes. Neither spoke a word. After gaining some composure Hal looked into her eyes and said, "Nancy, I feel a love for you right now like I've never felt before."

Nancy elected to have the safest surgery, a simple mastectomy. She says, "One of the hardest moments of all came when Hal and I had to leave each other as they wheeled me into surgery. He went one way and I another. When it's just you, the surgeon, and the Lord, you feel a tremendous vulnerability."

After the successful surgery, Hal slept in her hospital room both nights. He had to help her out of bed and support her to the bathroom. Some disagreeable medicine made her nauseous, and he cleaned up for her. He showed his love in a thousand ways.

"We felt a new closeness," says Nancy. "For the first two months we would just hug and hold each other all the time. Hal said to me, 'You'll never know how much I love you and how courageous I think you are.' That really ministered to me. I realize how precious life is every day. I look at my husband and kids differently. I thank the Lord for giving me life!"

Some illnesses are routine and short, like colds and flu. One illness, morning sickness, is even a sign of joy. But other diseases—like cancer—are terrifying and may cause disability, infirmity, and death. Some strike in the prime of life. Heart attack. Stroke. Cancer. Mental disorders. Chemical dependencies. Alcoholism. Hepatitis. Chronic Fatigue Syndrome.

When the body of the wife is sick, so is the body of the husband. They are one flesh. When the body of the husband takes ill, so does the body of the wife. They are one flesh. We belong to each other, as we belong to the Lord. How important it is for your mate to have an assurance that you will be there in the dark hour of illness.

DISCUSSION

Both answer: Have you faced a major illness, surgery, or injury in your marriage? If yes, what are the ways your mate demonstrated her/his love to you that you appreciated? If your mate was the one needing attention, what are the ways you wish you would have been more attentive? How can having an assurance that your mate will "be there" for you strengthen your marriage?

APPLICATION

Both: Express out loud your commitment to be there for each other when the need arises.

PRAYER

Either: Lord God, thank You for the good health You have enabled us to enjoy by Your grace. We ask that You would protect us from sickness and disease. Help us to show such love to each other that we each have an assurance that we will always be there for each other. Amen.

IN PLENTY AND IN WANT

I know what it is to be in need, and I know what it is to have plenty. I have learned the secret of being content in any and every situation, whether well fed or hungry, whether living in plenty or in want.
PHILIPPIANS 4:12

*H*e always had a big job. The Lord had occupied his heart and mind with gladness. He rarely reflected on the days of his life. Then, after twenty-two years, he was caught in the corporate "downsizing" craze.

Middle-aged. Never without a job before. Difficult job market. Down economy. Unemployed.

Week after week went by. Nothing. Weeks turned into months. His predicament clung to him like a bad case of flu. Sometimes he was just overwhelmed by the agony of it all. In his quiet times he would call out to God in groans that he could not put into words. After six months without employment, he forgot who he was. He had lost his identity.

We all find much of our identity in our work. Granted, it should not be so, but it is nevertheless true.

His wife could not understand why he couldn't find work. She knew he was putting in the hours and going on some interviews, but openly wondered if there was something wrong with him. "Why can't you convert an interview into a job? Are you expecting too much? Maybe you are acting too anxious. Maybe you should read a book on interviewing. We are running out of money. How will we pay the kids' tuition? I was able to find work in two weeks; I can't understand why after eight months you still haven't found something."

Each question, each insinuation, each doubt, each worry pierced his heart like a razor-edged, white-hot saber. His self-esteem began to flutter. On those occasions when his wife would doubt him, he would slip below the line that separates positive from negative. Each time it was harder to come back. By the end of the eighth month, his confidence was gone.

In our culture a man's *identity* usually comes from his work, yet a major chunk of his *self-esteem* comes from his wife. Both, of course, should instead come from Christ. However, if a man loses both his work and the support of his wife at the same time, he trembles on the brink of destruction.

When a man and woman tie the nuptial knot, they make a pledge to be there for each other in joy and sorrow, in plenty and want, in sickness and health, for better or worse, till death do they part. Unfortunately, none of us really understands ahead of time all that this entails. Some of us find it more difficult than we ever imagined.

The apostle Paul, our brother, said, "I know what it is to be in need, and I know what it is to have plenty. I have learned the secret of being content in any and every situation, whether well fed or hungry, whether living in plenty or in want." What was Paul's secret?

The secret of being content in any and every situation is to so completely surrender every desire of your heart to the Lord Jesus that whatever happens the peace of God remains with you.

- "Be content with your pay" (Luke 3:14).
- "But if we have food and clothing, we will be content with that" (1 Tim. 6:8).
- "Keep your lives free from the love of money and be content with what you have" (Heb. 13:5).

Husbands and wives need to be there for each other in daylight and darkness. When the dark hour comes, remember your vow. Keep the faith. Finish the race.

DISCUSSION

Both answer: What times of plenty and want do you remember in your marriage? Are you content with your circumstances now? Why or why not?

APPLICATION

List on paper everything that is blocking you from being content. Surrender each item by name to the Lord Jesus.

PRAYER

Each pray: Lord Jesus, I confess that sometimes I let my desires for security or luxuries tear at our marriage. Help me to be like Paul, content in any and every situation, whether well fed or hungry, whether living in plenty or in want. May my mate know that I am always here for him/her. Amen.

IN JOY AND IN SORROW

Jesus wept.

JOHN 11:35

*I*n our wedding vows we pledged ourselves to each other "in joy and in sorrow." Sometimes, though, we may feel neither joy nor sorrow, as this story about a friend's parents illustrates.

This couple, whom I'll call John and Nancy, had been good Christian stewards. Frugally managing John's income from the state highway department, they had acquired some rental properties. Between his job and taking care of the rentals, he kept busy.

John was not the kind of man to make a large display of affection. In fact, he never cried, but sometimes he would shake with bottled up emotion. He never set foot in the kitchen. Old school.

One day as John was driving down the freeway it suddenly occurred to him how emotionally dry he had become. He didn't feel like he cared about anything. As one thought tumbled over the next, he began to pray about it. "Lord, I'm just so emotionally dry. Lord, give me tears."

Within a few days he learned that Nancy had a terminal cancer. John retired from his job at the highway department to take care of her. Within a year doctors discovered that he had a type of cataracts that rendered him legally blind.

As Nancy's condition worsened, John became the family cook. Before, he had never set foot in the kitchen; now John worked in the kitchen joyfully.

One day my friend walked in on his parents unannounced to find them sitting on the couch, holding hands, gazing into each other's eyes.

John was no longer emotionally dry. In fact, he often wept openly. He was learning to accept and experience his emotions.

Interesting. Before their adversity he had found himself emotionally dry, feeling neither joy nor sorrow. Now, through tragedy, he experienced a deep sense of both joy and sorrow at the same time.

To be pledged to each other "in joy and in sorrow" only has meaning to the extent we share in each other's lives. Intimacy comes through connection. When we are two separate people living two separate lives, though we share a common roof, we will not experience the joy and sorrow of life together. In fact, we will become emotionally dry.

A huge part of joy is sharing the experience with someone else. The first thing I do on hearing good news is tell Patsy. Unshared joy is like letting choice food go to rot.

Likewise, a huge part of sorrow is sharing the experience with someone else. The first thing I do when I'm down is talk it out with Patsy. Unshared sorrow can lead to a depressed state. In short, unshared joy and sorrow will make us emotionally dry. We need each other for emotional balance. The shared life is the emotionally stable life.

Jesus shared His life with others. Jesus openly shared His emotions. Because He had people with whom He shared His life, Jesus never ran the risk of running emotionally dry.

The sisters, Mary and Martha, sent word to Jesus, "The one you love is sick." By the time Jesus arrived He found that Lazarus had already been in the tomb for four days. When Mary reached Him she fell at His feet and said, "Lord, if You had been here, my brother would not have died."

When Jesus saw her and the Jews who had come along with her weeping, He was deeply moved in spirit and troubled. The Bible records that "Jesus wept" (John 11:1–35).

The shared experiences of both joy and sorrow are what stir the emotions within us. Share your lives together, both the joy and the sorrow.

DISCUSSION

Both answer: Are you emotionally dry? Why or why not? Have you been sharing your sorrows with each other? Have you been sharing your joys with each other? As Oswald Chambers said, "Many will confide to you their secret sorrows, but the last mark of intimacy is to confide secret joys."[1]

APPLICATION

Because we live on this side of the Fall we experience sorrow. Because we live on this side of the Cross we experience joy. Every believer's life is chock full of tales of joy and sorrow. Take a few minutes and tell each other the things that are bringing sadness into your lives right now. Then take a few minutes to tell each other the things that are bringing joy into your lives right now.

PRAYER

Both: Lord, in faith we thank You for both the joys and the sorrows of our lives. Help us to share deeply our lives with one another. Help us, we pray, to live up to our pledge to love one another "in joy and in sorrow." Amen.

THE GOOD AND BAD OF MARRIAGE

He who finds a wife finds what is good
and receives favor from the LORD.
                                        PROVERBS 18:22

*T*he Bible declares that marriage is a good and holy estate. Marriage is the deepest, most profound of all human relationships. Marriage is the only human relationship that includes a spiritual and physical unity of a man and woman. Marriage is more than communion; it is a union in which two people mysteriously become one.

The world declares that marriage is a difficult and temporary estate. The world says that marriage is for "a while." The world says marriage partners are disposable. It is not that the world has only recently said these things. Throughout history the world has derided marriage:

- "Marriage, if one will face the truth, is an evil, but a necessary evil"
  —Menander, fourth century B.C.
- "Marriage is an evil that most men welcome"
  —Monostikoi.
- "Marriage is a noose"
  —Cervantes, sixteenth century.
- "Marriage happens as with cages: the birds without despair to get in, and those within despair of getting out"
  —Montaigne, sixteenth century.
- "Marriage is a desperate thing"
  —John Seldon, seventeenth century.
- "Marriage is like life in this—that it is a field of battle, and not a bed of roses"
  —Robert Louis Stevenson, nineteenth century.

The world is correct. Marriage is a difficult estate. Marriage has always been a difficult relationship. But that is not the end of it, for the Christian marriage holds out the hope of the deepest human joy a man and woman can drink. Though marriage can be difficult, it can also be a good and holy estate.

What the world has missed is that marriage is a spiritual enterprise. Marriage was established by God. And God said that marriage would be a good thing. Yet, because of the Fall our sinful natures constantly put stress and strain on our marriages. We are weak people married to weak people, and the closer we come to one another the more our weaknesses become visible to each other. Tiny hairline cracks and fractures appear. Without maintenance the estate of marriage can crumble.

The secret of a happy, fulfilling marriage is found in the approach. The world approaches marriage to see "what I can get" from the marriage: my needs, my wants, my desires, my plans, my hopes, my dreams, my ambitions, my expectations. The Christian approaches marriage to see "how I can serve" my partner: her needs, her wants, her desires, her plans, his hopes, his dreams, his ambitions, his expectations.

The problem of marriage is solved by the surrender of one's individual (selfish?) aspirations to the greater good of the couple. Something must give, and it should be you. To require your spouse to give goes against the grain of New Testament love. New Testament love is *giving* love, not *getting* love. Our Lord Jesus gave Himself once for all as a sacrifice for our sins. Have you made a sacrifice lately for your mate?

DISCUSSION

Both answer: In your heart of hearts, have you considered marriage good, or have you had some reservations toward it? How have you been approaching marriage—as a giver or a taker?

APPLICATION

Make the choice to have a spiritual view of marriage and not a "worldly" view. If you have been a taker and not a giver, plan some specific ways you can begin to be more of a giver.

PRAYER

Either, as applicable: Heavenly Father, I confess that I have let the world's negative views of marriage seep into my own thinking. I acknowledge that marriage is a good and a holy estate. I rejoice that my mate and I have been mysteriously joined together into one flesh. Help me to be a giver and not a taker. Amen.

WALLS

"For this reason a man will leave his father and mother and be united to his wife, and the two will become one flesh." So they are no longer two, but one. Therefore what God has joined together, let man not separate.
MARK 10:7–9

wall *n.* 1. An upright structure serving to enclose or divide. 2. A structure built as a defense. 3. Something virtually impenetrable.
wall *vt.* 1. To enclose, surround, or fortify with or as if with a wall. 2. To divide or separate with or as if with a wall. 3. To enclose within a wall. 4. To block or close with or as if with a wall.

We live in a world of walls. Walls are everywhere. Brick walls, stone walls, wood walls. Graffiti-covered inner-city walls. Gated walls surrounding luxury developments.

Sterile prison walls, the granite walls of a high rise building. High walls, low walls, wide walls. Walls with curls of barbed wire. The Berlin Wall, the Great Wall of China. Canyon walls, Wall Street. Broken down walls, impenetrable walls. Emotional walls. Walls of misunderstanding. Walls of routine. Walls of difference and indifference. Backs to the wall. Pushed to the wall. Up the wall. Off the wall.

A wall is simply an upright structure that encloses, protects, divides, or separates. People build walls for defense. People build walls to control passage. Some walls keep people in, other walls keep people out.

Some walls are visible, many are not. The most impenetrable walls are constructed in the mind—walls that represent prejudices over cultural or racial differences, the fallout from injuries and insults, and emotional self-protection.

When walls go up in marriage, someone is hurting. Walls are defensive structures. Someone feels injured. Someone feels the pain of neglect. Someone can no longer bear to feel the sting of insult. Emotional wounds cut far more deeply than physical blows. So walls go up for defense. Passage into the inner being needs to be controlled or stopped.

What are the reasons we build walls, those barriers that keep out the person to whom we should feel closest? Here are a few:

1. *Neglect.* My mate is busy with many things. I don't feel I'm a top priority.
2. *Injury.* My mate's critical spirit has left me feeling wounded.
3. *Insult.* Unkind words have shaken my confidence and jarred my self-esteem.
4. *Abuse.* I have been physically or mentally harmed, possibly as a young person.
5. *Guilt.* I have done something I'm ashamed of and don't want my spouse to know.

6. *Fear*. I'm afraid my spouse will not love me if he or she *really* knows who I am.
7. *Selfishness*. My ambition to gain power, possessions, money, popularity, success, or security has hurt our relationship.
8. *Pride*. I'm unwilling to admit my weaknesses, fears, doubts, worries.
9. *Fear of betrayal*. If I share my deepest thoughts, secrets, and longings, will my spouse tell all?
10. *Grudge*. I have allowed a past offense by my spouse to grow way out of proportion.

Can you think of some other reasons we build walls?

Jesus Christ came to destroy the barrier that separates people. By His death and resurrection He has given us power to eliminate the walls we build between us, which are the fruit of living by our flesh. Any walls between us now are of our own making. The walls we construct in our marriages are built in the flesh, not the Spirit.

No matter how high or seemingly impenetrable the walls between us are, they are ready to come tumbling down like Jericho's walls, if we will use the Lord's power. May each chapter of this book crash into your walls like a velvet-covered wrecking ball.

DISCUSSION

Both answer: What are some of the walls you have built in your marriage? How do you think this book can help tear down those walls? What else do you hope will happen in your relationship as a result of sharing this book together?

APPLICATION

Each: Put a check mark by any of the ten walls listed above you feel you have caused your mate to construct. You should come back after completing the book to see how Christ has helped you bring those walls tumbling down.

PRAYER

Either: Lord Jesus, thank You that You have destroyed the barrier that separates us, the dividing wall of hostility, by Your death and resurrection. Help us now to do our part to bring the walls tumbling down through faith and hard work. We ask You to give us a marriage without walls. Grant us Your peace. Amen.

SOMETHING I'VE ALWAYS WANTED TO SHARE

A gossip betrays a confidence,
but a trustworthy man keeps a secret.

PROVERBS 11:13

*P*atsy and I share everything with each other. Well, almost everything.

For the first sixteen years of our marriage I carried around a burden to tell Patsy something I had done wrong as a young man. Though I had experienced God's full measure of forgiveness, I longed to share my mistake with my most intimate friend. But I didn't.

What keeps us from sharing our secrets with the one we love? First and foremost, we fear betrayal. We wonder, "Can I trust my mate to keep my secret?" I believe this is the single greatest reason we don't share with each other. Above all else, we must learn to be an utterly trustworthy mate. Are you?

Second, we fear that what we say will damage our relationship. We ask ourselves, "What effect will this have on us?" This reason is a close second. It is the fear that my mate will think less of me as a result of what I share. We must learn to accept our mates for who they are: fallen sinners saved by grace. We call this, of course, unconditional love. Tough stuff. We must learn to listen nonjudgmentally when our partners do share with us. If not, they will close up. Do you accept your mate as is? Do you listen nonjudgmentally?

The common thread through both of these reasons is fear. There are only two ways to get past this fear: 1) Both partners must be willing to risk sharing deep thoughts, and 2) both partners must be utterly committed to trustworthiness.

In the process of building trust we take small risks to see how our spouse will react. Does he/she get angry? Does he/she blab to friends? Does he/she dismiss what we share as insignificant? Does he/she withdraw? Here is the key: Your response to the small risks your mate takes with you will determine how many secrets there are in your marriage. If we betray or demean our mates on a small thing, how can we expect them to trust us with a big thing? Deep sharing will only come after our mate has experienced safe sharing.

Do we share every single secret with our mates? No, we must be wise. For example, you must know your mate's level of spiritual maturity. The time may not be right. Or, do you really need to share sins committed before you met for which you have asked God's forgiveness? Maybe, but maybe not. Here are some questions to first ask yourself, assuming that you trust each other:

- Has the Lord impressed me to share this?
- Will it edify or encourage my mate?
- Will it deepen our connection to each other?
- Will it clear the air between us?
- Is not sharing this standing in the way of a right relationship?
- What will happen if I don't share this?

We must learn to trust and be trustworthy. Share your secret joys, your secret sorrows, your failings, your feelings of inadequacy, your fears and doubts, what makes you feel guilty. Do it in love and for love. Do it for your mate. Do it for yourself.

After sixteen years I finally took the risk one day and told Patsy my secret. We were driving (I couldn't look her in the eyes). I remember the exact spot our car was passing when I told her. What a relief! I felt a complete and fully satisfying release. No secrets. No regrets. She still accepted me, still loved me, didn't judge me. Thank God. Praise God!

DISCUSSION

Each answer: What makes you hesitate to share things with your mate?

APPLICATION

Is there something you've always wanted to share with your mate? Go ahead, take the risk. And may I say to the one who hears the secret, don't be judgmental, just listen. Affirm if you can. Be trustworthy. Accept. Love. Grow. Learn. May the Holy Spirit mysteriously knit your hearts together in a deeper way than you ever imagined possible.

PRAYER

Either: Lord Jesus, thank You for giving me a mate I can trust. Thank You for giving me a husband/wife who accepts me as I am (or is at least willing to try to accept me as I am). Help me to be worthy of that trust and acceptance. Lord, help us mature to the point that we have no need of any secrets between us. I ask this in Your name. Amen.

FRUSTRATION WITH LIFE

He has made everything beautiful in its time. He has also set eternity in the hearts of men; yet they cannot fathom what God has done from beginning to end.

ECCLESIASTES 3:11

*E*arly in our marriage I went through a period of deep frustration with life. Ironically, I was meeting all the goals I had set for myself: income, new luxury car, expensive suits, beautiful home, fabulous wife, starting my own business. Yet, I discovered an age-old truth: Success doesn't satisfy. Instead, those met goals tended to become an unrelated string of hollow victories, increasingly frustrating as more and more was accomplished.

What does it all mean? Surely there must be some higher purpose to life than simply accumulating more and more stuff? The enormity of these questions drove me to the brink of total despair.

I vividly recall driving home one day, pulling into our garage, putting the garage door down, getting out of the car, then in anger and frustration, repeatedly kicking the inside wall. I desperately wanted to expiate the cauldron of frustration with life boiling within me. When we later sold the house I was embarrassed to think that someone might ask why there were footprints on the garage wall!

Men and women who become frustrated with their lives do not become frustrated because life itself has no meaning. No, it is precisely because God *has* set "eternity in the hearts" of people that they have a built-in sense that life *does* have meaning. Their frustration is that they have not yet found it.

We each long for life to have meaning and purpose. We each have an intuitive sense that we are part of a larger plan, something bigger than ourselves. We sense that there is value and purpose to life beyond the immediate needs of our own small circle. We crave to be part of something bigger than ourselves. That something is eternity.

God has put eternity in our hearts. It is a built-in desire to know God and make Him known. Until we know God personally the meaning and purpose of life remains shrouded in frustration. Until we are in some way involved in doing the work of God in the world, we will experience a cauldron of frustration with life.

Patsy handled me with a delicate touch during those days. We were not at the same point on our spiritual pilgrimages. I could not "fathom what God had done from beginning to end." Patsy had begun to understand. The difference was that she knew God. I didn't. I knew *about* God, but I didn't *know* God.

Through her patience, wisdom, and prayer, God used Patsy to help me unlock the mysteries of meaning and purpose in due time. He made "everything beautiful in its time."

Many husbands and wives find themselves at different points on their spiritual pilgrimage. Frustrations and disillusionments come. "What's it all about? What does it mean? What is the point?" Through patience, wisdom, and prayer, God will use us to help each other *know* Him—not just know *about* Him.

DISCUSSION

Each answer: (There is no right or wrong answer to this question.) Where do you think you are on your spiritual pilgrimage? When do you believe you moved from knowing *about* God to actually *knowing* God?

APPLICATION

Give your mate wholly over to the Lord. Offer patience, wisdom, and prayer as the Lord leads you. If you are frustrated with your life, do you know *about* God or do you actually *know* God in a personal, real way? (If you have doubts, the next devotional will help you sort out your thoughts.)

PRAYER

Either, if applicable: Dear God, I am experiencing deep frustration with my life. I believe that life does have meaning and purpose, but I have yet to find it. Instead, I wonder, "What's it all about? Is this all there is?" Help me not only to know "about" You, but to know You—personally—for I sense that You have set eternity in my heart. Amen.

VALUES OR CHRIST?

The life I live in the body, I live by faith in the Son of God, who loved me and gave himself for me.

GALATIANS 2:20

*H*as it ever seemed to you that some people have the "inside story" on Christianity—that there is another whole dimension to Christianity you have not yet discovered?

When we were dating, Patsy frequently asked me religious-sounding questions. I quickly realized that my answers were not all that satisfying to her. This bothered me, since I had always considered myself religious.

Being a salesman, I simply stopped answering her questions. Instead, I would answer her questions with questions until I felt I understood the answer she was looking for. When I thought I had zeroed in on the answer she wanted, I would lie. I would tell her whatever I thought she wanted to hear. After all, I loved her and wanted to spend the rest of my life with her. Making her happy was at the top of my list. Though I don't recommend lying, it worked. We've been married over twenty years!

Soon after our wedding, however, it became clear we did not have the same understanding of what it meant to be a Christian. She seemed to know something I didn't know. On one hand, I was committed to a set of Christian values. I was surprised, however, to learn that Patsy was committed to a Person, Jesus Christ. I had always viewed Christianity as a task, something I did for God. Patsy taught me that, no, Christianity is a relationship, based on something God did for us.

We are not Christians because we live by a certain set of values or principles. Neither are we Christians because we go to church. As Billy Sunday said, "Sitting in a church doesn't make you a Christian any more than sitting in a garage makes you a car." Today's church pews are filled with well-intentioned people confused about how to know God.

Rather, we are Christians when we acknowledge our sins and ask Christ to forgive us and grant us eternal life. Certainly, as a result of placing faith in Christ, we will want to live by certain values and principles, and we will want to go to church. But these are the *result* of establishing a personal relationship with Jesus Christ, not the *cause* of it.

Jesus Christ is the issue, not religion. The question is not "What will you do with religion?" but "What will you do with Jesus?"

When I finally was able to draw this distinction in my mind I gave my life to follow Jesus Christ, not a set of values. The meaning and purpose came as quickly as the frustration melted away. Now I know: It is a Person who lives in me, not a set of values. We don't invite principles to live inside us. We invite the living Lord. Are you committed to a personal relationship with Jesus Christ for your salvation, or have you been depending upon a set of values?

DISCUSSION

Each answer: Upon what or whom have you been depending for your salvation? Have you been depending upon the person of Christ, or a list of values?

APPLICATION

If you have a personal relationship with Jesus Christ, thank Him. If not, you can receive Him right now as your Savior and Lord by repenting of your sins and by inviting Him to come into Your life. Use the following prayer, or one similar, to receive Jesus Christ as your Savior and Lord.

PRAYER

Either, if appropriate: Lord Jesus, I confess that I have erred in my understanding of how to be saved. I now see that *You* are the issue, not *religious behavior*. I may have been committed to living by Christian values and principles and to attending church, but I have never really established a personal relationship with You. By faith I now turn from my sinful ways, and ask You to forgive my sins and give me eternal life. Thank You for giving Your life for mine. Take control of my life and make me into a follower of You. Amen.

ROBBED OF THE BLESSING

Leah became pregnant and gave birth to a son. She named him Reuben, for she said, "It is because the LORD has seen my misery. Surely my husband will love me now."

GENESIS 29:32

*W*hen John Trent was pursuing his doctorate degree in counseling and working with couples in therapy, he saw people daily who were depressed and in emotional distress. One day, while preparing to teach a Bible lesson, the bitter cry of Esau leaped off the pages of Genesis, "Bless me, even me also, O my father!" (Gen. 27:34 NASB).

At that moment, John realized that all the heartache and pain Esau had felt when he did not receive the blessing that rightfully belonged to him was echoed over and over in the lives of those he counseled.[2]

In their wonderful book, *The Gift of the Blessing*, John Trent and Gary Smalley show how difficult it can be to lead a fulfilled, meaningful life without receiving the blessing from our parents and giving the blessing to our own children and mate. What is the blessing in marriage? The blessing is a genuine acceptance of each other; it is attaching high value to your mate; it is providing a sense of security for one another; it is visualizing a positive future for the two of you together. The blessing is another metaphor for filling our mate's emotional bank account.

The Bible provides a snapshot of a marriage in which the husband did not bless his wife and the terrible pain that came as a result. (Read the account of how Jacob married the two sisters, Leah and Rachel, in Genesis 29.)

Rachel was beautiful, and after he married her, Jacob began to ignore Leah. When the Lord saw that she was not loved, He enabled her to become pregnant, and she gave birth to four sons. Note her lament after each son was born. Feel the pain of this woman who felt unloved. See how her husband robbed her of his blessing, and how her emotional bank account was empty. (This is how our mates feel if we rob them of the blessing.)

1. *Depressed.* "Leah became pregnant and gave birth to a son. She named him Reuben, for she said, 'It is because the LORD has seen my misery. Surely my husband will love me now'" (Gen. 29:32). The Hebrew word translated "misery" literally means "depression." She was depressed. A spouse who does not feel loved is on the dark road to depression.

2. *Hated.* "She conceived again, and when she gave birth to a son she said, 'Because the LORD heard that I am not loved, he gave me this one too.' So

she named him Simeon" (Gen. 29:33). The Hebrew words translated "not loved" literally mean "to hate." She felt hated by her husband. Far from feeling indifferent when a woman's husband does not demonstrate love toward her, she actually feels hated by him. The opposite of love is not neutrality, but hatred.

3. *Unattached.* "Again she conceived, and when she gave birth to a son she said, 'Now at last my husband will become attached to me, because I have borne him three sons.' So he was named Levi" (Gen. 29:34). The Hebrew word "attached" literally means "to twine." The image is of threads twisted together, stronger together than if apart, but all are broken if one is broken. She did not feel joined together as one with her husband.

4. *Filled with regrets.* "She conceived again, and when she gave birth to a son she said, 'This time I will praise the LORD.' So she named him Judah. Then she stopped having children" (Gen. 29:35). *Surely now,* she must have thought, *my husband will bless me and I will be able to praise my God.* She remained hopeful.

These verses illustrate how devastated a wife can become when the blessing of her husband is withheld. And surely husbands, too, can feel this pain. It is in the heart of God that husbands and wives be a blessing to one another.

Give your mate the blessing. Nothing will deepen your relationship with each other more. The next devotional offers ten suggestions on how to bless your mate.

DISCUSSION

Each answer: Have there been times in your marriage, past or present, in which you have felt like a Leah? Refer to each of the four responses of Leah, and relate how you are doing personally in each area. Do you feel depressed, unloved, unattached? Are you filled with regrets?

APPLICATION

Give your mate the blessing. Commit yourself to genuinely accept your spouse, to attach high value, to give a sense of security in your marriage, to visualize a positive future. Determine to fill her/his emotional bank account.

PRAYER

Either or both: Lord, thank You for the many ways in which my mate has blessed me. Help me to be a blessing to her/him. Amen.

TEN WAYS TO BLESS EACH OTHER

Be completely humble and gentle; be patient, bearing with one another in love.

EPHESIANS 4:2

*A*s we saw in the last devotional, to give each other the blessing is a most powerful way to glue us together as husband and wife. Here are ten ways to bless each other. Elsewhere in this book we will explore these subjects more fully.

1. *Touch each other.* Successful couples touch each other. They hug, squeeze, embrace, pat, hold hands, put arms around each other, and sit close enough to touch when sitting anywhere together. Nonsexual touching leads to genuine intimacy. And they enjoy sex, too, and often.

2. *Listen to each other.* Communication invariably shows up as the number one problem in marriage surveys. We attach high value to our mates when we listen deeply to each other without giving any overly quick response that criticizes or gives advice. Listening lubricates marriage and reduces the friction.

3. *Spend time together alone.* The issue is time—who gets it? How we spend our time reveals what is really important to us. Successful couples spend time together. They pray together. They read the Bible together. They develop shared interests, like bowling, reading, hiking, or seeing plays.

4. *Encourage each other with words.* Encouragement is the food of the heart. We all need to be lifted up when we are blue, but the most successful couples go another step—they create a positive environment. They verbally affirm each other at every opportunity. They try to catch each other doing things "right." They pass along compliments others make about their mate. They never pass up an opportunity to express appreciation: "I love the way you look today." "Thank you for being such a good provider." "That was a great new recipe you tried." "You did a super job of listening to the kids describe what happened at school today."

5. *Unconditionally accept each other.* Unconditional love and acceptance form a crucial foundation in successful marriages. Happy couples don't feel like they have to perform to be loved. They don't feel like they will be rejected if they don't meet a set of standards. Jesus accepts us just as we are, and smart mates accept each other "as is" too.

6. *Be committed to each other.* Successful couples have a commitment to work through troubles. The word "divorce" is not uttered, no matter how upset one becomes. They have an agreement on how to "fight fair" under peaceful conditions. They try to let the little irritations go. They make an

active commitment to want the best for their mate, to help him or her grow as a person.

7. *Take care of your financial future together.* Money problems create more stress on marriage than any other outside threat. Successful couples have resolved to live within their means. They do not live so high today that they fail to provide for tomorrow's unexpected needs, retirement, and premature death. They are very careful about taking on debt.

8. *Laugh with each other.* The antidote for boredom in marriage is lively humor. If your partner tells a joke, laugh! (Even if he isn't Bob Hope or she isn't Carol Burnett.) If neither one of you is funny, make sure to watch funny movies and be around funny friends.

9. *Make each other your top priority.* The only one you can fully count on to be there for you is your mate. The rule of rules for successful marriage is this: After God, but before all others, make each other your top priority. Don't let anyone—not even your children, and especially not your parents—come between you.

10. *Be each other's best friend.* Happy couples commit to spend time together as friends. They share secrets with each other. They enjoy each other's company. They realize they are the only ones who are really in this thing "together." Everyone else is for themselves to some degree, even kids. But couples are "one flesh."

DISCUSSION

Both answer: Have you enjoyed each other's company in the ways mentioned in today's devotional? Which ones? Which ones would you like to improve?

APPLICATION

Beside the "Ten Ways to Bless Each Other" listed above, make a mark by the ones which you would really like to improve on. Ask your mate what you could do to show improvement in each of those areas.

PRAYER

Both pray: Lord God, I thank You for my mate. I pray that we will have a successful, happy marriage all our days. Lord, I confess that I need to work on the following areas (name them). Grant me the desire and the power to be the kind of mate I know You and my husband/wife would like me to be. Help me to be a blessing. Amen.

LOVE ALWAYS PERSEVERES

Love . . . always perseveres.

1 CORINTHIANS 13:6–7

*T*aking a midweek afternoon off turned into a delightful break from the normal pressure of daily duties. The sun filtered gently through the leaves of the tree under which I was sitting, forming delicate shadows that danced like carefree nymphs on the pages of my opened book.

Except for our dog, Katie, I was all alone. A subdued quiet engulfed the entire neighborhood. After lying in the sun for a while, Katie turned playful. Actually, crazy. She began to run around the yard from corner to corner to corner as fast as she could.

"Katie! What in the world are you doing?"

That only egged her on. She began to crisscross the yard at full gallop. Then she started reversing direction at the midpoint and backtracking, again, at full steam. Next she picked up her favorite ball with her teeth, tossed it herself, and then ran to fetch it.

This was all too much for me. I burst out laughing. Then something strange happened. A tidal wave of feelings welled up from the depths which words could not express. An incredible sense of love and joy overpowered me.

How could I ever live without Katie? I wondered. *I simply cannot imagine what it would be like for her not to be around.* I wondered how heavy the silence would have been that day without Katie in my life. I wondered how carefree the shadows could have danced on my book were I alone.

Yet life with Katie involved travails and disappointments. As with every puppy—and she'd become a large dog—we had endured the digging, bills, chewed furniture, shed hair, etc. Our relationship with Katie required perseverance.

To persevere means "to remain constant in the face of discouragement or opposition."

My mind turned to other relationships, especially mine with Patsy. In spite of the differences and misunderstandings that come with marriage, I couldn't help but reflect on the myriad ways she blesses me. How great the travails and disappointments I'd brought to her kind, gentle soul. How many times had she overlooked my weaknesses? Served without seeking recognition? Forgiven? Yes, she had persevered with me. Love always perseveres.

The natural tendency is to think only how we have persevered. Consider also, however, how your mate has persevered. Weaklings are we all. We

36

disappoint each other. We let each other down. The Fall has infected us all, producing the putrid odor of smugness. We tend to remember all the good we do to our mate and all the bad they do to us. Likewise, we tend not to remember the bad we do to them nor the good they do to us.

Yes, we have persevered. But our mates have persevered, too, though differently. Every person's discouragement visits them in a different way. Let us each choose never to knowingly discourage each other. Instead, let us persevere. It is the loving thing to do.

When we consider the incomprehensible grace of our Lord Jesus Christ in persevering with us, can we offer anything less to the mate He entrusted to our care?

DISCUSSION

Both answer: What are some of the ways your mate has persevered with you?

APPLICATION

Make a pledge to persevere with your partner. What will that look like in day-to-day living?

PRAYER

Either: Lord Jesus, how could we ever live without each other? I simply cannot imagine what it would be like for my mate not to be around. In spite of occasional disappointments, this marriage is worth it. Help us both, I pray, to remember all the good we do for each other while forgiving and forgetting any bad. Grant us that supernatural love that always perseveres. Amen.

IN SUMMARY

*A*t the end of each section, some of the key ideas which have been presented will be summarized.

APPLICATION

Read these out loud to each other meditatively. One of you read a point and the other make a comment. Then reverse roles, and so on, until you have read and commented on each idea. Conclude in prayer.

- God has given couples no greater gift than the ability to laugh at life together. The joy of sharing humorous secrets and private jokes breathes energy into a marriage.
- Some walls are visible, most are not. Most walls are constructed in the mind. When walls go up in marriage someone is hurting.
- You and I have no greater need than the need to feel wanted. Each of us longs to be significant in the life of another person. We yearn for a sense of being valuable to our mate for who we are.
- We each have an emotional bank account into which our partner makes deposits and withdrawals.
- The secret of a marriage made of two-part harmony is to fill each other's emotional bank accounts to overflowing.
- If simple chores are left undone, it may also be that more important matters—like time spent with the children—are being left undone too. To succeed at work but fail at home is to fail.
- Nothing our spouse can do for us can touch us so deeply as faithfully praying for us day after day—long after another person would have moved on to something new.
- When we pray for each other, the attitude of our own heart becomes softer and more forgiving toward our mate. It is impossible to hate others when we're earnestly praying for them.
- It is easier to pray *for* each other than it is to pray *with* each other. To pray with each other is a brave step toward intimacy.
- In our culture a man's *identity* usually comes from his work, yet a major chunk of his self-esteem comes from his wife. If a man loses both his work and the support of his wife at the same time, he trembles

on the brink of destruction. Both, of course, should instead come from Christ.

- When a man and woman tie the nuptial knot, they make a pledge to be there for each other in joy and sorrow, in plenty and want, in sickness and health, for better or worse till death do they part. Unfortunately, none of us really understands ahead of time all that this entails.

- When we are two separate people living two separate lives, though sharing a common roof, we will not experience the joy and sorrow of life together. In fact we will become emotionally dry. Intimacy comes through connection.

- When a husband and wife wear wedding rings, they tell the world, "I am committed to a person. This person has taken a vow to be faithful and I, in return, have also vowed to be loving and faithful. This ring is a symbol of love and affection both given and received."

- Without maintenance, the estate of marriage can be made to crumble.

- Your response to the small risks of disclosure your mate takes with you will determine whether or not there are secrets in your marriage. We cannot fail or break a confidence with our mates on a small thing and then expect them to trust us with a big thing.

- Men and women who become frustrated with their lives do not become frustrated because life has no meaning. No, it is exactly because God has set eternity in the hearts of human beings that they have a built-in sense that life does have meaning.

- Through patience, wisdom, and prayer, God will use us to help each other *know* Him—not just know *about* Him.

- We are not Christians because we live by a certain set of values or principles. Rather, we are Christians when we enter into a relationship with Christ by acknowledging our sins and asking Him to forgive us and grant us eternal life.

- Jesus Christ is the issue, not religion. The question is not "What will you do with religion?" but "What will you do with Jesus?"

- Money problems create more stress on marriage than any other outside threat. Successful couples have resolved to live within their means.

- Happy couples don't feel like they have to perform to be loved.

- The rule of rules for successful marriage is this: After God, but before all others, make each other your top priority.

DIFFERENCES IN COMMUNICATION

My dear brothers, take note of this: Everyone should be quick to listen, slow to speak and slow to become angry.
JAMES 1:19

"*D*o you think it's okay for Jamie to ride his bike to the bowling alley?" she asks.

"Yes, I think that will be fine," he responds.

Twenty minutes later. "Are you sure you think it's okay? Aren't you worried about him crossing the highway on his bike?"

"No, I think it's fine."

Ten minutes later. "I'm concerned about Jamie riding his bike to the bowling alley."

"Don't worry, everything is all right."

Five minutes later. "Are you sure it's okay?"

"Argh! How many times do I have to tell you? It's okay!"

She withers and slinks away, never to ask again.

This all-too-common scenario plays out in millions of homes each week. What is the dynamic at work in these conversations? The basic problem is that men and women communicate differently and often for different reasons. They have different desired end results in mind.

Men speak to communicate information and facts. For men, communication is rational. Men speak for function. Their communication relates to the real, tangible, physical world all about them, which they are trying to manipulate and control. Men, of course, also express feelings, but their main thrust is information.

Women speak to express feelings, emotions, and inner moods. For women, communication is emotional. Women speak to clarify. Their communication relates to the emotional, psychological, relational world to which they are trying to bring harmony and peace. Women, of course, also communicate information, but their main thrust is feelings.

You can begin to see the potential for miscommunication when man and woman are joined together as husband and wife. When the wife repeats herself over and over again (assuming her husband *is* listening to her), it doesn't mean she didn't hear her husband the first time. Rather, she is trying to discharge the emotional tension that has built up in her heart. Only by going over the matter again and again can she assuage the feelings that make her uneasy. Since communication for her primarily is to clarify, she feels (emotionally) the need to repeat herself.

The husband who understands why his wife repeats herself takes a giant step forward in accepting his mate. The husband who doesn't understand why his wife does what she does will become very frustrated, angry, and will gradually withdraw from her.

When the husband grunts and says he doesn't want to talk about it, he isn't necessarily trying to shut out his wife. What he is communicating is that he believes he has already done everything possible to resolve the matter and sees no need to belabor it. Since communication for him is functional, he thinks (rationally) that there is no need to say more.

The wife who understands why her husband isn't more chatty takes a giant step forward in accepting her mate. The wife who doesn't figure out why her husband does what he does will become very frustrated, hurt, and will gradually withdraw from him.

The key principle is this: Men and women have different needs and purposes in communication. However, when their needs are unmet they experience the same result. They become frustrated, hurt, and gradually withdraw from one another.

DISCUSSION

Both answer: How does today's devotional help you to better understand your mate? Why?

APPLICATION

The next time you find yourself beginning to withdraw from your mate because she repeats herself or he grunts, take a few moments to talk it over. True love will listen.

PRAYER

Either: Dear God, thank You for the wonderful ways in which You have made us different. Help us to be a complement to one another. Help us to appreciate the way You designed our needs for communication. And help us to sacrificially be sensitive to each other's needs in communication. Amen.

BRIDGES

Was it not you who dried up the sea,
the waters of the great deep,
who made a road in the depths of the sea
so that the redeemed might cross over?

ISAIAH 51:10

bridge *n.* 1. A structure spanning and providing passage over an obstacle. 2. Something resembling or analogous to a bridge.

In a primitive land, far away and long ago, villagers placed slabs of stone in the stream to get over to the other side. Thus began the first bridge. To build a bridge is a most natural thing to do.

For as long as people have been separated they have been trying to bridge the gap. To get connected. To come together.

Branches laid across a stream. Timber, stone, and brick. Concrete, iron, and steel. Long suspension bridges, and arch, and girder. The Golden Gate Bridge. Brooklyn Bridge. "Bridge Over Troubled Waters." *The Bridges of Madison County. The Bridge Over the River Kwai.*

Bridges that span deep gorges. Bridges across wide rivers. Bridges over the bay. Train bridges. Covered bridges. Car bridges. Foot bridges. Bringing people together.

When I was in Army infantry training we learned that troops can't go wherever they want. They have to find the bridge. If the enemy wants to control passage, they guard the bridge. If we want to cut them off, we blow up their bridges.

Walls are everywhere, but so are bridges. Whether you build a wall or a bridge depends upon your purpose. Do we want to let our mates in, or keep them out?

The motivations to build a wall are fear, anger, and disappointment. The motivations to build a bridge are the desire for intimacy, to give and receive love, and to have a friend. Walls keep us apart; bridges bring us together.

The most important bridge in marriage is communication. Words are the slabs of stone in the stream that get us over to the other side. Listening is the bridge that draws our mate over to us. Whatever obstacle we may have in our marriages, it is communication that spans the gap. Let the redeemed cross over to one another.

A marriage without walls is a marriage with bridges. Walls artificially keep us apart, but to build a bridge is a most natural thing to do.

DISCUSSION

Both answer: Do you agree that the most important bridge in marriage is communication? Why or why not?

APPLICATION

From your perspective, describe the communication bridge between you and your mate—how wide, how long, how sturdy, how well repaired? Now describe what you would like the bridge between you to look like. In this section of the book you will find the building materials to build the bridge you want.

PRAYER

Both: Lord Jesus, thank You for building a bridge between us. We sense that we have (or are beginning to have) a marriage without walls, a marriage that is constantly getting better. Show us where the bridges are washed out. Show us where to make repairs. Show us where new bridges need to be built. We ask this in Your name. Amen.

TWO TOOLS TO TEAR DOWN WALLS

Do not let any unwholesome talk come out of your mouths, but only what is helpful for building others up according to their needs, that it may benefit those who listen.

EPHESIANS 4:29

*I*n my experience working with men whose marriages face problems, there are two perennial problems couples face in meeting each other's needs.

- *Time*: First, we don't carve out enough time just to be with each other.
- *Talk*: Second, when we are together our talk is not meaningful.

The first problem is not what happens when we are together, but that we are not together enough. This is the problem of *time*. One or both of us is not making the relationship a top priority.

Second, when we are together we don't connect. This is the problem of *communication*. A failure to communicate constitutes the number one marriage problem cited by most marriage surveys. Even when we are together we are often not really "together."

The wife or husband with a "time and talk" deficit will inevitably feel like his/her emotional bank account is empty. The principal value of "time and talk" is that it fills our mates up with emotional love. These actual comments by wives from a marriage survey I conducted illustrate the emotional neglect many wives feel, even when they rate their marriages as good or great.

- "I feel taken for granted."
- "I am never shown that I'm important."
- "I feel like he is on another planet—he has to be told how I feel."
- "I am vulnerable to attention by others who make me feel desirable."
- "My personal needs don't seem important."
- "I need to feel like my mate really sees and recognizes my strengths—others do!"
- "My mate pulls me down rather than builds me up."

Women need emotional love, not just physical love. Husbands do, too, they just don't recognize it so readily. The things we say and do when we make room for "time and talk" fill the emotional bank accounts of our mates.

The concerns wives express are basically always the same, no matter how good or bad their marriages: Not having enough time alone with their husbands, a lack of meaningful conversation, stress from money pressures, little intimacy in sex, no help around the house, not enough help raising the children, and so on.

There is, however, one major difference between a good and bad marriage. Wives in the best marriages say that even though they have struggles, they can communicate with their husbands. In other words, though a wife in a good marriage may struggle with the same problems as any other wife, her husband's willingness to communicate compensates. They work it out. Consider the answers wives gave to these questions: "How would you rate your marriage—poor, average, good, great, or superior? Why?"

- "Superior: We have known each other a long time and understand one another very well. We stick together no matter what."
- "Great: We are close because of our faith, because we laugh and kid each other, because we share almost everything with each other."
- "Good: There are some areas yet to deal with, but we do communicate and have a healthy, fun marriage."
- "Average: We can have fun together but it is all superficial. I'm tired of forty years of chitchat."
- "Poor: No communication."

The better the communication, the better both of you will feel about your marriage, even if you can't explain exactly why. Spend time together and talk things over. Do this, and watch the walls come tumbling down.

DISCUSSION

Both answer: Do you spend enough time together? Why or why not? When you spend time together, do you communicate well? Why or why not?

APPLICATION

Both: Pick one activity you can sacrifice this week and give the time to your spouse.

PRAYER

Either: Our Father and our God, thank You for the time together and conversation we are able to have during these devotionals. We pray that You will direct us to fill each other up with emotional love by the time and conversation we invest in each other. Amen.

FRANKNESS

There is a time for everything,
and a season for every activity under heaven: . . .
a time to be silent and a time to speak.
                                        ECCLESIASTES 3:1, 7

*I*n a television interview about her marriage, I heard Ruth Graham quote a Chinese writer and philosopher, saying "In the West, in America, marriages start at a boil and gradually cool off. In the East it starts cool and gradually reaches a boil."

Why do our marriages cool off? When we dated our mates we shared every dream, every hope, every aspiration. We also shared our fears, our doubts, our worries. We were fervently interested in each other. What happens as time passes?

In his jewel of a book, *To Understand Each Other*, Paul Tournier writes that the single most frequent fault he sees while counseling marriages is a lack of complete frankness. Behind the marital difficulties he invariably sees a lack of mutual openness, a loyal and total openness to one another. As he points out, we cannot understand each other if we have begun to hold back.[3]

Why do we begin to hold back? Over time two great fears that we all have begin to seep into the marriage. First is the fear of being judged or criticized.[4] After a few years faults appear that love's first blush concealed. As our mate mentions these blemishes we are hurt. We begin to withdraw. And we see their faults, press them, and they withdraw. No one likes to be criticized, especially for something they cannot change. (We'll discuss the fear of criticism at greater depth in the next devotional.)

The second fear is that of receiving advice. When the wife, for example, too quickly gives a ready-made answer to her husband's business problem, he may feel she simply does not understand the complexity of the situation. He wanted to talk through a delicate problem, but she short-circuited communication by replying too quickly. Often it's simply best to console each other without words at all.[5]

People are without exception more sensitive than we first think. Men are often hurt as easily as women, though we men try to hide it.[6]

Has a lack of complete frankness seeped into your marriage? Have you been too hasty in making reply? Here is Tournier's solution. Give it a try:

In order really to understand, we need to listen, not to reply. We need to listen long and attentively. In order to help anybody to open his heart, we have to give him time, asking only a few questions, as carefully as possible, in order to help him better explain his experience. Above all we must not give the impression that we know better than he does what he must do. Otherwise we force him to withdraw. Too much criticism will also achieve the same result, so fragile are his inner sensibilities.[7]

What makes a marriage boil? Conversation, affection, interest, time, and a willingness to listen—really listen. Remember, it's a whole lot easier to bring a pot back to a boil than to start over with a cold pot. Listen attentively, and watch the temperature rise.

DISCUSSION

Both answer: Do you feel there is a high level of frankness and openness in your marriage? Explain your answer. If the answer is "No," what would it take to achieve greater openness?

APPLICATION

Based upon your mate's answers to the discussion questions, evaluate the following:

- Do you reply too quickly?
- Do you listen attentively?
- Do you judge and criticize your mate?
- Do you give your mate advice where you shouldn't, or do you give it too quickly?

Commit by God's grace to make appropriate changes.

PRAYER

Each, as appropriate: Dear God, I had no idea how much I have cut off frankness and openness in our marriage. I am grieved by what I have learned about myself. Help me, O God, to be the kind of husband/wife to whom my mate will be eager to open up. Restore the joy of our early days together. May You receive praise and glory for the changes I now commit to make. Amen.

THE FEAR OF CRITICISM

Do not let any unwholesome talk come out of your mouths, but only what is helpful for building others up according to their needs, that it may benefit those who listen.

EPHESIANS 4:29

*W*hat's wrong with this picture? It has been a long day. He has had many disappointments. He looks forward to getting home and kicking back. When he walks through the door he observes that the house is a wreck. "Why can't you keep this house clean? You are not a very good housekeeper." She just got home from work herself and remembers how he agreed last weekend to help more with household chores. She's hurt and feels the bile of anger rising in her throat.

What's wrong with this picture? She writes the checks to pay the bills. He thought it would be good for her in case anything ever happened to him. But the money just doesn't seem to go far enough. She struggles month after month to make ends meet. Finally, in exasperation she cries out, "You are not making enough to pay our bills. Why can't you make more money?" His heart sinks, and blistering words form on his tongue.

The trouble here in both "pictures" is that the focus is on the *person* rather than the *problem*. A first principle of counseling is never to criticize or judge the other person but, rather, to express how the event or situation makes you feel. Criticism threatens; discussing your own feelings is nonthreatening. We each fear criticism from our closest companion. It is tantamount to rejection.

Husband, telling your wife she is not a very good housekeeper is an attack on her competence. It claws away at her self-worth. Nevertheless, you still are upset by a messy house. Instead of criticizing, express how seeing the house that way makes you feel. "Honey, when I come home from a long, hard day at work and walk into a cluttered house, it really makes me feel irritable. How can we solve this together?" Notice how the focus is transferred from her perceived shortcoming to how it makes you feel. This approach helps remove the emotionally charged atmosphere and allows for mature dialogue over the subject.

Wife, to tell your husband he isn't making enough money is a blow to his confidence and, said often enough, will break his spirit. Nevertheless, you are still concerned about finances. Instead of criticizing, express how it makes you feel when there is still month left over at the end of the money. "Honey, when I can't seem to ever get these credit card bills paid off, I feel so frustrated—even worried. Is there something we can do together to solve this?" Do you sense the release of tension in this approach? Open, nonthreatening communication in which you both do not fear criticism will lead to productive solutions.

Finally, never bring up at all something which your mate cannot change. This is an important part of loving unconditionally. For example, she may have fat ankles or he may be going bald. Not only should we not criticize in such cases, neither should we bring up our feelings at all. As today's verse says, "Do not let any unwholesome talk come out of your mouths, but only what is helpful for building others up according to their needs, that it may benefit those who listen."

When we criticize each other we drive each other to withdraw. Our wounded mates will not feel like they live in a safe, nonthreatening place. They will keep secrets and protect themselves.

DISCUSSION

Both answer: How do you communicate when there is a problem? Do you criticize, or express your own personal feelings? To what extent do you make your spouse withdraw?

APPLICATION

When you have a problem to discuss, make a conscious effort to distinguish between criticizing the other person versus sharing your own feelings.

PRAYER

Either or both: Heavenly Father, we desire to create a safe environment for each other to express our innermost thoughts and feelings. Help us to speak constructively to each other. Help us to focus on our own reactions and feelings, rather than our mate's behavior. Amen.

THE FEAR OF CRITICISM, PART 2

Do not let any unwholesome talk come out of your mouths, but only what is helpful for building others up according to their needs, that it may benefit those who listen.

EPHESIANS 4:29

*I*n the last devotional we saw the importance of focusing on the *problem,* not the *person.* Two kinds of statements in particular become barriers to open and nonthreatening communication because they focus on the person: "You" statements and "Why" questions. We saw both of these in the last chapter. Let's look at them again:

> Finally, in exasperation she cries out, "You are not making enough to pay our bills. Why can't you make more money?" His heart withers, and a small piece of his courage dies.

> When he walks through the door he observes that the house is a wreck. "Why can't you keep this house clean? You are not a very good housekeeper." She's hurt and feels the bile of anger rise in her throat.

"You" statements and "Why" questions are the very heart of criticism. Let's look at each of them more closely.

1. "You" Statements.

"You" statements feel like an attack while "I" statements keep the focus on the problem. Which of the following would you rather hear?

- "You make me so angry!" or "I am so angry!"
- "You don't love me!" or "I don't feel loved!"[8]

Obviously, none of us likes to hear someone draw a conclusion about how we think or feel, even more so if we disagree with their conclusion. If you tell me, "You are stubborn!" I will revolt and argue back: "I'm not stubborn!" It is a personal attack. But if you tell me, "I don't feel my opinions matter to you," then I am moved by compassion and conviction to respond maturely. Now I want to heal your hurt. Instead of defending my "honor," I feel it is safe to minister to you. You have set me free to respond maturely.

2. "Why" Questions.

"Why" questions are simply "You" statements at a higher volume. Not only does the "Why" question sting like a "You" statement, it demands a response. The emphasis is still on the person, not the problem. Which of the following would you rather hear?

- "Why can't you make more money?" or "I'm afraid because our paycheck isn't covering all of our bills."
- "Why can't you keep this house clean?" or "I feel irritable when the house is messy."

No mate wants to answer a question not asked in love and respect. A question intended to cut and degrade will only provoke your mate to anger. And anger will only lead to an argument or withdrawal.

Learn to avoid "You" statements and "Why" questions. Instead, make "I feel" statements. Then both of you will feel safe.

DISCUSSION

Both answer: Do you agree that "You" statements and "Why" questions are the very heart of criticism? Why or why not?

APPLICATION

Pick one area in which your mate has made you feel hurt or angry. Express how that made you feel without using any "You" statements or "Why" questions.

PRAYER

Both: Heavenly Father, we confess that we have criticized each other. We have focused on the "person" and not the "problem." We have made "You" statements and asked "Why" questions, largely because we have not known any better. Help us, we pray, to use the principles in this devotional to express ourselves in a mature, nonthreatening way that fosters communication. Amen.

The Fear of Receiving Advice

My dear brothers, take note of this: Everyone should be quick to listen, slow to speak and slow to become angry.
JAMES 1:19

*T*he second fear that stifles communication is the fear of receiving advice.

What's wrong with this picture: Supper is over. Her face is long. He asks her, "What's the matter?" She hesitates, then begins to explain how their daughter is being hurt by the barbs of a supposed friend at school. He quickly rolls his eyes, knits his brow, then says, "Honey, that's life. She will have to get used to it sometime. It might as well be now. Besides, it's good training for life. Don't you agree it's better for her to learn these lessons now when she has someone as wonderful as you to console her and show her how to cope?"

What's wrong with this picture: Supper is over. His face is long. She asks him, "What's the matter?" He hesitates, then begins to explain how his boss keeps criticizing his work but never shows appreciation. After two more sentences she enters into the conversation. "I think it's high time for you to start looking for a new job. You deserve better than that! Who does he think he is, anyway? Look at how hard you have worked for that ungrateful man. You have so many excellent skills. You would have no trouble getting a better job."

At first glance, both of these responses seem like reasonable arguments. The major problem, however, is not in the quality of the response but its speed. The mistake in both examples is the overly quick response. Good intentions must be seasoned by wisdom. There is no greater loss than the right advice given at the wrong time.

When he says do this, this, and that, and everything will turn out all right, he misses the purpose of her communication. She isn't looking for a response. She wants to release the emotional tension building up in her heart. She wants to express her feelings. She likely has already handled her daughter well, but the residue of hurt feelings remains. He has missed the signal entirely. She wants consolation, not advice. She will respond to his quick response in one of two ways. She will become verbally angry with him or withdraw from him. And she will think twice before making herself vulnerable again. Eventually, this scene repeated over and over will bring a halt to sharing altogether.

When she gives him a quick-fix formula to solve what he views as a complex problem, she misses an opportunity to be his soul mate. Since she has not listened deeply, he dismisses her advice as shallow, half-baked, and inappropriate. He wants consolation, not advice. He will dismiss her angrily with a wave of his hand, or he will withdraw from her, thinking, *I simply cannot share with her. She doesn't understand. She isn't really hearing me. It's no use trying.*

In both examples the spouse sincerely sought to be helpful but hindered rather than helped. The way to be helpful is to listen without giving advice. It can be taken as a general rule that when your opinion is not asked for it is not wanted. Learn to be each other's soul mate—the one person in whom you can confide, the one person who can share anything with you in safety.

DISCUSSION

Both answer: In your communication with each other, do you feel like you are too quick to respond to your mate? How do you feel when your mate responds too quickly?

APPLICATION

It is difficult to be a good listener, especially if you think you have a helpful answer. We become good listeners by practice. From now on, earnestly try not to respond when your mate begins to share concerns. Instead, listen attentively. Try not responding at all, unless and until your mate asks your opinion.

PRAYER

Either or both, as appropriate: Lord God, we each confess that we have been too quick to respond to each other's sharing. We have given opinions when none were desired. We have offered advice when we really have not understood what was going on. We have angered and hurt each other. Help us, Lord, to listen to each other without feeling compelled to respond. Amen.

LISTEN FOR AND EXPRESS FEELINGS

A gentle answer turns away wrath,
but a harsh word stirs up anger.

PROVERBS 15:1

*T*he brass ring of marriage is intimacy and oneness. The skill that enables us to achieve these lofty goals is the ability to communicate effectively with one another. It is by meaningful conversation that we scale the heights and plumb the depths of marriage. Conversely, if our communication skills are rusty or dull we can get stuck in marital mediocrity.

In addition to being completely frank, not giving quick advice, not criticizing, avoiding "You" statements and "Why" questions, what else can we do to communicate better?

Another important ingredient is to listen for and express feelings. Husband, this comes more naturally for her. Nevertheless, men have feelings, also, but may think it is unmanly to express them. In truth, your wife will never connect her heart to your heart if you only speak to her through your head. You must speak from the heart too. Intimacy is the work of the heart, not the head.

Wife, since you are naturally gifted in expressing feelings, you may not easily understand why your husband can't. It hurts you, and makes you feel angry. Actually, he can speak to you from his heart, but he will never be quite like you no matter what. Learn to accept this.

How can we better listen for and express our feelings?

1. *Listen for feelings.* She says, "I just cannot accept the fact that you can't call me when you are going to be late. What if you were in an accident? How would I know? In fact, I can't understand why you have to be late at all." Normally, he responds, "I'm sorry. I'll try not to let it happen again. Can't we just drop it?" In this case no communication has taken place. The question is, What is the burden in her heart? She feels like she is unimportant, not his top priority, and has not been treated courteously. She is at least mildly angry.

A better response would be, "I guess you feel pretty disappointed with me right now, don't you?" This response opens the gate for interaction, while the first response builds a wall. The idea is to listen for the feelings behind the words. Then ask questions to see if you are reading the feelings correctly. Restate what you think you are hearing in terms of the feelings behind the words. In this way, you have put things in a nonthreatening manner and your mate can begin to dialogue with you to clarify the feelings. This says, "I care for you. How you feel is important to me. I want to be your soul mate. I want to minister to your heart."

2. *Express feelings.* He says, "You never show me any appreciation. I work my fingers to the bone, and all I hear about is how much better off the Smiths down the street are doing." At first blush this looks like acceptable communication, but it is wanting. This statement has a built-in invitation to engage in argument. He would do better to keep the focus on "I" instead of "you." He could say, "I am really feeling unappreciated. When I work hard and don't receive positive feedback at home it makes it all feel worthless. When you tell me how much better off the Smiths are than us, it makes me so angry I want to scream! I feel like I am working as hard as I can."

Discussing facts enables you to connect at the head level. Discussing feelings enables you to connect at the heart level. Connecting at the level of the head will get the task done, but only by connecting our hearts to each other can we become the intimate soul mates of our dreams.

Anyone who wants a more intimate marriage can develop the skills of listening for and expressing feelings. It will keep the focus on connecting your hearts rather than winning the battle of the minds.

DISCUSSION

Each answer: Do you feel like you have been connecting in your communication? Why or why not? If not, how can today's devotional about listening for and expressing feelings help you?

APPLICATION

The next time you are feeling enough emotion to speak about it to your mate, try to express yourself in terms of feelings rather than facts. Keep the focus on yourself and the problem, not your mate.

PRAYER

Either, as applicable: Dear Lord, we have done a good job connecting at the head level. We are getting the task of marriage done. We confess we have not done as good a job connecting at the heart level. We long to be each other's soul mate. Help us, we pray, to listen for each other's feelings and help each other articulate our feelings better. Help us also to express ourselves by keeping the focus on our own feelings and the problems at hand. Amen.

DEEP LISTENING: THE ULTIMATE DEPOSIT

Husbands, in the same way be considerate as you live with your wives, and treat them with respect as the weaker partner.
1 PETER 3:7

*T*hrough the process of writing this book, I have become more and more aware of my own shortcomings in marriage. No area needs more work by me than the area of *deep listening.*

Deep listening means to take an all-consuming interest in building up your mate. It demonstrates that you are "for" your mate. It is the consummate deposit into her/his emotional bank account. It is a desire to understand where your mate is coming from—the motives, unmet needs, and feelings that are also being expressed. It is wanting to know the real meaning behind her/his spoken words. Deep listening is hard work. It takes concentration and a willingness to block out distractions. It is the ultimate expression of concern for your mate. It says, "I care." It cannot take place when we are preoccupied or in a hurry. Deep listening is not something done on the run.

Recently Patsy began expressing some thoughts and feelings to me. After a minute or so she paused, intuitively knowing the length of time I typically wait before offering a comment. However, I simply looked back into her eyes as if to signal, "Yes, I understand. Please continue."

Somewhat surprised, I think, she continued to talk and I labored to listen deeply. After another intuitively timed period she paused again, waiting once more for me to offer a comment. I restrained myself and, after a moment of silence, Patsy continued.

We went back and forth like this several times. Each time I held my tongue but signaled with my eyes that I was interested in what she was saying.

Interruption could easily have made this just another surface conversation. Instead, it became an opportunity for Patsy to clarify and shape deep feelings that she would otherwise not have been able to get in touch with and articulate. She was grateful to see her (until then) inexpressible thoughts find expression. I was grateful to learn about my wife at a deeper level. It gave me a greater appreciation for the quality of her walk with God, the purity of her motives, and the wisdom of her thinking.

We, especially men, can quickly quench the sparks of deep sharing. Whether by a raised eyebrow, hurried body language, a terse reply, an unsolicited piece of advice, or an apathetic display of interest, we can quickly douse the flame of sharing from the depths by our marriage partner. Deep sharing depends upon deep listening.

Men, our wives have things to share. Some of these things are for our mutual benefit. Listen deeply. Other times you may not receive an immediate benefit, but you will have been considerate of her. A dividend will certainly come in the natural course. Your wife is the weaker partner (see today's verse again), but often the wiser. Therefore, respect her. Listen deeply and learn. It will be a wonderful deposit into her emotional bank account.

Wives, most husbands are not familiar with deep listening. He often runs on a fast track and may not know how to go soft or slow. Teach him. Wives, too, need to listen deeply to their husbands. Sometimes you will need not only to be willing to listen deeply, but also to skillfully, gently question your husband to evoke his sharing.

DISCUSSION

Both answer: Do you listen deeply to your spouse? Explain your answer. Spouse, help your mate fine-tune her/his answer.

APPLICATION

The next time you want to share something with your mate, elevate the moment by changing the normal "scenery." You may want to move to the living room, or even go out to dinner! Explain that you have something important to share—that you would appreciate it if you could talk out the problem/feeling/doubt/concern/worry or whatever it is on your mind. Ask for deep listening and for help in thinking it through. Partner, listen deeply.

PRAYER

Either or both: Heavenly Father, thank You for giving me such a wonderful mate. I want to be a good listener, a deep listener. I want to understand my wife/husband. Help me, I pray, to take the time to build up my mate through deep listening. I pledge to do whatever it takes to make these types of deposits into my partner's emotional bank account. Amen.

THE POWER OF WORDS

A new command I give you: Love one another. As I have loved you, so you must love one another.

JOHN 13:34

A woman sent me the following:

> Why can't he say "I love you" to me and the kids? Why can't he at least try to say it? I am greatly disappointed over this. He didn't seem to have a problem with this before we were married. I guess then he realized he had to let me know. I need to hear "I love you." More than anything this has pulled me away from him. I don't feel very happy, satisfied, or loved. I know I sound like a broken record, but if I could hear him say "I love you" on a regular basis it would mean so much to me.

How many wives, and husbands, are there in the world who long for more verbal affirmations of love? Who can tell, but it must be a huge throng.

Most husbands readily admit they struggle with love. They can't see it, analyze it, or explain it. They often don't feel it, and quite frequently have a hard time expressing it. To them love is a mystical, romantic notion that wears off after the wedding day like the gradual retreat of a fragrant perfume.

Wives crave to hear their husbands express feelings of love in words. Without frequent verbal reassurance, wives can begin to doubt if their husbands even love them at all. He may not sense the same need for verbal affirmations of love as does she. This tends to make him assume she must feel the same way he does.

On the other hand, many husbands do express their love by doing kind things for their wives. The husband who surprises his wife with a new television is trying to communicate his love, only not in words.

Wives need to be more alert to the nonverbal ways in which their husbands do signal their love and affection. Properly understood, these kindnesses can be received by the wife as important deposits into her emotional bank account. By the same token, husbands need to verbally express their love often. The relative value of a verbal deposit far outweighs a nonverbal deposit. In truth, wives need both.

And wives, don't neglect expressing your love through words of appreciation for your husband's hard work for the family. As you know from your own work, it's a jungle out there! If he is a help around the house, tell him so. Any word of encouragement means so much to a man, even if he doesn't seem to appreciate it.

Both husband and wife need to know that verbal expressions of love left unsaid are a withdrawal. Not only is a deposit not made, but unspoken love depletes the account balance.

DISCUSSION

Each answer: How often do you express your love for each other verbally? Is it enough? Why or why not?

APPLICATION

Make a concerted effort to tell each other "I love you" at least once each day.

PRAYER

Either: Lord Jesus, help us to love each other the same way that You loved us. Help us to verbally affirm each other by regularly expressing in words the love we feel. Forgive us for the times we have left unsaid what should have been said. Make our nonverbal expressions of love more real to each other as well. In Your name we pray. Amen.

THE MINISTRY OF WORDS

There is a time for everything, and a season for every activity under heaven:
. . . a time to be silent and a time to speak.
ECCLESIASTES 3:1, 7

*W*ords are the window into the soul. Words escort my mate into my inner being, and usher me into her innermost thoughts. Words give form and expression to our deepest thoughts. Words are valuable.

We use words to paint the portrait of our love for each other. "I love the way you do your hair." A few sincere words skillfully clumped together can lift the spirit of your partner high into the heavens. Words are beautiful.

Words capture the raw intensity of our passion. Mark Twain said, "A powerful agent is the right word." Words can be like the pressure valve on a steam cooker that lets off steam. Or the arrow through the bull's-eye that heals a wounded mate. Words are powerful.

Sometimes, though, words don't come. We cannot find the words to express our deepest feelings. Language can be inadequate to get across our meaning. Sometimes the right word eludes us altogether. Other times, it teases us by buzzing around our head, never landing long enough to be captured. And sometimes, the word that comes just doesn't measure up to the beauty of the feeling. Mark Twain also said, "The difference between the right word and the almost right word is the difference between lightning and the lightning bug." Words can be inadequate.

There are times we groan inwardly in joy or sorrow but the right words will not come. Our souls ache with anguish that remain ambiguous, obscure, and inarticulate. Other times, inexpressible joy wells up in our hearts, but air never passes over our vocal cords to form the sounds that capture the moment. Why can't we express our deepest feelings clearly? Why can't we communicate our exact meaning?

Of course, many times we have not developed the categories in our minds to express ourselves. Our vocabularies may simply need expanding. Sometimes, however, our feelings are of such a deep, spiritual nature that words cannot express them.

It is the duty of every husband and wife to know the times they should speak words of encouragement, comfort, challenge, and inspiration to their spouses. We have responsibility for each other's nurturing. It is likewise the duty of every husband and wife to know when to remain silent. There are times of silence when the highest form of love we can express may be a hand laid gently on our mate's shoulder or hand.

When words won't come when you need them, you can still communicate with your mate. Try these ideas.

- Express what you can, acknowledging you have deeper feelings and thoughts you cannot quite reach at that moment. Your mate will appreciate the effort.
- Ask your mate to help you talk out your feelings.
- If you can't express the thought at all, at least identify what the topic is for later reflection and meditation. It may yet come to you.
- Do things that reflect how you feel. If you are ready to explode with love, grab your spouse and hug him/her tight!

Never leave a thought or feeling left unsaid that may build up and encourage your mate. It is the ministry of words. Conversely, never say something better left unsaid. There is a time for everything.

DISCUSSION

Both answer: Do you feel you are able to express yourself to your mate or not? Describe a few topics about which you wish you could better express yourself.

APPLICATION

The next time you have difficulty expressing yourself with words, work through the four ideas mentioned above.

PRAYER

Either: Heavenly Father, thank You for the gift of words and language. Thank You that our language does not always have to be words, but that we can still express ourselves by what we do for each other. Give us, we pray, a more intimate relationship through ministering to each other through our words. Amen.

LET THE LITTLE ONES GO

A man's wisdom gives him patience;
it is to his glory to overlook an offense.
PROVERBS 19:11

- She forgets to write down a phone message. He forgets to phone that he will be fifteen minutes late for dinner.
- He doesn't put the garage door down when he leaves for work. She doesn't mark down the checks she writes in the register.
- She eats more ice cream than he would prefer. He spends more time hammering away in his workshop than she would like.
- He thinks she talks on the telephone too much. She thinks he needs to get more exercise.
- She likes to go shopping, but never calls ahead to see if the store carries the product she wants. He hates to go shopping so he never lends a hand getting groceries or household items.

In every marriage, each day produces many small offenses. A great secret of successful marriage is learning to let the little ones go. The more we must adjudicate every small infraction of our self-styled rules and regulations, the less room we will find for love and affection in our marriage. We should laugh more and legislate less.

We must be patient with one another. Humans are odd creatures. It is not only our partners who are funny ducks at times. We ourselves have many foibles that can grate on the nerves of our mate. We have many weaknesses that our spouse did not see in the early days of the honeymoon. We have many quirks that can be taken as insensitivity.

Wisdom leads to patience—to letting the little ones go. "A man's wisdom gives him patience; it is to his glory to overlook an offense." To grow in our marriage we must grow in maturity and wisdom. Overlooking an offense is not the work of the spiritually immature. Each day we see and read of countless conflicts, most of which would never happen if people would let the little ones go.

Pride leads to impatience. Pride is the fruit of folly. Folly is the opposite of wisdom. The foolish strut about, puffed up in their self-importance, pushing too hard and telling people off. It is better to be humble and let the little ones go.

Notice that this devotional's opening verse says that "it is to his glory to overlook an offense"—the individual's glory, not God's glory. This is a rare occasion when glory is ascribed to people. The principle of overlooking offenses is so important to our Lord that He lets human beings receive glory when they do so. Surely this is not the same kind of glory that God receives, yet nevertheless the wife or husband can receive a type of glory by letting the little ones go.

A great secret to this principle is always to strive to raise the threshold of what you deem "little." In other words, constantly seek to let bigger and bigger offenses become smaller and smaller.

Wife, if his smallest offense that grates your nerves is that he does not put down the garage door, try putting it down yourself and letting it go. You will receive glory.

Husband, if the smallest offense that rubs you the wrong way is that she forgets to call ahead to the store to see if they carry the product she wants, try accepting this as a little one to let go. You will receive glory.

DISCUSSION

Both ask: What are the little things I do that bother you? Both answer: Why do you think we take these small matters so seriously?

APPLICATION

From the matters discussed, pick two or three little things and decide by the help of the Spirit that you will begin to let these go as little ones. Also, make up your mind to intentionally broaden the spectrum of what you call "little things."

PRAYER

Either: Dear Father, forgive us for being so petty, so small, so little. Help us to become more spiritually mature. Help us to let the little ones go. Help us not to be so touchy. And help us to remember what is really important, our love for You and each other. Love covers over a multitude of sins! Amen.

Don't Let the Sun Go Down on Your Anger

"In your anger do not sin": Do not let the sun go down while you are still angry, and do not give the devil a foothold.
EPHESIANS 4:26–27

*E*arly in our marriage, Patsy and I had a horrible argument one afternoon. The following day our next door neighbor sheepishly said to Patsy, "Did you know your windows were open yesterday afternoon?"

Ahh, the embarrassment of anger. What would we do without air conditioning?

Everyone becomes angry, of course. Jesus certainly became angry. In this devotional's theme verse the Bible actually encourages us to be angry. In the King James Version it reads, "Be ye angry, and sin not." The key principle is not that we shouldn't be angry, but that when we are angry we should not sin. We must express our anger constructively, not destructively. Dr. David Seamands offers this explanation:

> Be angry, but be careful. Anger becomes resentful and bitter when you don't know proper ways to express it. This is exactly what happens to the perfectionist who can never even allow himself to express anger; who won't even allow himself to be aware that he is angry. He denies it and pushes it down deep into his inner self where it simmers and festers and comes out in various kinds of disguised emotional problems, marital conflicts, and even in forms of physical illness.[9]

I believe a lot of Christians are a whole lot more angry than they would dare imagine. We believe anger is a sin (it is not), and so we suppress it. We are angry at work, but we suppress it. We are angry at inconsiderate drivers, but we suppress it. We are angry because our friend didn't show up for tennis, but we suppress it. We are angry because our paycheck doesn't go far enough, but we suppress it. Finally, we erupt and dump on our mate because we can't withhold all this anger any longer. Unfortunately, rather than constructively expressing feelings of anger, we lose our temper.

When is our anger sin? Because we don't deal with it constructively, the answer is "most of the time." We do not take advantage of our legitimate opportunities to be angry and instead push down the feelings. Later, we explode at our spouse or children. They, of course, have nothing to do with why we are angry. They are innocent bystanders, caught in the line of fire.

The healthy way to handle anger to keep from sinning is to 1) acknowledge it, 2) think it through, 3) express it appropriately to the offending party or a confidant, 4) turn it over to the Lord as you are able, and 5) go on to the next thing in your life. For some, the reasons for an angry spirit are so deeply entwined with their past that it may require a qualified Christian counselor to help sort through the causes.

How do we sin when we are angry? First, we can lose our temper. There is a right and a wrong way to express anger. Restrict yourself to express-ing—as calmly as possible—how the event or offense makes you feel. (If you can't speak in a normal tone of voice, you probably haven't cooled down enough yet!) Don't yell and berate your mate. Don't attack his/her person-ality. Don't lose your self-control. Wait until you cool down.

Second, you sin when you "let the sun go down while you are still angry." The most explicit biblical instruction about anger is that we never go to bed angry. We must clear the air that same day. An angry person will sleep fitfully. Time lets bitterness seep in. Hearts harden. Positions become inflexible. We cut ourselves off from fellowship with God. Forgiveness is held at bay. Repentance is postponed.

Never go to bed angry. Why give the devil a foothold?

DISCUSSION

Each answer: Are you an angry person? If yes, do you really understand why you are angry? When you are angry, do you clear it up the same day, or do you make it a practice to go to bed angry? How does the verse from Ephesians affect your thinking about that?

APPLICATION

If you have hurt your mate by your anger, ask his/her forgiveness right now. Discuss how both of you can begin to express anger constructively without attacking your mate. Commit to one another to not go to bed angry. Note: If anger is a huge issue in your relationship, why not consider seeking outside help from a trusted friend, pastor, or Christian counselor?

PRAYER

As applicable: Heavenly Father, we desire to never be destructive to one another with anger. Lord, forgive me for expressing my anger in inappropri-ate ways against my beloved mate. Help me, I pray, to express my anger in appropriate ways. If we could have our way we would never go to bed angry with each other. Give us grace as we work toward that end. Amen.

TEN PRINCIPLES FOR RESOLVING CONFLICTS

*I*n other devotionals we've looked at what causes conflicts and how to manage or avoid them. If you can, it is better to drop a matter before a dispute breaks out, but no marriage escapes conflict altogether. Let's look at ten principles for how to resolve conflicts, and in the next chapter we will review a few practical ideas to implement these principles.

1. *Be patient.* "A man's wisdom gives him patience; it is to his glory to overlook an offense" (Prov. 19:11). The best resolution to many conflicts is to never let them get started. It takes two to tango. If your mate wants conflict and you don't, then don't!

2. *Remain calm.* "If a ruler's anger rises against you, do not leave your post; calmness can lay great errors to rest" (Eccl. 10:4). Don't return fire. Be a thermostat, not a thermometer. Everyone gets upset occasionally. If your mate is just blowing steam, let her/him ventilate without getting rattled. If you answer humbly and calmly, there may be no real conflict and the issue will simply disappear.

3. *Listen carefully.* "My dear brothers, take note of this: Everyone should be quick to listen" (James 1:19). Many conflicts result from faulty perceptions of what our mate really said. The best way to listen carefully is to ask a lot of questions. This will help you understand the "real" problem.

4. *Don't respond too quickly.* "My dear brothers, take note of this: Everyone should be quick to listen, slow to speak." (James 1:19). "A man who lacks judgment derides his neighbor, but a man of understanding holds his tongue" (Prov. 11:12). Let things cool off before responding. In the flare of the moment you may say things you will regret.

5. *Speak gently.* "A gentle answer turns away wrath, but a harsh word stirs up anger" (Prov. 15:1). To be gentle is to be considerate and kind; it is not to be harsh, severe, or violent. Let gentleness season your talk. This is a product of patience and wisdom. Don't speak when you are in emotional turmoil. Try taking a walk instead.

6. *Do not speak rashly or recklessly.* "He who guards his lips guards his life, but he who speaks rashly will come to ruin" (Prov. 13:3). *Rash* means marked by ill-considered boldness or haste. Rash responses can ruin a relationship if they become habitual. "Reckless words pierce like a sword, but the tongue of the wise brings healing" (Prov. 12:18). To be reckless is to

take no heed for the consequences. Our words do have consequences which must be considered before uttering them.

7. *Do not escalate the conflict.* "He who covers over an offense promotes love, but whoever repeats the matter separates close friends" (Prov. 17:9). To escalate means to increase in intensity or scope. It is to turn up the volume. Do not bring other parties into your quarrels, whether family members or outsiders, in the heat of the moment. Later, if the conflict remains unresolved you may want another couple or counselor to act as a mediator, but not unless and until you both agree you need outside help.

8. *Do not return injury.* "Do not say, 'I'll do to him as he has done to me; I'll pay that man back for what he did'" (Prov. 24:29). It is the ultimate sign of immaturity to keep score. Jesus says to turn the other cheek. If you cannot, and the offense requires redress, look for resolution, not retribution.

9. *Do not say everything that comes to mind.* "Without wood a fire goes out; without gossip a quarrel dies down" (Prov. 26:20). Many arguments, quarrels, and conflicts continue because we keep thinking of things we wish we had said—and then we go and say them! Put a muzzle on your tongue.

10. *Trust the Lord to solve your conflicts.* "Do not say, 'I'll pay you back for this wrong!' Wait for the LORD, and he will deliver you" (Prov. 20:22). If your conflict is not resolved to your satisfaction, turn to God and ask Him to put the burden of reconciliation on your spouse's heart, or show you where you have erred.

DISCUSSION

Each answer: Which of these ten principles are you pretty good at applying? What is your weakest point?

APPLICATION

Both: Review the ten principles and encourage your mate by telling her/him which ones she/he is doing a good job of applying. Think about what changes you should make in resolving conflicts appropriately.

PRAYER

Either: Heavenly Father, thank You for the way my mate desires to resolve conflicts for Your glory. I ask You most sincerely, Lord, to help me become a more spiritually mature, wise mate when it comes to resolving conflicts. Help me not to have such a short fuse. Amen.

PRACTICAL IDEAS TO RESOLVE CONFLICT

If a ruler's anger rises against you,
do not leave your post;
calmness can lay great errors to rest.

ECCLESIASTES 10:4

*I*n the morning my wife's top priority is to launch our two kids toward school on time. This requires culinary skill in making breakfast and lunches, supervisory skill in keeping the children on schedule, mediating skill to resolve the conflicts of a shared bathroom, and psychological/sociological skill to keep everybody in a good mood.

On the other hand, my top priority in the morning is our family devotions. I believe this is one of the most important investments I can make. But family devotions ended up becoming a point of high tension, because Patsy and the children are on a schedule, but I am not. I made the children late several times, and this became a major friction point between Patsy and me. What were we to do?

Here are some suggestions for ironing out marital conflicts like this one.

1. *Commit to deal with your conflicts head-on.* Every couple has conflicts. If you try to ignore them they will only continue to build up a wall. A callus develops because of repeated friction. The skin toughens and develops a thick layer to protect your body. The larger the callus the more it hurts. It's the same when we ignore friction points between us. "Patsy, could we talk about why family devotions are not working?"

2. *Ask questions to learn how your mate feels.* By asking questions and then listening deeply you can learn 1) your mate's view of the problem, 2) how the problem makes him/her feel, and 3) the intensity of those feelings. "Patsy, I feel like you are angry with me about how I'm leading devotions. What am I doing wrong?" (Keep the focus on how "I feel" and what "I" am doing wrong—not your mate.)

Patsy's response: "I sure am angry. I am responsible for getting the kids to school on time, but you have control of the last, crucial fifteen minutes. And you don't seem to pay attention to the clock."

3. *Restate what you understand your mate to be saying.* "I understand you to be saying that I make you angry because I don't pay attention to what time it is. Is that correct?"

4. *Continue stating and restating yourselves until the issue is clear.* Patsy: "Not exactly. What I am saying is that I don't feel like you respect me when you don't pay attention to when the kids need to leave."

"I understand you to be saying that when I don't pay attention to the time we should end that you feel angry and don't feel like I am showing respect for you. Is that closer?"

"No, still not exactly. It's more that I don't feel like you are taking responsibility for the kids in the same way I do."

"So, I understand that you feel angry because I am not taking responsibility to finish on time. It also makes you feel like I don't have respect for your job in getting them off on time."

"Yes. That about sums it up."

Notice the themes at first were *anger* and *leaving on time*. These were the surface problems. The real problems were *respect* and *shared responsibility*, which were only revealed by going deeper through questioning. Give this a try.

5. *Decide how to resolve the conflict.* Accept your share of the blame, apologize, and ask forgiveness as necessary. "I'm sorry, I can see how I have not been very sensitive. I want to make a commitment right now to end on time. How can we solve this problem?"

Patsy: "Why don't you put that old travel clock you don't use any more—the one with the large digital display—in the drawer of the lamp stand next to where you sit during devotions? You can pull it out and glance at it to make sure you end on time."

"Done."

DISCUSSION

Do you have a predetermined method for resolving your conflicts? Do you think this method is effective? What are its advantages and disadvantages?

APPLICATION

The next time you have a conflict, use the steps in this devotional to resolve it. If it feels awkward, don't worry about it. A few times through and it will become second nature.

PRAYER

Either: Lord, thank You for giving us the ability to communicate and express our feelings to each other. We pray that You will enable us to use these principles to resolve our conflicts in the most positive ways. Amen.

IN SUMMARY

*T*he single most important skill in building a harmonious marriage is the delicate art of communication. Hopefully this section has informed your mind and inspired your heart to seek more frequent, deeper contact with each other. Let's review what we have learned.

DIFFERENCES IN COMMUNICATION

	Men	*Women*
Main Thrust	Information	Feelings
Principle Use	Transmit info, data, facts	Express feelings, emotions, moods
Main Purpose	Function	Clarify
Relate To	Physical world	Relational world
Starting Point	Rational	Emotional
Irritating Tendency	Grunting	Repeating

BARRIERS TO COMMUNICATION

The single greatest obstacle to understanding each other is a lack of complete frankness. This is brought about by two fears:

- The fear of criticism
- The fear of receiving advice

GATES THROUGH THE WALL

The two main gates to good communication are listening and speaking and, more specifically, being "quick to listen and slow to speak." We developed the following eight principles for effective communication:

Listening:
1. Never give an overly quick reply.
2. Listen for feelings.
3. Listen deeply by asking questions.

Speaking:
1. Avoid making "You" statements.
2. Avoid asking "Why" questions.
3. Learn to express your feelings with "I feel" statements.
4. Focus on the problem, not the person.
5. Never criticize your mate for something she/he cannot change.

IMPORTANT THOUGHTS

- When a wife repeats herself over and over again, it doesn't mean she didn't hear her husband's response the first time. Rather, she is trying to discharge the emotional tension that has built up in her heart.
- Wives in the best marriages say that even though they have struggles, they can communicate with their husbands.
- What makes a marriage boil? Words, affection, interest, time, and a willingness to listen—really listen.
- We each fear criticism from our closest companion. It is tantamount to rejection.
- Learn to avoid "You" statements and "Why" questions. Instead, make "I feel" statements. Then both of you will feel safe.
- There is no greater loss than the right advice given at the wrong time.
- It can be taken as a general rule that when your opinion is not asked for that it is not wanted.
- The wife will never connect her heart to her husband's heart if he only speaks to her through his head.
- Discussing facts enables you to connect at the head level. Discussing feelings enables you to connect at the heart level. Connecting at the level of the head will get the task done, but only by connecting our hearts to each other can we become the intimate soul mates we dream about.
- Deep listening means to take an all-consuming interest in building up your mate.
- Wives crave hearing their husbands express feelings of love in words.
- A few sincere words skillfully clumped together can lift the spirit of your partner high into the heavens.
- In every marriage each day produces many small offenses. A great secret of successful marriage is learning to let the little ones go.
- The most explicit biblical instruction about anger is that we never go to bed angry.

UNDERSTANDING EACH OTHER

For as woman came from man, so also man is born of woman. But everything comes from God.

1 CORINTHIANS 11:12

*I*n one sense, we have so much in common it is remarkable we don't understand each other better. As Adam said of Eve, "This is now bone of my bones and flesh of my flesh; she shall be called 'woman,' for she was taken out of man" (Gen. 2:23). We are of the same flesh. Not only that, "so also man is born of woman." Every man first lived in the warm safety of a woman's womb.

Warm-blooded mammals, we are of the same species. We are genetically and biologically connected. Every woman receives half her DNA from a man. Every man receives half his DNA from a woman.

Yet, in another sense, men and women are as different as night from day, as beauty from the beast, as sandpaper from silk, as rose from thorn. In fact, husbands and wives are virtual opposites in almost every significant area of comparison—exactly the way God intended. Rather than a disadvantage, our diversity works the miracle of God in the sacred institution of family.

In this section we will explore how to understand each other better. The chart on page 73 compares the differences between husbands and wives. The chapters that follow will unpack the important concepts suggested on this chart.

DISCUSSION

Both answer: Why do you think God made you so different from one another? What are the advantages and disadvantages? In what ways are you alike?

APPLICATION

Study the chart until you begin to see the connections. Notice, for example, how his principal weakness relates to her principal strength, and vice versa.

PRAYER

Either: Lord God, thank You for the wonderful diversity in our marriage. Thank You also that we have so much in common compared to any other creature in Your kingdom. We celebrate our differences—how they complement Your plan for the family. Every good thing comes from You, O God, and we thank You in Jesus' name. Amen.

UNDERSTANDING EACH OTHER
A COMPARISON OF THE DIFFERENCES BETWEEN HUSBANDS AND WIVES

	Husband	*Wife*
1. Because of the Fall . . .	Painful Toil	Painful Birth
	Ground Cursed	Desire for Husband
	Gen. 3:17	Gen. 3:16
2. As a Result,	Task	Relationship
Orientation Is to . . .	Doing	Being
3. Therefore,	Significance	Intimacy
Greatest Need . . .		
4. Resulting	Providing	Nurturing
Principal Activity . . .	1 Tim. 5:8	Titus 2:4–5
5. Creativity Directed	Work	Home
Toward . . .		
6. Principal Concerns . . .	Money, Meaning	Family, Security
7. Deepest Fear . . .	Failure to Provide	Something Happen to Child
8. Principal Struggle . . .	Pressure	Worry
9. Principal Need	To Be Respected	To Be Cherished
in Marriage . . .		
10. Principal Command . . .	Love Wife	Submit to Husband
	Eph. 5:25	Eph. 5:24
11. Disobedience Is . . .	To Hate,	To Resist
	Be Indifferent	
12. Principal Strength . . .	Wisdom	Humility
13. Principal Weakness . . .	Pride	Folly
14. Principal Temptation	Anger	Fear
in Daily Living . . .		
15. The Three	Love	Love
Mutual	Eph. 5:25	Titus 2:4
Commands . . .	Respect	Respect
	1 Pet. 3:7	Eph. 5:33
	Submit	Submit
	Eph. 5:21	Eph. 5:22

HIS GREATEST NEED

The LORD God took the man and put him in the Garden of Eden to work it and take care of it.

GENESIS 2:15

*P*atsy and I took a snorkeling trip while on vacation one year. We had a great time exploring coral reefs and viewing exotic tropical fish. We were by ourselves, but the boat carried several other young couples vacationing together.

After several hours it was time to head back. A fun, full day in the water and sun had mellowed us out. The soft breeze in our faces and the gentle, rocking motion of the sailing catamaran caused eyelids to droop everywhere.

As the vessel anchored in the cove, a small boat headed out from shore to transport everyone to land. Suddenly, one of the men in the other group yelled, "Last one to shore buys dinner tonight."

In an instant six bodies bounded into the water and started splashing away toward the shore, some 300 yards away. Their wives looked at each other with that knowing look and rolled their eyes.

Patsy always marvels at what the male hormones will do to a man! She can't believe how competitive men can get. I tell her it's nothing compared to women's team tennis!

Why do men like to compete so feverishly? Why will they take on almost impossible challenges? What drives a man? A man is driven by his greatest human need—to be *significant.*

Man was made for the task. In the breast of every breathing male beats the pulse of a doer. God has made man with an intense longing to perform meaningful work. "The LORD God took the man and put him in the Garden of Eden to work it and take care of it."

Men strive to make a mark, to live with purpose, to make a contribution, to make a difference. The highest calling of a man is to conquer, to achieve, to excel. There are mountains to climb, seas to explore, and frontiers to master. Men want their lives to count, to be somebody, to do something important.

Men have an innate need to seek after significance. Yet, this need must be balanced against the other priorities in a man's life, like marriage, fathering, church, recreation, and his personal relationship with Christ. Nothing devastates Christian families more than a man's desire to be significant run amuck.

Properly managed, God can use a man's greatest need for great good. The world needs great thinkers, administrators, merchants, engineers, pilots, plumbers, electricians, lawyers, teachers, and technicians. Even more, the world needs great husbands and fathers.

Is it possible for a man to find the total significance he longs for in his family apart from his work? I think not. God put Adam in the *garden* to work and care for it. He put Adam in *marriage* so that he would have a helper in his calling. Together they are to fill the earth and subdue it. A man will not be happy if he does not work at his calling. When we tally a man's contributions we must count the children he raises and the wife he cherishes. But that alone is not enough for a man. Trust me. Wife, help him achieve his significance. As your husband satisfies his longing to be significant, he will bless you for being his encourager and helper along the way.

DISCUSSION

Wife: Is your husband someone who would take the dare and swim for shore? Have you thought before about his need to be significant, as discussed in today's devotion? If not, what have you learned?

APPLICATION

Husband, take a pad of paper and list your priorities. How balanced are your career and family responsibilities? Wife, find an opportunity this week to encourage your husband to fulfill his dream.

PRAYER

Wife: Lord, I can see that my husband has a need to do something significant with his life. Help him to be the best he can be. Help me to be his best cheerleader. Amen.

HER GREATEST NEED

Your desire will be for your husband.
GENESIS 3:16

*I*n the last chapter we saw how a husband's greatest need is his need for significance, to make a difference in the world.

What, then, is a wife's greatest need? Her greatest need is *intimacy.* Intimacy means *I know who you are at the deepest level, and I accept you.* (More on this in the next devotional.)

Let's contrast these two needs: significance and intimacy. First, the need to be significant is a *task* orientation, while the need to be intimate is a *relationship* orientation. This captures the principal distinction between men and women. This doesn't mean that women don't want to be significant or that men don't want intimacy. What it does mean is that given a choice, generally speaking, men will gravitate to pursuing the task and women to pursuing the relationship.

When a woman makes a phone call she may talk for twenty minutes and never ask for anything. When a man makes a phone call, typically he has an agenda, a purpose, something he wants to ask or complete. Women will speak on the phone just to build relationship; men want to know, "What's up?" For wives the relationship *is* the task.

Second, the need to be significant is about *doing,* while the need to be intimate is about *being.* Dr. Larry Crabb says a significant way to describe maleness is "movement." Conquering, achieving, climbing, overcoming—these are words that describe men. Wives are doers, too, but not principally. For wives the key motivation is "nurturing." Words to describe wives? Listening, caring, nurturing, loving, mothering. Men are certainly capable of these traits also, but not principally.

Where does her need for intimacy come from? The need for intimacy is God's design for wives.

Because of the Fall this need was corrupted so that "Your desire will be for your husband, and he will rule over you" (Gen. 3:16). Because of the "corruption," this desire for intimacy must be managed. The Hebrew word *desire* literally means "a desire bordering on disease." In other words, her need for intimacy can make her sick of heart when her husband does not give her enough of himself or manipulates her emotions. Not only can the husband rob the wife of intimacy but, because of the flesh, she herself can fall prey to possessiveness, jealousy, pettiness, and oversensitivity. The wife must manage her need for intimacy by walking in the Spirit.

Husbands, to fail to satisfy her need for intimacy is to fail in love, consideration, and respect. It is sin. We are not separate beings but have been mysteriously fused into one flesh. It is a sin against her, and it is a sin against our own bodies.

Because the wife's greatest need is for intimacy, then the husband's greatest responsibility is to satisfy that need. How? Through mutual love, mutual respect, and mutual submission. The husband can satisfy his wife's greatest need by knowing who she is at the deepest level, and accepting her.

DISCUSSION

(Husband, listen patiently and hold your response.) Wife: How intimate is your marriage? Rank the level of intimacy you feel on a scale of 1 (low) to 10 (high), and explain why you chose that number. Husband: Respond to your wife's remarks in love. What surprises you about her answer? Have you sinned against her? Wife, are there any ways your need for intimacy has made you too self-centered, possessive, or oversensitive?

APPLICATION

Husband, make it a task to move your wife's intimacy rating up by 1 point per month (or whatever time period suits you) until you reach a 10. Wives, encourage your husband as he makes progress.

PRAYER

Husband: Lord, I want to be more intimate with _____ (wife's name). Grant me the courage and wisdom to meet my wife's need for intimacy. Show me creative ways to express my love to her. Help me to fill her emotional bank account. Amen.

Toward Greater Intimacy

"For this reason a man will leave his father and mother and be united to his wife, and the two will become one flesh." This is a profound mystery.
EPHESIANS 5:31–32

*T*he one thing most men lack is the one thing most women want: Intimacy. Why do women want intimacy? Why do men lack it? And what is intimacy, anyway?

Sigmund Freud, after thirty years of research into the feminine soul, said, "I have not yet been able to answer the great question, 'What does a woman want?'" The answer is actually quite simple. A married woman wants to occupy the first place in her husband's life in the same way that she seeks to give him the first place in her life.

If intimacy is the greatest desire of a wife, why then do most husbands lack it? Men often lack intimacy because it is contrary to what is most valued in most men's careers where the spoils go to the field generals—the ones who can get the job done. Task is valued more highly in a man's world than relationship.

Unfortunately, the ambition that drives men to succeed competes directly against the intimacy women desire. Let's be realistic. A man cannot be at the top of the corporate world and be the consummate family man at the same time. That man exists only in fairy tales. In other words, work can be number one or wife and family can be number one, but not both. If husbands are to be more intimate, wives will have to allow and help them to reevaluate their work and success priorities. This applies to career women too.

Just exactly what is this profound mystery called intimacy? Here are several definitions to consider:

- Intimacy means that I know who you are at the deepest level, and I accept you.
- Intimacy is reaching out to understand each other in the face of busy schedules, different personalities, embarrassing secrets, and past hurts.
- Intimacy is a block of time given freely or sacrificially to the one to whom you have made vows.
- Intimacy is opening up to your mate when he/she reaches out.
- Intimacy is being spiritually, intellectually, and emotionally familiar with the deepest nature of your partner in mind, soul, body, and spirit.

- Intimacy is the fusion of two distinct lives headed in two distinct directions into a single journey of one flesh.
- Intimacy with Christ is *communion*; intimacy in marriage is *union*.
- Intimacy is unconditional love.
- Intimacy is 1 Corinthians 13 love.

DISCUSSION

Both answer: Which of the definitions of intimacy is most meaningful to you? Why? Wives: Is intimacy with your husband what you most want in your marriage? Why or why not? Husbands: How does your wife's response make you feel? What has been first in your life, your career or your wife? Why?

APPLICATION

Men, when we don't give our wives first place—because we give our work, sports, hobbies, or some other interest first place—our wives have at least three choices. They can accept second place, press for first place and eventually win, or press for first place until they lose heart. Discuss together which of these three choices (or some other) the wife has made. Husband, what changes are you willing to make to build a more intimate marriage?

PRAYER

Either: Lord, we see seeds of complacency in our marriage. We have not been active enough in seeking intimacy with each other. We have let the good get in the way of the best. Help us to reclaim the level of intimacy we have shared in the past. Amen.

His Principal Activity

To Adam he said, "Because you listened to your wife and ate from the tree about which I commanded you, 'You must not eat of it,' cursed is the ground because of you; through painful toil you will eat of it all the days of your life. It will produce thorns and thistles for you, and you will eat the plants of the field. By the sweat of your brow you will eat your food until you return to the ground, since from it you were taken; for dust you are and to dust you will return."

GENESIS 3:17–19

*L*ife was good. Each new chapter of his career exceeded his expectations. After the children all started attending school, she went back to teaching. Her tender but firm style earned her a "Teacher of the Year" award her second year back. He was proud. Their children blessed them by getting good grades, finding good friends, and generally obeying their mom and dad.

Each of the children received Jesus Christ as their personal Savior and Lord to the deep encouragement of both parents. Each family member faithfully served the Lord, each in a different way.

They owned their own home and were able to purchase a new car for cash. Except for their mortgage they were debt-free. Their investment decisions all seemed to be paying off. Their insurance program alone promised a comfortable retirement. Indeed, life was good.

But even when life is good it is not easy. The pressures at work weighed him down. It was not so much the responsibility itself as the weight of the *knowledge* of responsibility. Demons preyed on his mind when he awakened in the middle of the night. He found it difficult to get people committed to projects. Once they were committed, he found it difficult to get them to follow through. He would plan his day carefully, but because of interruptions he often accomplished very little of his plan by the end of the day.

Sometimes he would be amused at how much toil came with a good life; other times his heart would pine for simpler days.

Keeping a family going is a tremendous challenge—one that can occasionally be terrifying to a man.

The principal activity of husbands is *providing*. It is God's call on the husband to make provision for the needs of his family. In the process of providing for their families, husbands alternate between intoxicating pleasure and excruciating pain. One moment the husband is working on his success, the next moment his survival.

The work husbands do to provide can at times produce a consummate satisfaction. Met goals, well-deserved appreciation, and projects completed on a timely basis yield a deep inner joy. At the same time, providing is not easy. Because of the Fall, "thorns and thistles" obstruct the way. There are grizzly bears, ferocious lions, terrifying tigers, and venomous snakes out there ready to devour a man who accidentally stumbles or, God forbid, wanders off the trail!

Providing is an enormous responsibility made difficult by the Fall. As a result, a pervasive worry often grips a man's heart. Men worry they will not be able to satisfy the wants of their family. Men worry they will not be able to meet their financial obligations. Men worry they will not be loving husbands and fathers. Men worry they will fail.

The great need for husbands is to trust God with their families—to turn their families over to the living Lord. Wives can help their husbands tremendously by understanding that beneath that brave facade of masculine strength is a little boy who sometimes wishes he could chuck the whole thing, or at least hear his daddy say, "Don't worry, son. I'll take care of it for you like I did when you were small."

DISCUSSION

Husband: How heavy is the weight of providing for your family on your shoulders? Do you feel like your wife understands your pressures? Wife: Are you aware of how terrifying it can be to be the provider?

APPLICATION

Some couples have created a lifestyle that puts an enormous amount of pressure on the husband. What changes, if any, should both of you consider that would make providing more of a joy for him?

PRAYER

Husband: My Father, the weight of the knowledge of my responsibilities weighs me down. It is a burden I sometimes can scarcely bear. I want to be a good provider, but it is hard. Help me to depend upon You to provide for my family instead of laboring in my own power. Let me experience deep joy alongside the sorrows of my sweat and toil. Amen.

UNDERSTANDING HIS PRESSURE

For you did not receive a spirit that makes you a slave again to fear, but you received the Spirit of sonship. And by him we cry, "Abba, Father."
ROMANS 8:15

*H*e has missed his quota every month for the last six months. In a special meeting the sales manager raked him over the coals.

The family charge cards register $15,000 in short-term, high-interest debt. For two weeks he couldn't bring himself to open the envelope that contained the payment notice for that stupid luxury car he just had to have. He is juggling a horrendous burden of growing bills and shrinking income.

Because of the pressure he grouses irritably when at home. Since he works so hard the last thing he wants at home are any more pressures. He has reneged on his part in child rearing. He retreats to his television and magazines. He hasn't engaged his wife in meaningful conversation for months. Frankly, he is deeply embarrassed by the whole situation, but doesn't know what to do.

By the time he finally sat down to discuss his concerns with his wife, his head felt like it would explode and his chest was tight and ached from the pressure. He labored to breathe, his blood pressure soared, his pulse raced. Caustic acids churned inside his stomach.

"I am just so tired, so overwhelmed with pressure," he began. "To tell you the honest truth, I'm scared. I've been hiding the truth from you. I don't know where the money is going to come from to keep providing for our lifestyle. I feel like I have let you down, let the children down, let myself down. I just don't think I can hack it. I guess I don't have what it takes."

"Honey," his wife replied, "I don't care if we have to live in a tent. All I want is to have you healthy and back as a husband and father. I knew you were really struggling, but you've always kept things to yourself. I only wish you had told me sooner. We can pull together. We can work this out. You don't have to go through this alone."

Most men are deeply concerned about the image they portray to the world. The world crushes and ridicules runners who fall behind. *Let them whip and beat me, but never let me fall back in the race,* a man thinks. He feels caught in a performance trap. This unhealthy view creates enormous pressure on a man. It would be far better, of course, to run a different race—the race that Paul finished in 2 Timothy 4:7—a race in which everyone can be a winner. But few make the change, even among Christians.

As a result men are afraid. They are terrified that they will not be able to keep it up. Men like to say of this fear that they are "under a lot of pressure." In truth, the pressure men feel is nothing less than raw, naked fear.

A wife can help her husband two ways: First, she can be a nonjudgmental listener while expressing love and acceptance. She can help draw her husband out—get him to open up. She can help him see that God has always brought them through tough times; He is trustworthy. She can help him sense her unconditional love. She can bring him to the foot of the cross where he can cry out, "Abba, Father." He no longer needs to be a slave to fear. He is God's son.

Second, she can suggest and agree to changes that will lower his pressure. She can assure him that his health and happiness are more important to her than a large house and a new car, and she'll support lifestyle changes.

Wives often do not truly understand the pressure and fear their husbands feel. Often husbands skillfully hide these feelings until they're ready to blow. But they can work together to build a healthier, more satisfying lifestyle.

DISCUSSION

Him: Do you feel like you are under a lot of pressure right now? Explain your answer. Her: Do you think you understand the pressure he feels to be a good provider? Can you think of things you or other family members do to increase this pressure? How might the two of you together be able to lower the amount of pressure he feels?

APPLICATION

If you are living under too much pressure, decide together the lifestyle sacrifices you are willing to make to return the husband to his optimum level of joyful productivity in the marketplace.

PRAYER

Him, if it applies: Lord, it is true that I feel like I am under a great deal of pressure. I admit that I have not thought of my pressure as fear, but I can see that this is true. I am afraid. I pray You will enable us to settle on a lifestyle that I can comfortably support. Release us, O Lord, from the desire to always be moving up. Amen.

Her Principal Activity

To the woman he said, "I will greatly increase your pains in childbearing; with pain you will give birth to children. Your desire will be for your husband, and he will rule over you."

GENESIS 3:16

She struggled desperately over the decision about whether to go back to work or not. On one hand, the family really needed the money. College tuition for the kids was not too far off and, besides, what was she going to do with her life when the children were gone? Would anybody still need her when they were off on their own? The thought of not being wanted and useful to her family so disturbed her that she labored to block it from her mind.

She cherished every opportunity to help her children grow. She listened attentively as they rambled on about their friends. She played nurse to all their scrapes and bruises. When their first teenager started liking boys, she relished explaining the ins and outs of courtship. Her shoulder provided the comfort for her daughter's first broken heart.

She took pride in the cheerful home environment she created, a place of rest and retreat for her husband and children. Each day he looked forward to arriving home and flinging his arms around such a loving wife.

The principal activity of wives is *nurturing*. It is God's call on the wife to feed, to nourish, to train, to educate, to sustain, to help grow and flourish. She creates an environment in which every member of the family can meet his/her full potential in Christ.

The wife is like the keel of the family ship, which provides balance and stability in troubled waters. The husband may be the captain of the ship, but it is the wife who keeps the family boat from running aground on rocky shoals.

A wife can experience no deeper joy than when her family is happy and in harmony with God. At the same time, nurturing is tremendous work. Raising children and building a relationship with a husband require diligence, patience, understanding, and faith. Children sass and rebel and disobey. Husbands can be insensitive and selfish and withdrawn.

Nurturing is an enormous responsibility made difficult by the Fall. Women are often gripped with paralyzing fears for their children's safety. Women fear their children will abandon their faith. Women fear there will not be enough money to send the kids to college. Women worry that their husbands spend too much time at work and do not know their children.

The great need of wives is to trust God with their families—to turn their husband and children over to the living Lord. Husbands can help their wives tremendously by understanding that the feminine soul has a certain fragility and must be handled with care. A husband can do nothing greater for his wife than to listen—*really* listen—when she expresses her fears and concerns for the family welfare.

DISCUSSION

Her: In what areas do you feel your nurturing of the family is working well? Where is it not working so well? Do you feel like your husband understands and appreciates your role as the family glue? Him: Have you fully appreciated the tremendous energy your wife expends to keep the family on an even keel? Do you really listen and not half-listen when your wife approaches you about a family matter? Are you aware of the gripping fears that nurturing a family can produce?

APPLICATION

Him: Concentrate on really listening to your wife as she goes about the business of nurturing you and the children. Express appreciation to her vocally the next time you observe her making life better for the family.

PRAYER

Her: Dear Lord, I love the job of nurturing my family, but sometimes I don't feel very appreciated by my husband and the children. Sometimes I feel that I bear the burden of everyone's well-being on my own. Help me to depend upon You for the well-being of my family instead of my own effort. Please help me trust in You alone, and to experience the pleasure of energy well-spent. Amen.

Understanding Her Fear

Have no fear of sudden disaster
or of the ruin that overtakes the wicked,
for the LORD will be your confidence
and will keep your foot from being snared.
                                                    PROVERBS 3:25–26

*W*hen the first baby was born she just knew he wasn't breathing right and rushed him to the emergency room for an overnight stay. When the children crawled around the house she was petrified they would pull a lamp over on themselves.

When they became toddlers she worried that they would be struck by a car. When they entered school she was concerned that they would not be able to make friends. When they started to drive, horrible scenes sometimes played in her mind. A distant siren would make her heart leap into her throat. When they started dating she was frightened they would be victimized by irresponsible dates.

If men as a general rule tend toward anger, then women tend toward fear. The male ego cannot bear to call fear "fear," so instead men say that they are "under a lot of pressure." Women are more honest and realistic. Women call their fear "worry." The "worry" women feel is the same "pressure" men feel, but it is directed in different directions. Men experience their fear in the role of providing, while women experience their fear in the role of nurturing/protecting.

The wife feels responsible to manage the nest and has two principal concerns: the family and security.

The welfare, safety, education, and nurture of her children stand supreme for the Christian wife. She arranges activities. She drives the car pool or drops off the children at day care. She schedules the visits with teachers. She monitors the doctor's appointments. She comforts the downcast. She explains bullies. She wipes away the tears.

The other main concern of the wife is the security of her nest. Whether the family income is $100,000 or not isn't that important to her. Generally speaking, what she wants is the security of a steady paycheck. And if she's married to someone on commission, she may accept it but never fully gets used to it. She doesn't care if the home is a palace, as long as it belongs to her family.

A husband can help his wife in three ways. First, he can learn to accept his wife just as she is. That's exactly what Jesus Christ did. Husbands who chide and demean their wives for worrying would do well to remind themselves that the "pressures" they feel are merely a euphemism for their own raw, naked fear. Give her a break!

Second, a husband can help his wife learn to trust God. The Bible says, "Have no fear of sudden disaster or of the ruin that overtakes the wicked, for the LORD will be your confidence and will keep your foot from being snared" (Prov. 3:25–26). God loves the wife, the husband, and the children. The husband can help his wife to increasingly trust in the character of God.

Third, if the husband will listen to his wife express her fears, the very act of letting her give verbal shape to her fears helps her to exorcise them. God has given husbands and wives to each other to make sacrifices for each other, and listening ranks at the top of the list. To feel understood by just one person is the greatest blessing of all.

DISCUSSION

Her: What are the worries that you find most gripping? How rational or irrational are they? Him: Do you think you understand the worry she feels as she nurtures the family? In what ways have you been insensitive toward her concerns? How can you help your wife make progress in conquering her fears?

APPLICATION

Spend some time praying together for the Lord to release both of you from your worries, pressures, and fears. Place your faith in Him daily to do good and not evil in your lives.

PRAYER

Both: Dear God, I pray that You would work in our hearts to help us *really* know that not even a sparrow falls to the ground apart from Your will. We already know this in our heads, but please plant it deeply in our hearts. Help us conquer our fears so we can love You and each other better. Amen.

THE PRUDENT WIFE

Houses and wealth are inherited from parents,
but a prudent wife is from the LORD.

PROVERBS 19:14

prudent *adj.* 1. Using good judgment or common sense in handling practical matters. 2. Careful with respect to one's own interests. 3. Careful about one's conduct.

What makes a prudent wife? It is that she understands something of how men are, and that she handles her own man well, as this tongue-in-cheek piece from *Anniversary Waltz* by Chodorov and Fields accentuates:

I'll tell you the real secret of how to stay married. Keep the cave clean. They want the cave clean and spotless. Air-conditioned, if possible. Sharpen his spear, and stick it in his hand when he goes out in the morning to spear that bear; and when the bear chases him, console him when he comes home at night, and tell him what a big man he is, and then hide the spear so he doesn't fall over it and stab himself.[10]

A prudent wife is a great blessing to both herself and her husband. She does not chafe at being her mate's helper but rather finds purpose and pleasure in helping him stay in motion. Ladies, we men often tend toward pride and think ourselves more important than we should. Thank you for not finding it necessary to point out at every opportunity that you are the one who keeps the ship on a steady keel! This approach is nothing more than using your faculties of good judgment and common sense to the maximum. It has been said by some that a man's greatest fear is that he will not be a good provider. In truth, most men are terrified that they will not be able to meet the obligations they have taken on by marriage and childbirth. Men will do everything within their power to avoid this fear, including complete denial.

A prudent wife recognizes that her husband is afraid, even though he may look fearless in his battle regalia and war paint. She knows he needs her support in an offhanded, side-door way. He will not take well a frontal assault which constantly exposes his weaknesses and infirmities. Encourage him, and he will bring home the bear, eventually.

Husbands, we must see that we are much too touchy. All such touchiness is born in our pride. A real man must become aware of himself. Through observation and self-examination we must see ourselves as we are—with fears and the pride that keeps us from admitting them—and not as we have re-created ourselves in our imaginations. We are not conquerors—not really. Rather we are more like worms, like dust on the scales, tiny fleas, vapors that appear for a little while and then vanish. We stand naked before God—and our wives. They know us as we are. They are being prudent with us: 1) Using good judgment or common sense in handling practical matters; 2) being careful with respect to one's own interests; 3) being careful about one's conduct.

A prudent wife is a gift from God whom He uses to meet the needs of the husband. She deserves much love and respect in return. She is, after all, a gift, and her responsibilities as keeper of home and family equal his in depth and importance.

DISCUSSION

Husbands: Have you given much thought to the role your wife has played in keeping you going? What are some specific things she does to keep you in motion? Wives: Have you been prudent in the way you have handled your husband? Or have you "man-handled" him instead of using a woman's touch?

APPLICATION

Husband, name several specific things your wife does to "sharpen your spear, put it in your hand," and to make sure you "don't fall on it and stab yourself" when you come home empty-handed. Now, express appreciation to your wife for the ways that she keeps you moving. Wife, name several specific ways in which you have not been gentle with your husband. Purpose to be more prudent—satisfied to play a wise, supporting role.

PRAYER

Her: Lord Jesus, I long to become everything You intend for me as the wife of my husband. Help me to understand him better as he seeks to better understand me. Give me the wisdom to be prudent, and the grace to keep my man in motion. Amen.

HIS DUTY TO LOVE

Husbands, love your wives, just as Christ loved the church and gave himself up for her. . . . In this same way, husbands ought to love their wives as their own bodies. He who loves his wife loves himself.

EPHESIANS 5:25, 28

*I*n the mind of God love is the most important thing. The greatest commandment is to love God. The second greatest commandment is to love people (Matt. 22:36–40). The Living Bible says, "Keep only these and you will find that you are obeying all the others" (Matt. 22:40).

The Bible tells all people to love one another, all people to love their neighbors, all people to love their enemies, and husbands to love their wives.

As great as the emphasis the Scriptures place on loving one another, it is rather interesting that the only specific type of people singled out for direct biblical instruction are husbands. Could that be because task-oriented, world-changing husbands don't naturally gravitate toward demonstrating love? It is also quite interesting that the command for husbands to love their wives is the only "love" instruction upon which the Bible goes into detail. We find that detail in this devotional's verses that shows husbands four ways to love their wives.

1. *As Christ loved the church.* Who is the church? We are—not some building. How did Christ love us? He loved us with intensity. We are His top priority. Everything He did was to build up His bride, the church. Husbands have a duty to love their wives with intensity.

2. *As Christ gave Himself up for her.* How did Christ give Himself up? He lived a life of denying Himself and living for others. He even sacrificed His actual life. He loved us sacrificially. Why? Because we are His top priority. Husbands have a duty to love their wives sacrificially.

3. *As your own body.* To look at some of us this wouldn't appear to amount to much! Think, though, of how we love our bodies—no matter how big the paunch. Think of the time spent in front of the mirror scraping your face with a blunt instrument, scrubbing your teeth, preening your hair, checking yourself out from different angles. "No one ever hated his own body, but he feeds and cares for it" (Eph. 5:29). We do love our bodies, and husbands have a duty to love their wives the same way.

4. *As you love yourself.* At first blush this may seem like splitting hairs with number three. Yet, this is a broader concept. By nature every human has a love of self. It is the instinct which fuels our struggle to survive. We

do have a natural love for self, and husbands have a duty to love their wives the same way.

Husbands have a duty to love their wives by imitating the example of Christ loving His church. In His demonstration, Christ makes the church His top priority. The only way for a man to really love his wife is to make her his top priority, after God, but before all others.

Husband, what is your top priority? Is it your wife? Or have you been too busy changing the world?

DISCUSSION

Husband: If you have made your wife your top priority then you are to be commended. If not, what do you think God wants you to do? What might be standing in the way of making her your top priority?

APPLICATION

Both: Reflect on each of the four ways men are instructed to love their wives. Husband, rate yourself on a scale of 1 (low) to 10 (high) in each area. Wife, encourage and affirm him where you can.

PRAYER

Wife: Lord, I thank You for _____ (husband's name). I pray that you will help me to meet his needs as he helps me to meet mine. Give him the strength and courage to bless his family. Help me to be an encouragement to him as he strives to balance his priorities. Amen.

Husband: Lord, I thank You for _____ (wife's name). I confess that I have not always kept her as my top priority. Help me to love her by imitating the way You loved the church and gave Yourself up for her. Help me to love her as I love my own body and as I love myself. I see that if I am to really love my wife I must make her my top priority. Amen.

HUSBANDS: ANOINTED SPIRITUAL LEADERS

Husbands, love your wives, just as Christ loved the church and gave himself up for her.

EPHESIANS 5:25

*T*oday, let's focus on the word "Christ" in our Scripture passage. Husbands are told to love their wives as *Christ* loved the church—not as the Lord or the Son of Man might. What's the difference? How was it that Christ loved the church?

Many people mistake Christ for Jesus' last name. I'm Pat Morley, he's Bill Smith, and that's Jesus Christ. Actually, Christ is not a name but a title for Jesus, the most frequently used title in the Bible. The Old Testament term is "Messiah." Christ, or Messiah, literally means "anointed one." In the Old Testament there were many types of anointed ones. In the New Testament, as we shall see, husbands become a type of anointed ones.

Jesus loved the church as its Christ, or Anointed One. Since husbands are to love their wives in the same way as the Anointed One loved the church, it will be immensely valuable to know exactly what Jesus was anointed to do.

Christ occupies the classic, threefold office of prophet, priest, and king. In the same way, God has anointed every husband to lead his wife as her prophet, priest, and king. Let's briefly review these three offices:

1. *The role of a prophet.* A prophet represents God to people. In the Old Testament a prophet would face the people and speak. Jesus was a prophet who spoke the Word of God to the people and was, in fact, the Word incarnate. A prophet speaks for God.

A husband is to be the family prophet. He represents God to his wife and children. When his wife is weary and stressed, he calms her with his wisdom. He proclaims the gospel to his family. He provides biblical instruction and training without becoming legalistic. He prepares family devotions and encourages private devotions. He is the arbiter of family values. He insists on regular church attendance. He is a messenger from God to his family. This is a ministry of guidance.

2. *The role of a priest.* If a prophet represents God to people, then a priest represents people to God. In the Old Testament a priest would turn his back to the people and mediate for them before God. Jesus is the High Priest who mediated between people and the Father by the sacrifice of His life. A priest mediates before God.

A husband is to be the family priest. He represents his wife and children to God. He spends time in prayer each day remembering the needs and concerns of his wife. He prays for the salvation of his children. He sets the spiritual temperature in the home. As with all persons redeemed through Christ, he can mediate directly with God for others—in this case for his family. This is a ministry of understanding.

3. *The role of a king.* A king takes responsibility for the welfare of his people. He provides both justice and mercy to his people. Jesus is a king from the line of David. David ushered in a golden age for his people. Under his leadership Israel knew its most prosperity, its greatest military strength, its best culture, tremendous religious reform, and became a major world power. A king provides for his people.

A husband is to be the family king. He provides for the needs of his family. He works diligently to earn enough for food and shelter. He administers discipline with fairness. He quickly forgives and overlooks offenses. He acts in a manner worthy of receiving honor. He treats his wife with consideration and respect. He is careful not to be harsh with her or to frustrate his children. He is a provider for his family. This is a ministry of blessing.

In the same way Jesus is the anointed leader of the church, husbands are to be the anointed spiritual leaders of their wives. God has anointed you to lead your wife as her prophet, priest, and king.

DISCUSSION

Both: Jesus was the Christ, the Messiah, the "Anointed One." As such, He loved the church as its prophet, priest, and king. What are some practical ways a husband can be a prophet, priest, and king in his relationship with his wife?

APPLICATION

Husband, select one of the three roles discussed in which you desire to improve. What is one change you would like to make in that area?

PRAYER

Him: Lord Jesus, Messiah, thank You for the roles You play in our lives—prophet, priest, and king. In the same way, help me to provide guidance to _____ (her name), increase my understanding of her needs, and be a blessing to her. Help me to be a successful messenger, mediator, and provider. In Jesus' name I pray. Amen.

THE NATURE OF SUBMISSION

Do not be a man who strikes hands in pledge
or puts up security for debts;
if you lack the means to pay,
your very bed will be snatched from under you.
PROVERBS 22:26–27

*T*he economy had gone sour, and Ed's business failed. In the aftermath of cleaning up, he had to negotiate with a creditor over a $12,000 outstanding debt for which he had personal liability.

The only substantial asset Ed and Betty had left was their home, which had significant equity. The creditor demanded that Ed and Betty execute a second mortgage on their home and both sign personally on the promissory note. This meant that if the $12,000 was not repaid on schedule the creditor could not only foreclose on their home but also sue both Ed and Betty personally for repayment.

Betty was deeply troubled by all of this. She had never been involved in the business. The thought of losing her home grieved her spirit. Early one morning she walked to a small pond near their home. She cried out to God, asking for His guidance. Tears began to flow. She sobbed for a long time. She told the Lord that if He wanted her to sign the note and mortgage that she would.

When Betty returned home she told Ed that she felt impressed by the Lord not to sign the note. No amount of pleading moved her.

Ed scheduled a meeting with the adamant creditor and told them, "I'm sorry, but my wife simply refuses to sign a mortgage on our house. I don't know what else to do."

With that the creditor ranted and raved for a while, threatening to put Ed into bankruptcy. After ventilating, he settled for a simple note without security. Over the next two years Ed was able to satisfy the debt completely.

For twenty years Betty has lived with a sense of guilt that she had not been submissive to her husband in this matter—even though the outcome had been a blessing to her husband.

The Greek word for "submit" is *hupotasso*. The clear meaning of this word is to subordinate or to obey. It is used in Scripture to establish who has the authority. Submission to God (see James 4:7) and to one another (see Eph. 5:21) is a foundational concept of the Christian faith.

The Bible further amplifies specific relationships in which people are to submit, perhaps because submission is more difficult there. Included are servants to masters (or employees to employers), children to parents, all people to rulers and authorities, and wives to husbands.

There are no exceptions to submission, but what on the surface appears as resistance may well be submission. For example, a submissive employee is not a "yes man" who blindly obeys. Instead, he looks out for the best interests of his employer. In the same way, a submissive wife is not a servile doormat who blindly follows her husband. Instead, she looks out for the best interests of her husband. She uses her good judgment to advance the cause of her husband. As Larry Crabb has said, "A 'submissive wife' is one who takes all her resources and, understanding the unique opportunity of femininity, uses them to bless her husband."[11] Sometimes this means firmly reminding him of God's ways. This kind of active submission benefits the husband, even when he cannot immediately see it.

Actually, Betty was perfectly submissive to Ed in refusing to sign that note and mortgage. The Scripture says that we should not strike our hands in pledge or put up security for our debts, for if we cannot pay they will snatch our beds out from under us! In other words, Betty had listened to the Word of the Lord and benefited her husband by directing him away from an unwise decision.

DISCUSSION

Both answer: What has been your view of submission? How does today's devotional "stretch" your thinking? Can you think of an example in your relationship that on the surface seems to be resisting, but which on further reflection is actually submitting for the benefit of the husband?

APPLICATION

The next time you disagree about the best course to follow, examine whether the wife is simply following her own ideas or is in touch with the heart of God on the matter. This will help you solidify this concept.

PRAYER

Her: Lord God, in my heart I desire to be wholly devoted to You and to my husband. I know that to do this I must submit myself to both You and him. Give me, I pray, the wisdom and grace to understand what it means to submit and the power of Your Spirit to do it. Help me to benefit my husband in everything we do. Amen.

TO RESPECT HER

Husbands, in the same way be considerate as you live with your wives, and treat them with respect as the weaker partner.
1 PETER 3:7

*I*t was going to be the first time Patsy had met my parents. As a potential life mate, Patsy broke all the records as far as I was concerned. She was perfect! My nerves were a bit on edge, though, as to whether Mom, Dad, and my brothers would see it the same way. Hands clammy, I opened the door of my family's home.

"Mother, this is Patsy. Patsy, this is my mom. What's for dinner?"

Things went well, or so I thought. Driving back to her apartment, Patsy pointed out that I spoke disrespectfully to my mother several times during the evening. I had been totally blind to this, but I soon saw what she meant. Patsy will tell you today that I never did it again.

Patsy was right to be concerned. How I treated the most important woman of my youth was sure to affect how I treated the most important woman of my manhood.

The Bible tells the husband to "respect" his wife as the weaker partner. The Greek word for respect means "to value, to esteem to the highest degree, to give honor, to show dignity."

Why did God think it necessary to point this out? In history the weaker party has always suffered at the hand of the stronger. "Might makes right." Generally speaking, the wife is the *weaker partner*—the Greek word literally means "strengthless." This Greek word can be used in various applications, but surely the first thing that comes to mind is physical strength.

We each have a place in our mind that Carl Jung called "the shadow." It's a dark place where every sort of sordid thought lurks. The Bible calls it the flesh. When we meet someone new we want to impress him or her, so we keep our shadow in check. But familiarity often breeds complacency, if not contempt. Once married the social checks and balances of unfamiliarity don't exist. Life is up close and personal. The tendency is to live by the Spirit in public but walk in the flesh in private. When this happens the stronger partner lords over the weaker.

Because a wife is usually the weaker partner, God defends her. He says, "Treat her with respect, give her honor, show her dignity." How can a husband show respect to his wife? Here are five suggestions.

1. Never force your wife to do anything because you hold a physical advantage.
2. Consider your wife as better than yourself (Phil. 2:3).
3. Worship your wife. Not in the same sense as we worship God, of course. Little "w" versus big "W." The Greek word for "worship" paints one of the most beautiful word pictures in all Scripture. "Worship" comes from the word meaning "to kiss, as the way a dog licks his master's hand." Oh, the affection from a dog! So be it from husbands to wives.
4. Honor your wife privately and/or publicly, as she prefers. To compliment or pay tribute to your wife for her fine qualities will fill her emotional bank account to overflowing. Be sure to not embarrass her. I know Patsy does not like to be complimented lavishly in public.
5. Bless your wife by your everyday actions. Listen to her as attentively as you would to your boss. Ask her to do things the same way you would ask a respected peer. Don't treat secretaries and waitresses with the kindness reserved for royalty, and then treat your wife like a servant.

DISCUSSION

Both answer, wife first: Does he treat her with respect as the weaker partner? Give an example. Don't be combative.

APPLICATION

Husband, which of the five suggestions for how to respect your wife do you need to work on? Write them down, tape them to your mirror or stick them in your Bible, and commit to treat your wife with respect.

PRAYER

Him: Lord, I confess that I have let familiarity breed complacency and have not shown my wife the respect she needs and deserves. By faith I now commit to never force her to do anything simply because I am stronger and "I said so"; to consider her as better than myself; to worship her; to honor her; and to bless her in my everyday actions. In Jesus' name. Amen.

THE OVERARCHING GOAL: ONENESS

For this reason a man will leave his father and mother and be united to his wife, and the two will become one flesh.
EPHESIANS 5:31

oneness *n.* 1. The state or quality of being one. 2. Uniqueness: singularity. 3. The condition of being undivided: wholeness. 4. Sameness of character. 5. Agreement: unison.

In their highly acclaimed marriage seminar, the FamilyLife Ministry of Campus Crusade for Christ makes "oneness" the centerpiece of their teaching. "Oneness" forms the thread of continuity in Larry Crabb's book *The Marriage Builder* as well.

Oneness captures in a single, pregnant word the overarching goal of a Christian marriage. Oneness marks the summit of marital union. It is the peak toward which we climb. It is the idea that summarizes scriptural teaching on marriage: "And the two will become one flesh."

Oneness is a state of harmony in which the husband and wife lovingly meet each other's needs and fulfill God's purpose for their marriage. Oneness is the sublime state of marital union that is the goal of every newlywed. Oneness is to make a third entity of two who forsake themselves for each other. Oneness is symbolized by the formula on my wedding band: "$1 + 1 = 1$." Oneness means that through all we'll be one.

Unfortunately, after the honeymoon these poetic thoughts often get packed in the attic with all the unusable wedding gifts. Noble ideas take a backseat to jobs, mortgage payments, starting a family, and busy calendars. Why does the honeymoon end? It ends because the self-sacrifices we are willing to make for our mate cool off. The prize is won. There are other mountains to climb. The routine is demanding. The body is tired. The tongue is loose. Selfishness sets in. The "one" becomes two again. The marriage knot unbraids.

The question is, how can two distinct people from two distinct backgrounds with two different sets of needs, priorities, drives, and motivations make one life together?

The difference between a great marriage and a poor marriage is the degree to which each partner is willing to meet the appropriate needs of the other. According to a survey I conducted, in marriages people rated "average" compared to "good," these characteristics seemed to boil to the surface: lack of connectedness; lack of respect; lack of cooperation; independent; on different tracks with different goals and a different way of thinking about things.

The secret of oneness lies in the biblical command to deny ourselves, take up our cross, and follow Jesus. To really love someone—anyone—requires self-denial and sacrifice. Compromises must be made. Unless we have our cross in hand, these self-denials, sacrifices, and compromises create petty resentments and bitterness.

When both the husband and wife are committed to sacrificially loving and serving the other, a fantastic oneness—as becoming one flesh—occurs.

Have you ever said (*really* said), "I will give up what I want to meet the needs of my life mate"?

DISCUSSION

Both answer: Do you agree that the overarching goal of marriage is to create oneness? Why or why not? In your mind's eye, which direction do you see your marriage headed:

1. The two are becoming one.
2. The one is becoming two.

APPLICATION

Have you ever said (*really* said), "I will give up what I want to meet the needs of my life mate"? If yes, congratulations! Keep up the good sacrifice. If no, why not say so right now out loud to your mate in your own words.

PRAYER

Either: Lord, I can see from Your Word that oneness is the ultimate, desired end result for marriage, that it captures what a biblical marriage is all about. Help us to move toward each other in a greater way. Help us to do this with giving in mind, not getting. Help us to live more sacrificially for each other. Help us to become one flesh in the deepest sense. Amen.

HIS NEEDS, HER NEEDS

However, each one of you also must love his wife as he loves himself, and the wife must respect her husband.

EPHESIANS 5:33

*I*n the last devotional chapter we developed the thought that oneness is the overarching goal of marriage. We based the conclusion on Ephesians 5:31, "The two will become one flesh."

The next verse (32) notes that this is a profound mystery, this oneness. This devotional's verse shows us the "action consequences" of becoming one flesh with each other. In other words, as a result of our marriage God wants us to do something for each other. Marital oneness may be mysterious, but while we're trying to figure it out, we can still be doing something: He wants us to meet each other's needs.

Love and respect are umbrella concepts which summarize meeting all the needs of both husband and wife. Love your wife, and you will find you are meeting all of her needs. Respect your husband, and you will find you are meeting all of his needs. What are those needs?

In his skillfully written, highly readable book, *His Needs, Her Needs*, Willard Harley identifies five needs wives tend to have and five needs men tend to have. Her needs are identified as affection, conversation, honesty and openness, financial support, and family commitment. His needs are identified as sexual fulfillment, recreational companionship, attractive spouse, domestic support, and admiration.[12]

Wives and husbands basically have the same needs, of course. The difference is in the degree of importance each attaches to a particular need. What other needs—or variations of needs—can you think of in addition to Harley's list? Here are some ideas:

Her

Emotional, romantic love
Nonsexual touching
Intimacy: to really know her husband
Security: home, income, and retirement
Understanding her needs
Help around the house
Time with husband
Help with the children

A soul mate
Flowers, glances, looks, smiles, eye contact,
    winks, "I love you"

Him
Physical love: wife takes initiative too
Hugs and kisses
Understanding
Respect
Trust
Significance
Intimacy
A confidante
Orderly, clean home
Humor
Glances, looks, smiles, eye contact,
    winks, "I love you"

The degree of harmony in a marriage will be in direct proportion to ways in which these needs are met or not met. These are the items we should put on our "do lists" to make each other happy.

DISCUSSION

Both answer: From the lists of needs mentioned, which ones are best being met for you? Which ones would you like your mate to concentrate on improving?

APPLICATION

Both: Write down your spouse's answers—the needs you have met (for your encouragement) and those needs you have not met (so you can work on them). Try to do one thing today that demonstrates you are genuinely interested in meeting your mate's needs.

PRAYER

Either: Heavenly Father, thank You for the unique way You have crafted our lives to have needs that can only be met by each other. Thank You for the ways my mate meets my needs. Help us both to "do" better. Lord, we commit to meet each other's needs for Your glory. Amen.

EMOTIONAL VERSUS PHYSICAL LOVE

Let him kiss me with the kisses of his mouth—
for your love is more delightful than wine.
                                    SONG OF SONGS 1:2

*T*hough he never said so aloud, he felt like he could never satisfy her. She was almost clingy. She seemed to need constant reassurance. She wanted to talk about everything. She worried excessively about trivial matters. She wanted him to cuddle and whisper sweet nothings.

His career demanded maximum concentration. By the end of a typical day he was mentally and emotionally exhausted. He wanted rest and relaxation, not conversation. He needed some space. He was confident and self-assured, so he couldn't understand her need for constant reassurance. His family never made showy displays of affection, and he chafed whenever she suggested they spend time embracing or touching in a nonsexual way. Though he would certainly confess his love for her if asked, he just couldn't bring himself to volunteer it.

She was hurt that he was not more demonstrative. She needed more affection, but began to believe she was never going to get any from him. Problems from her work and with the children troubled her, and she yearned to resolve them by talking things out. But he was too busy for that. She found her sexual interest in him decreasing.

He resented that his wife had become disinterested in sex. He felt he always had to be the initiator. He assumed she didn't like sex and wanted only to do the minimum to get by. This spilled over into the way he felt about her on a day-to-day basis. Resentment gave way to anger; anger became bitterness.

Over a period of years he cut her off emotionally, and she 'cut him off physically. It created a cold, vicious down draft.

There are two kinds of romantic love: *emotional* and *physical*. Both husbands and wives need both kinds of love. However, the priorities are different. A wife needs to be loved emotionally so that she can love physically, while a husband needs to be loved physically so that he can love emotionally.

The husband has a raw, sexual energy that is unlike that of a woman. It is impulsive, quick, sudden, intense. The husband views sex the way he views everything: It is an *event*.

The sexual desire of a wife comes bubbling forth from the deep wells of intimate sharing with her husband. It is meditative, slow, earned, a by-product of affection and tenderness. As Ed Wheat said, "It's what you do with the entire week that determines the quality of your love life."[13] The wife views sex the way she views everything: It is a *relationship*.

For him sex is an event; for her sex is a relationship. He wants to have sex as another task on his checklist, while she wants to have sex in the context of their relationship. He says, "Let's make love, and then we'll talk about it." She thinks, *Let's spend time learning to really know each other, and then make love to celebrate.* You can see the potential for trouble.

Sexual fulfillment for both partners comes on the wings of mutual sensitivity. As he invests himself emotionally into her, she will want to love him more physically. As she invests herself physically into him, he will want to love her more emotionally. Wife, romance him physically. Husband, romance her emotionally. Understand each other's priorities, and you both will enjoy a sex life more delightful than wine (Song 1:2).

DISCUSSION

Both answer: A wife needs to be loved emotionally so that she can love physically, while a husband needs to be loved physically so that he can love emotionally. Do you agree/disagree? Explain your answer.

APPLICATION

Her: Ask your husband if you are satisfying his physical needs for love. What changes can you make to improve your relationship? Him: Ask your wife if you are satisfying her emotional needs for love. What changes can you make to improve your relationship? *Be careful to be extremely sensitive to each other's feelings as you do this application.*

PRAYER

Both: Heavenly Father, thank You for the gift of sexual union. We pray that we will be more sensitive to how we can meet each other's sexual needs. Help us to see how our respective task and relationship orientations carry over into the realm of our sexual relationship. Help us to love each other both physically and emotionally. Amen.

HOW TO ACHIEVE ONENESS

For this reason a man will leave his father and mother and be united to his wife, and the two will become one flesh.
EPHESIANS 5:31

*O*neness is the promised outcome of loving each other. We achieve oneness by sacrificially loving each other three ways: morally, emotionally, and physically. Let's briefly examine each of these three kinds of love.

1. *Morally.* Moral love is *agape* love. According to *Strong's Concordance*, agape love is "an assent of the will to love as a matter of principle, duty, and propriety." Agape love is the "right" thing to do. It demonstrates responsibility and commitment. To not love in this sense is morally wrong. Agape love is to love in a moral sense.

We achieve oneness by loving each other morally.

Guess what? It will come as no surprise to you that agape love is not the only thing your mate is looking for! She/he wants romantic love, too, which is both emotional and physical.

2. *Emotionally.* Emotional love is *phileo* love. *Strong's* says phileo love is "to be a friend, to be fond of, to have affection for." It denotes personal attachment as a matter of sentiment or feeling. We phileo love because we "want" to. It demonstrates that we really care. Phileo love is to love in an affectionate sense.

Agape means willing, choosing. Phileo means preferring, inclined to. First the head, then the heart. Agape comes from the mind; phileo comes from passion. This kind of passion is nonsexual, but represents extreme affinity. In marriage it is romantic.

Emotional love includes nonsexual touching—hugs, kisses, pats, squeezes, and holding hands. Are you a toucher? Do you come from a family of touchers? If not, you can experience a whole new world if you will begin touching each other.

Emotional love means small, routine kindnesses. Husbands, when is the last time you held the door for her? Or opened her car door? Wives, when is the last time you rubbed his back? Or made his favorite dessert?

How do we achieve this? Frankly, if we will simply treat each other like we would treat a stranger! Think of the attention, common courtesies, and interest we show perfect strangers. Or a prospect, a secretary, or a delivery man.

We achieve oneness by loving each other morally and emotionally.

3. *Physically.* Physical love is *eros* love. Eros love means sexual love. We eros love because it is God's gift, even command (see 1 Cor. 7:3–5), to married couples. It is the consummate expression of intimacy, the icing on the cake. Eros love is to love in a sexual sense.

We achieve oneness by loving each other morally, emotionally, and physically.

When each partner will commit to unconditionally love his/her mate morally, emotionally, and physically without depending on the mate's response, then the emotional bank account balances will begin to register surpluses.

DISCUSSION

Each answer: Which of the three kinds of love do you think you have best demonstrated? Why? What is the area in which you would most like to improve? How?

APPLICATION

Follow this seven-part plan to add more romance to your marriage. 1) Make a list of everything you appreciate about each other. Be specific. 2) Husband, call your wife today from work and ask her out to dinner. 3) Husband, send her flowers or, as a friend of mine does, pick wildflowers and bring them home in an empty Coke bottle! 4) Wife, pull out all the stops in getting ready. 5) Go out to dinner and engage in meaningful conversation. Share your appreciation lists with each other. Discuss each item. Ask each other three questions: "Is there anything you would like me to stop doing or change? If you could change one thing about your life, what would it be? If you had no one else to answer to, what would you like to be doing in five years, ten years, in retirement?" 6) Go home and enjoy each other romantically and physically. 7) Do it again next week with your own twist!

PRAYER

Either or both: Lord God, thank You for the gift of Your plan for our marriage. Help us to achieve the oneness You long for us to possess. We commit to love each other not only morally from a sense of duty, but also emotionally with our time because we like each other, and physically because You want us to enjoy each other's bodies. Amen.

THE RADICAL EFFECT OF THE FALL

The man and his wife were both naked, and they felt no shame.
GENESIS 2:25

*T*his devotional's verse captures the essence of intimacy. Adam and Eve, the first husband and wife, were naked and they felt no shame. They knew each other at such a deep level, that even their nakedness posed no problem to each other. As already mentioned: Intimacy means that I know who you are at the deepest level, and I accept you.

Do we have that kind of relationship between husband and wife today? No, of course not. Why? It's because in the very next verse mankind falls. "Now the serpent was more crafty than any of the wild animals the LORD God had made" and so on (Gen. 3:1). A corruption takes place.

Is it possible for a husband and wife to so share in each other's lives that they would be able to restore the kind of intimacy that existed before the Fall? Do you think it is possible?

We have a tremendous problem. As the saying goes, "You can't unscramble an egg." We can't rewrite history. The mind has been darkened by sin's deceit. We have sinful desires. The flesh inside of us wars against the Spirit, and the Spirit wars against the flesh. We can't communicate our ideas clearly. We have these beautiful, lucid thoughts, but somehow we just can't seem to articulate them to each other. And so, there are misinterpretations, misunderstandings.

Yet you and I know that we have had crystalline, clear moments of joy, communion, and intimacy with our mates—moments we wish we could suspend and make last forever. That was the kind of intimacy that existed before the Fall.

A lot of water has gone under the bridge since the Fall. The domino effect of the Fall has left the world bound in a pervasive, sticky web of sin and deceit. I do not think it is possible to fully recover the kind of oneness that existed in the garden before the Fall. I believe it will always be somewhat elusive, always somewhat just beyond the grasp.

On the other hand, I believe that a man and woman can pledge themselves to a lifelong pursuit of oneness and see the sun break through the mist most of the time. Still, there is a tug of war. Inattention will pull us away from each other, not push us together.

We cannot underestimate the radical effect of the Fall. It permeates the world like a colorless, odorless poison dissolved in water. It clouds our

thinking like black thunderheads. It jades our perceptions. We must acknowledge that now we are sight-impaired and "see through a glass, darkly."

Yes, we are naked and ashamed. Yes, the whole world is a prisoner of sin.
And yes, relationships tend toward atrophy and decay. But God has exalted
marriage to be a haven of enjoyment in this life.

The Fall is a great barrier to intimacy, but through awareness and focused
effort, the sun can shine brightly each and every day.

DISCUSSION

Read today's verse again, and both answer: Do you personally think it is
possible to fully recover the kind of oneness that existed in the garden before
the Fall? Explain your answer.

APPLICATION

Together, make a pledge to each other to a lifelong pursuit of oneness.
Then, enjoy each other every day, and watch the sun burn through the mist.
Always be on the lookout for those precious, memorable moments when you
are able to simply, yet profoundly, express your inmost thoughts and feelings
in transcendent, clear, lucid words.

PRAYER

Lord God, we thank You for the gift of marriage. We pledge ourselves to
a lifelong pursuit of oneness. Help us to simply and profoundly enjoy each
other. Help us to express our inmost thoughts and feelings in beautiful words
that build each other up. Amen.

INTROVERT OR EXTROVERT?

A new command I give you: Love one another. As I have loved you, so you must love one another.

JOHN 13:34

*L*ate one Friday afternoon I was speaking on the phone to one of my closest friends. We commiserated over the difficult week we both had limped through.

Suddenly my friend belted out, "Say! I've got a great idea! Why don't we get our families together and go spend the weekend at our beach house?"

"Bill, you've got to be kidding. The *last* thing in the world I feel like doing right now is spending the weekend with people. What I need to do is go crawl in a hole somewhere for a couple of days and lick my wounds."

> **introvert** *n.* A person concerned primarily with his own thoughts and feelings rather than with the external environment.
>
> **extrovert** *n.* A person concerned primarily with the physical and social environment rather than with one's own thoughts and feelings.

Introverts and extroverts. Most people assume that the difference between an extrovert and an introvert is that extroverts love people and introverts don't. Nothing could be further from the truth. There are many extroverts and introverts alike who don't enjoy people much. Likewise, introverts love people every bit as much as extroverts.

What is the difference, then? The difference between an extrovert and an introvert is not a question of love but of how we restore our energy. Introverts find that people use up their energy and wear them out. It isn't for lack of love, but it is work to be around people. Hence, they need time alone, away from the crowd. Extroverts, on the other hand, gain energy from being with people (there are really very few pure extroverts, you know). They actually find that other people recharge their batteries while introverts find that people run their batteries down.

Many husbands and wives unwittingly think their spouse does not love people because he or she prefers large blocks of quiet time away from the crowd. This is simply not true. Rather, he is an introvert who finds that people wear him out. To remain emotionally healthy he must recharge in the quiet.

Conversely, many husbands and wives feel like their spouse is killing them with social engagements. He, the introvert, feels like they must do everything together as a couple, so he tends to stifle her need to be among friends. Instead, he must accept that she, the extrovert, needs more social contact than he does. To remain emotionally healthy she must recharge in the crowd.

Some fortunate couples are both extroverts or both introverts. Even then, they may have different appetites for the quiet or the crowd.

Whether alike or opposite, it is important to do two things. First, recognize whether you are an extrovert or an introvert, and realize what your spouse is too. Remember that it is not a matter of love but of how we gain fresh energy. You must realize that God has made each of you what you are and has joined you together. God doesn't have accidents.

Second, you must accept your mate as he or she is. You should discuss your differences and establish realistic guidelines. Patsy and I are both introverts. However, I need to be around people considerably more than she does. So we have agreed that I will do some things without her. It's as simple as that. And it works. I don't push her to go unless I think it is a "command performance," and she never tries to talk me out of going unless I am neglecting our agreed-upon priorities.

Be sure to give each other enough room to breathe. The only way to do this is to talk it out.

DISCUSSION

Both answer: Are you an introvert or an extrovert? How does being around people affect you—do you gain or use energy? How have you been trying to shoehorn your mate into being what he or she isn't?

APPLICATION

Discuss the "two important things" in the last paragraphs and set some mutually agreeable guidelines where you differ in the amount of time you need/want to be around people. Be sure to stretch a little in your spouse's direction.

PRAYER

Either: Dear Lord, thank You for the way You crafted our personalities. We ask that You give us wisdom to know how we gain fresh energy, and the good sense not to force each other into being something we are not. Give us each, also, a desire to sacrifice our own interests for the benefit of each other. Amen.

In Summary

*T*o understand and to be understood—every human heart aches for these two great goals. To understand our mates opens up a whole new world of opportunities to bless them. To be understood by our mate is like a tall, cool drink in the scorching heat of everyday trials. Hopefully from this section you have seen each other in new ways that will lead to greater understanding.

APPLICATION

Read these thoughts out loud to each other meditatively. One of you read a point and the other make a comment. On the next idea switch roles, and so on, until you have read and commented on each idea. Conclude in prayer.

- Properly managed, God can use a man's greatest need for great good. The world needs great thinkers, administrators, merchants, engineers, pilots, plumbers, electricians, lawyers, teachers, and technicians. Even more, the world needs great fathers and husbands.
- A woman wants to occupy the first place in her husband's life in the same way that she gives him the first place in her life.
- Intimacy means that I know who you are at the deepest level, and I accept you.
- Intimacy is reaching out to understand each other in the face of busy schedules, different personalities, embarrassing secrets, and past hurts.
- Intimacy is opening up and accepting your mate when he/she reaches out.
- Intimacy is being spiritually, intellectually, and emotionally familiar with the deepest nature of your partner in mind, soul, body, and spirit.
- Intimacy is the fusion of two distinct lives headed in two distinct directions into a single journey of one flesh.
- Intimacy with Christ is *communion*; intimacy in marriage is *union*.
- Wives can help their husbands tremendously by understanding that beneath that brave facade of masculine strength is a little boy who sometimes wishes he could chuck the whole thing, or at least hear his daddy say, "Don't worry, son. I'll take care of it for you like I did when you were small."

- "Honey," his wife replied, "I don't care if we have to live in a tent. All I want is to have you healthy and back as a husband and father. I knew you were really struggling, but you've always kept things to yourself. I only wish you had told me sooner. We can pull together. We can work this out. You don't have to go through this alone."
- The principal activity of wives is *nurturing*. It is God's call on the wife to feed, to nourish, to train, to educate, to sustain, to help grow and flourish. Husbands who chide and demean their wives for worrying would do well to remind themselves that the "pressures" they feel are merely a euphemism for their own raw, naked fear.
- A prudent wife is a great blessing to both herself and her husband. Knowing human nature, she accepts the differences between men and women. She does not chafe at being his helper but, rather, finds purpose and pleasure in keeping him in motion.
- Christ occupies the classic, threefold office of prophet, priest, and king. In the same way, God has anointed every husband to lead his wife as her prophet, priest, and king.
- A submissive wife is not a servile doormat who blindly follows her husband. Instead, she looks out for the best interests of her husband. She uses her good judgment to advance the cause of her husband. As Larry Crabb has said, "A 'submissive wife' is one who takes all her resources and, understanding the unique opportunity of femininity, uses them to bless her husband."
- Oneness captures in a single, pregnant word the overarching goal of a Christian marriage. Oneness marks the summit of marital union. It is the peak toward which we climb. It is the idea that summarizes Scripture: "And the two will become one flesh."
- The difference between a great marriage and a poor marriage is the degree to which each partner is willing to meet the needs of the other.
- A wife needs to be loved emotionally so that she can love physically, while a husband needs to be loved physically so that he can love emotionally.
- We achieve oneness by loving each other morally, emotionally, and physically.
- When each partner will commit to unconditionally love his/her mate morally, emotionally, and physically without depending on the mate's response, then the emotional bank account balances will begin to register surpluses.

THE NEED TO BE SIGNIFICANT MISPLACED

A wife must not separate from her husband. But if she does, she must remain unmarried or else be reconciled to her husband. And a husband must not divorce his wife.

1 CORINTHIANS 7:10–11

*D*ivorce is not an option for a Christian except in the case of adultery and desertion. Even then, it is better to work it out. God's design for couples does not include divorce. "'I hate divorce,' says the LORD God" (Mal. 2:16).

So why do so many Christian couples get divorced? The following illustration helps answer the question for a majority of cases.

When a young couple courts, they enchant each other with their hopes and dreams. Using fertile imaginations, they speak of immortal love, doting children, and meteoric career success.

Then that glorious, fateful date arrives and they are wed. The honeymoon, while not at all like television and the movies, is quite nice. They arrive back in town and set upon their adorable newlywed nest.

About two weeks later he leaves for work one day to begin pursuing his career and forgets to come home. There are mountains to climb, nations to conquer, deals to be made, and a brass ring to be had. In the blinking of an eye he forgets all the promises he made to his lovely bride. He abandons the place he said he would occupy to go off and pursue significance.

She notices that ambition preoccupies his mind. She misses him but knows how important it is to him to be successful. And she likes nice things too.

One month goes by, then two. One year goes by, then two. One day she says, "You know, darling, I thought we were going to spend the rest of our lives together."

"Oh, we will. We will. But I just have to get a few more deals put together. Then I can ease back."

Two years become three, and three become four. "This isn't right," she tells him. "You are not giving me enough of you. This is not what I expected. Besides, we have little Jessica to think about now."

"I'm almost there, honey, I'm almost there. I promise."

Four years become eight, and eight become twelve. Then one day she is paralyzed by an extremely lucid thought, "You know, I don't think he is ever coming home."

112

She broods over this thought. She mourns the death of her marriage, silently, alone. Then one day, after ruminating on her loneliness for many years, in the privacy of her thoughts, she purposefully, below the surface, severs all the lines that moor her to the dock.

Soon she begins to drift away, ever so slightly. He notices that she has not remained where she promised she would be. Distraught, he rushes back to the place where he said he would be when he took his wedding vows, then asks her why she has moved away. But to his surprise, instead of coming back she keeps slowly drifting away. No matter how much he pleads and weeps, nothing seems to persuade her.

What he failed to see, of course, is that she has completely disconnected from him. Slowly, over the years, he let their love burn down, never putting fresh fuel on the fire. One day, feeling cold and isolated, she made her choice, and now nothing will bring her back.

Our choices have consequences. When we make any person or ambition (except Christ) more important than our spouse, we run the risk of the fire going out.

DISCUSSION

Husband: (Be completely honest with yourself before answering.) Have you been showing up at home, or has some other pursuit captured your fancy? Wife: Has your husband been fulfilling his role as you expected?

APPLICATION

Husband: Recall the little things you did when you courted your wife. If you have trouble remembering, ask her. Try out two or three of those courtship ideas over the next few days. If you have seriously neglected your marriage and find it difficult to discuss, seek help from a friend or a good Christian counselor who can help you get in touch with your deepest feelings.

PRAYER

Him, as appropriate: Father, I plead guilty. I have been far too preoccupied with my ambitions. I have flirted with letting the fire go out. Forgive me, Lord, and grant me the courage and imagination to fulfill my vows and promises. Amen. Her, as appropriate: Father, I, too, plead guilty. In the process of building a life I have withdrawn when I should have spoken up. Amen.

Deep Frustrations

So I say, live by the Spirit, and you will not gratify the desires of the sinful nature.

GALATIANS 5:16

*E*arly in our marriage I found myself ranting and raving around the house one morning before heading to work.

An all-consuming, pervasive sense of frustration had enveloped my entire being. It was a deep angst about my life I could neither express nor suppress. I had this lingering feeling that something was profoundly wrong but I could not form the words on the tip of my tongue to express myself. So the feeling remained inarticulate, inexpressible, just below the surface of conscious expression.

Actually, this amorphous feeling had stalked me like a hunter for months. As I paced back and forth, waving my arms wildly, taking my frustrations out on my new wife, Patsy, I said things I never should have said.

I happened to look over at her only to see large tears rolling down her cheeks. She wasn't sobbing, she was just sitting there taking my anger. To be candid, making Patsy cry was not that unusual at that point in our marriage. However, something that day was different, and I was transfixed. I couldn't look away. I wanted to, but I couldn't. She has these captivating, beautiful, large fifty-cent-piece-sized eyes.

After she had held my gaze for what seemed like a very long time she asked me this interesting question. She said, "Pat, is there anything about me that you like?"

In the course of our lives all of us will go through several periods of deep, dark frustration. Not merely minor upsets over the day-to-day vicissitudes of life, these periods represent landmark turning points of self-examination, redirection, and change.

These periods often mark the borders between different phases of our lives. Some examples include: Adjusting to a new marriage or career. The stress of starting a family and raising children. The trepidation of starting a new business. The agony of closing a business. Sending your first child off to college. Marrying off your daughter. Settling into an empty nest. The wife returning to the job market. Realizing your dream is not going to come true the way you planned. Losing your savings in investments that go sour. Learning you have a health problem that requires a change in lifestyle. Taking a parent into the home. Burying a parent.

Each of these frustrating times is an opportunity for retreat or advance in our relationship with one another. We can tackle our frustration in the Spirit or in the flesh. If we take on our problems in the flesh our natural urge will be to exclude our partner. He or she will see us hurting and approach us. But because we are waging war in our own strength we repel any advances. We will not let anyone in to our agony. And by rebuffing them, we hurt them too. And the gap widens. The wall grows thicker.

If, on the other hand, we deal with our frustrations in the Spirit, our desire will be to include our mate in the totality of our pain. He or she will seek to listen to us, to draw us out, to build us up. Because we are in the Spirit we accept his or her loving concern. And an almost mystical intimacy develops on the back of shared sorrows.

How do you handle your deep frustrations? Are you getting the best of them, or are they getting the best of you? The next time waves of gloom and frustration wash over you, share them quietly with your mate. She/he is there for you, if you will let him/her in. You can rant and rave, or you can open up. You can take your frustrations out on your partner, or you can let her/him in on them. It's your choice, but remember, this is the one who married you for better or for worse. So what if it's a little worse just now?

DISCUSSION

Both answer: How often do you go through periods of deep frustration with life? Are you in such a period now? If so, describe what is happening. Is it your natural inclination to let your spouse in when you are frustrated, or to close your mate out?

APPLICATION

The next time (or now, if applicable) a deep sense of frustration washes over you, decide to do two things: 1) Respond in the Spirit and not the flesh and 2) share to the best of your ability the full extent of everything you are going through with your mate. Let your mate in to share your life, for better or for worse.

PRAYER

Either or both: Lord, I confess that I tend to take my frustrations out on my mate rather than try to work through them together. Help me to walk in the Spirit and not respond in my flesh. Help me to be a better communicator of my feelings. And help me to be more sensitive to the frustrations that my life mate is going through too. Amen.

"THERE IS A BIG WALL HERE"

Husbands, love your wives and do not be harsh with them.
COLOSSIANS 3:19

*B*ill's anger constantly rumbled just below the surface, like a volcano ready to erupt. Ten years ago he went to his pastor for prayer to remove his angry spirit. After talking and praying for some time the pastor looked up at Bill and said, "I don't think this is helping. There is a big wall here."

Bill didn't have a clue what that wall might be. No matter how much he probed his thoughts and feelings, he simply could not put his finger on the source of his free-floating, volcanic anger.

Recently Bill and a few other angry men started a small group to deal with their inner rage. Soon they started spending more time on their marriages than their anger. At a meeting one morning, without any advance warning, these words flowed from Bill's mouth: "I really think I hate my wife."

Bill elaborated, "I am just so angry over so many things. She won't ever argue with me, and it really irritates me. In thirty years of marriage we haven't had five heated arguments—not even warm. Her unwillingness to hammer things out has built up a tremendous wall between us. I have shut down my emotions toward her. I think I have finally discovered the identity of the wall my pastor found ten years ago.

"For nearly all our thirty years of marriage all conversation has been housekeeping—'What's for dinner? When are you going to mow the grass? What time are you getting up tomorrow?'"

One man in the group shared that recently he had started doing the dishes from time to time and making the bed. He related how these small acts of kindness had a tremendous impact on his marriage. Women feel appreciated when their men are considerate of them. It really helped thaw out his relationship with his wife.

"Oh my goodness," Bill chimed in, "I haven't done those things in years."

"Well, it really works," his friend responded.

The following week Bill did the dishes one evening. A tremendous sense of relief swept over him. It was a feeling much like repentance. It was tantamount to saying, "I've got a problem with my marriage, and I've got to start with me."

Since that first foray into the world of his wife's duties Bill has unloaded the dishwasher and made the bed several times. He is trying to spend more time listening, and he hopes to learn the questions to ask his wife.

Over the course of years the temperature of our romance with each other will slowly, quietly cool off without vigilant effort to keep it heated up. He needs to be able to express his frustrations (without making her a dumping ground), and she needs to be willing to act as his sounding board. To not do so has a chilling effect. She needs the reassurance of his love through small acts of kindness, and he needs to be willing to share in household chores and responsibilities. To not do so will cool off the relationship.

The deepest expression of our love comes through our willingness to share in the tedium of each other's daily routines and frustrations. It says, "I am here for you," in the minutiae of the repetitious and boring as well as the high moments. It says, "We are going through the daily grind together."

DISCUSSION

Both answer: Are you engaged with each other in the details of daily living? Can you share the frustrations of the day with each other? Do you cooperate with each other on household chores and responsibilities? If not, what effect do you think it is having on your relationship? Is it making either of you angry? Is it causing either of you to shut down your emotions?

APPLICATION

Wife: Ask your husband regularly to share his struggles, frustrations, and fears with you. Husband: Share in household chores and other responsibilities as a tangible expression of your love. Do it without asking or comment.

PRAYER

Him, if applicable: Lord God, I am humbled by this reminder of how self-centered I have been. Help me to be more of a partner to my wife. Prompt me to say, "I am here for you," in a thousand ways through both my words and actions. Lord, help me to love my wife. I confess that my wife is not the cause of my anger, but it is my selfishness. Forgive my sin, O Lord, and restore me to a right path. Amen.

SEXUAL UNION

But since there is so much immorality, each man should have his own wife, and each woman her own husband. The husband should fulfill his marital duty to his wife, and likewise the wife to her husband. The wife's body does not belong to her alone but also to her husband. In the same way, the husband's body does not belong to him alone but also to his wife. Do not deprive each other except by mutual consent and for a time, so that you may devote yourselves to prayer. Then come together again so that Satan will not tempt you because of your lack of self-control.

1 CORINTHIANS 7:2–5

A man in Bill's small group on anger related that after they had produced several children together, his wife decided not to have intercourse with him any more. Early on this brought about many heated arguments, but she would not change her mind.

Notwithstanding, he loved her and did not believe in divorce, so he settled into a platonic relationship. Essentially, they split up. She took the inside and he took the outside. Through the years he found that when he arrived home each day a deep, pervasive frustration would envelop him. Through his small group he discovered that the bedrock of his anger was his sexual relationship with his wife.

The Bible is clear that men and women are not to withhold sexual relations from each other unless two conditions are met. First, it must be by mutual consent. Unilaterally deciding to withhold intimate relations from your spouse is banned by the Bible. It is not your decision to make alone. The essence of marriage is a cooperative, joint effort to live for each other in the Lord. Any unilateral decision which goes against the intent of the Scriptures is not allowed. Such a decision requires the consent of both partners.

Second, any mutual abstinence from sexual union is to be only for an agreed-upon time, and only then so you can devote yourselves to prayer. No permanent abstinence from the act of marriage is ever contemplated in the Scriptures. Even temporary withdrawal is limited as to the purpose: for prayer. By extension, such a time could also be for fasting or spiritual retreat.

The operative principle is that our bodies do not belong to ourselves alone but also to our mates. Any decisions about the property of another person cannot be made without that person's consent.

Why are we not to deprive each other of the most intimate act of marriage? Positively, our sexual drive is a profoundly beautiful and strong urge. It is a gift from God for the joy of married couples. Also, by implanting sexual desire God assured procreation and the "fruitful multiplying" of the human race. God created sexual relations both for the enjoyment of His married children and the proliferation of humankind.

Negatively, when one marriage partner deprives the other of sexual union, *both* are subject to temptation by the devil. Because the drive is so strong, depriving each other tests our self-control. As the Bible says, "But since there is so much immorality. . . ." We live in an era of hyper-sexual stimulation. What was *Playboy* pornography twenty years ago is today the swimsuit edition of mainstream *Sports Illustrated*. Who among us is that strong?

A sexually satisfied husband or wife will not be sexually tempted as easily as someone unilaterally deprived and filled with resentment. Why? Because he or she will be empowered by his or her spouse to be self-controlled. It is our biblical duty, for we belong to each other and not only to ourselves.

DISCUSSION

Both answer: Are you satisfied with the level of sexual intimacy in your marriage? Why or why not? What would you like to change? (If you find this topic difficult to discuss, one or both of you may want to write out your thoughts and feelings in a letter to your mate.)

APPLICATION

In the next few weeks be especially sensitive to your spouse's sexual needs. Put him or her before your own interests. Remember, you belong to each other. It is your duty. Don't put each other in the position of being tempted by the devil.

PRAYER

Both: Dear God, thank You for the beautiful gift of sexual union. We ask You to help us to be more sensitive to each other's sexual needs and desires. I realize that my body does not belong to me alone and pledge to not deprive my mate unless by mutual consent, and then only for a time of prayer or spiritual retreat. Amen.

119

THE BRIDGES OF MADISON COUNTY

The husband should fulfill his marital duty to his wife, and likewise the wife to her husband.

1 CORINTHIANS 7:3

*T*he dust cover calls it "an experience of uncommon and stunning beauty." It soared to the top of the *New York Times* Best Seller List. *The Bridges of Madison County* is a lyrical fiction book that found a hungry audience.

Francesca Johnson, an Iowa farm wife, reached her mid-forties, proud of her two children and mildly content. Richard Johnson, her husband, offered her a sturdy kindness and steady ways. He gave her an even life. They met when he was a young soldier in uniform, she a vivacious young Italian woman looking for a way to America.

They lived an utterly predictable life: dinner at five, then the TV news, after that television programs. She would read books in the kitchen or on the porch. Occasionally Richard would call out, "Frannie, you've got to see this!" It was usually something like Elvis. Richard didn't approve of the Beatles.

Richard was interested in sex only every couple of months. It was fast, then over, an event. He showed no interest in warming things up, shaving, or her perfume. Something inside her ached for him to carry her away.

What's wrong with this picture? This is a woman starving to death emotionally. It is the story of a love-famished woman, desperate for romance.

She was hungry for some attention to the femininity deep in her emotional being. When Robert Kincaid pulled into the Johnson's driveway looking for directions, he saw that she was very lovely. A photographer for *National Geographic*, he had come to Madison County, Iowa, to capture their well-known covered bridges on film. He was no womanizer, but disaster was only a kind word away. She fought it—they both did, really. But when he met her emotional needs, a steamy, torrid affair followed like night the day.

Admittedly, *The Bridges of Madison County* makes adultery appear mystical, almost noble. Yet there is a message here. Both husband and wife yearn for a deep love from one another. It is a desire to be one entity, to feel that I am absolutely the most important person or thing in your life—not just because of moral duty, but because you like me, you really do like me. Tell me our marriage can be romantic, touching, intimate, physical, affectionate, and tender.

DISCUSSION

Both answer: How sensitive to and aware of your emotional and physical needs do you consider your mate? Be gentle but honest. What can you sincerely do to better demonstrate your love to your spouse?

APPLICATION

Read this devotional's verse again. Make a pledge to meet each other's needs for emotional and physical love.

PRAYER

Either or both: Our Father, we praise You for the marvelous gift of marriage. We thank You for each other. Help us to love each other in every way: morally, emotionally, and physically. We surrender our marriage to You. Work in us to meet each other's needs. May neither one of us ever hunger for something more. Amen.

Spiritual Leadership

If anyone does not provide for his relatives, and especially for his immediate family, he has denied the faith and is worse than an unbeliever.
1 TIMOTHY 5:8

*I*f you had a problem, this pastor was there. You could always depend on him to deny himself to meet your need.

He loved God with all his heart and served Him with abandon. His church flourished under his leadership and his zeal for God's house. He baptized their babies, he saw to the spiritual education of their young, he made sure their teens had alternatives, he married their young adults, he visited their sick, and he buried their dead.

The congregation loved this man deeply. They appreciated the sacrifices he made for them. They admired his dedication and commitment. They accepted his service and leadership as a gift from God.

His church became a leading light in the community. His stock rose to prodigious heights among the other church leaders. He was highly esteemed, a sort of wise man sitting at the city gate. His name was often called to chair important area-wide committees and meetings.

After forty years of self-sacrificing service he retired. What does a man want in retirement? To enjoy a few memories from time to time, to take up a few hobbies he has been putting off, to enjoy the friends he has made, to travel and spend some time with his wife, to deepen his relationship with his children at an adult level, and to spoil his grandchildren rotten. At the end of life what counts is not the accomplishments and accolades attained, but the people we have touched and the relationships we have developed.

Unfortunately, when he retired this man found that his children would have nothing to do with him. They were bitter because they had not known him when they were growing up. They resented the church that stole all their father's time away. They cut him off from both themselves and his grandchildren. No amount of discussing the matter could assuage their bitterness. He had not provided for them and they could not forget it. He had been the spiritual leader for his entire community, but he had failed to be the spiritual leader of his own home. Oh, the anguish he has had to endure.

The pressure of daily living weighs heavy upon us. It seems we vacillate between struggling to make ends meet one week to juggling too many opportunities the next. In the press of this demanding life many Christian families are not provided for properly. Choices are too often made based upon the murky criteria of financial reward, career advancement, and ego satisfaction. The needs of the family, which include but go far beyond finances, often go unconsidered.

It is the biblical responsibility of the man to be the spiritual leader of his wife and children. To be an effective spiritual leader is to actively think about and provide for all the needs—spiritual, financial, emotional, educational, recreational—of both the wife and the children. It is no small challenge.

It is the man who is to "provide for his relatives, especially his immediate family." How tragic when men succeed in the community but fail at home. How tragic not to hear the coos and to miss the cuddles of grandchildren. How utterly sad to grow old alone.

Husband, where are you known as a spiritual leader? The place that really counts is at home. It is your duty before God. Wife, have you assumed the role of spiritual leader? Give it back. Although your intentions may have been noble and sincere, you have usurped what God intended for your husband.

DISCUSSION

Both discuss: Who is acting as the spiritual leader of your home? If the husband has not been acting as the spiritual leader—whatever the reasons may be—what changes would you like to make because of today's devotional?

APPLICATION

On paper write a paragraph describing your "dream" retirement. Include information on where you would live, what you would do, whom you would see. Husband, what changes to the way you are leading your family would you need to make now to ensure what you both wrote down will become reality then?

PRAYER

Him: Lord, I have allowed myself to be deceived by the desires of the world, and I have not been the spiritual leader in my home as I should. Father, forgive me, and help us to rewrite the script for our marriage and family. Keep me from the pain of so many men who don't properly provide for their families. Don't let me grow old alone. Amen.

Spiritual Leadership: Another Angle

If anyone does not provide for his relatives, and especially for his immediate family, he has denied the faith and is worse than an unbeliever.

1 TIMOTHY 5:8

*M*ost men who fail to be the spiritual leader of their wives fail because they don't provide for them emotionally. Some, however, fail because they don't provide for them financially. A woman wrote the following in response to an anonymous survey I conducted:

> There hasn't been a book written about the man who doesn't provide financially for his family. The wife is either forced to go to work or use her own inherited means to keep a roof over their heads. I personally know of some twenty-plus women in this situation. The husband has a problem with authority, he is a dreamer, wants the easy dollar, has a big "get-rich-quick scheme." He makes promises of change but it never happens. His pride keeps him from getting a real job selling shoes, working at a lumber store, etc. She loses respect for him. She feels insecure, they don't have any or enough life insurance or retirement funds, and it goes on not just for a brief time but for a lifetime. Who needs it? I've already raised my kids, I don't need to raise another one! A wife also can't talk to anyone about her needs because it undercuts her mate and reveals his sin.

Yes, it is sin, as this devotional's theme verse points out. One counselor suggests that ten percent of men fall into this category. They simply don't meet the needs of their families. The husband has a biblical responsibility to provide for his family!

Contrast that with my friend, Steve. Steve was a high-powered, big-salary executive with a well-known national company. The victim of a massive layoff, he was out of work for twenty-two months. This put extra pressure on his wife, who was working. His self-esteem took a drubbing. After crying out to God, "Why me?" he became angry. He shook his fist at God. Finally, he so exhausted himself that he could only listen. The voice he heard told him to go get work doing anything.

Steve took a job washing golf carts at a country club. Humiliating? Yes, in one sense. But Steve began to find himself again. He witnessed to six young teenagers working there. There was a purity in doing manual labor to provide for his family. It cleansed his soul.

That season of Steve's life is over. He is once again a high-powered, big-salary executive with a well-known national company. He will always carry the satisfaction, however, that he provided for his family in the darkest hour of his career. As a result, his wife never lost respect for him. His children are proud of their dad.

It is better for a man to make a little with dignity than to bluff his way through and lose the respect of his wife. Husband, if the money runs out, you are the one who should find a job, regardless of its pay or status.

Wives, nothing deadens a man like unemployment. He is made to work. Much of his identity comes from his vocation. It is good for a wife to bear patiently while her husband struggles through the dark hour of unemployment. Comfort him in his unemployment, all the more so when he humbles himself to keep bread on the table.

DISCUSSION

Husband: Where between these two men would you place yourself? Explain to your wife the desire you have to be a good provider. Wife: In what ways has your husband been a good provider? In what areas would you suggest improvements be made?

APPLICATION

Wife: If your husband has been a good provider, frequently express your appreciation to him. If not, ask him to prayerfully consider this chapter. Husband: If you struggle to be a good provider, consider Christian counseling. Take a job doing something, anything really. Your self-worth will not go down, but up.

PRAYER

Her, if applicable: Lord, I thank You so much that You have given me a husband who is such a good provider. Help me to be more sensitive to just how hard it is to keep a family going financially. Let me be a blessing to my husband as he works to provide for us. Amen.

Him, if applicable: Lord, I can see that I have not been the provider I need to be. As a result, I have sinned against my wife and family. I can see how I could lose the respect of my wife. Without her respect I know my self-esteem will dwindle. It's a vicious cycle. Forgive me, Lord, and help me to take over the role of spiritual leader in my home. In Jesus' name I pray. Amen.

OVERCOMING BITTERNESS

For if you forgive men when they sin against you, your heavenly Father will also forgive you. But if you do not forgive men their sins, your Father will not forgive your sins.

MATTHEW 6:14–15

*H*appy-go-lucky. That's the only way to describe him. Never met a stranger. Loves everyone. Quick with a smile. Hard worker.

Bitter. That's the only way to describe her. An angry person. Shriveled up like a prune. Rarely has a good word about anyone. Really unhappy with her life. She can't seem to let any offense go, no matter how petty. Every single thing her husband does wrong rankles her, no matter how minor. She rarely forgives and certainly never forgets.

At middle age she had to have some surgery that put her in bed for several weeks of convalescence. With time on her hands, she decided to write down every slight offense, wrong, and sin her husband had ever committed against her. Instead of feeling better she became more bitter than ever.

Admittedly, this example pushes the limits of bitterness. Yet, if we are completely honest, in every marriage there are roots of bitterness that take hold—some seen, some unseen. Sometimes we know what makes us bitter. Other times, the reason remains obscure. Sometimes we may even enjoy feeling like a martyr.

Bitterness is a sinister enemy of marriage. Bitterness strangles the life-blood out of a marriage—literally dries up our bones—and makes the words of our mate like fingernails on a chalkboard. Bitterness and intimacy cannot grow in the same heart. The one is poison to the other.

Where does bitterness come from? Bitterness is the fruit of a harbored grudge, the odor produced by pettiness, the product manufactured in the factory of unforgiveness. Like a field gone fallow, an unforgiving heart will yield to weeds of bitterness.

The root of bitterness, however, cannot take hold in a forgiving heart. Feelings of bitterness toward our mate send us a signal that we have something yet to forgive. What is it? We may not even know. It may require much thought, meditation, and prayer to come to grips with the source of bitterness against our mate.

Not only does an unforgiving spirit make us bitter, it cuts us off from fellowship with God. Jesus said, "If you do not forgive men their sins, your Father will not forgive your sins." Why? Because not forgiving each other is sin. (For a thorough explanation of this truth see Jesus' words in Matthew 18:21–35. Sobering.)

You may have been hurt deeply by your spouse. No one may know or understand how you feel. As the proverb says, "Each heart knows its own bitterness, and no one else can share its joy" (Prov. 14:10). The only way out is to forgive. When Peter asked Jesus how many times he must forgive the brother who sins against him, Jesus said, "I tell you, not seven times, but seventy-seven times." Jesus used hyperbole to say, "However many times it takes." Don't be bitter; forgive. Will you?

If you have hurt your spouse, you can make this process exceedingly easier by saying you're sorry and asking forgiveness. Will you? I think Mark Twain said, "Forgiveness is the fragrance the violet sheds on the heel that crushed it."

DISCUSSION

Each answer: Is there anything your mate has done over which you have become bitter? Can you share it? If not, what will it take to make it possible for you to share? (A word to the one listening: Please, please, don't be defensive. Even if you don't understand why the bitterness developed, apologize for the hurt it caused your life mate.)

APPLICATION

(Note: It is certainly possible that this application could be hurtful. Yet I know of no idea more powerful for healing and bonding a relationship. If you find it too difficult, just do part of it.) List what you have done wrong to your mate and what your mate has done wrong to you to the best of your recollection. Only list matters not already resolved. Next, each of you read your list of how you recall wronging your mate, apologize, and ask forgiveness. Mate, offer your forgiveness. Next, each of you read the list of how you recall your mate wronging you and forgive—outright without strings. (No need to repeat items covered in the first round.) Mate, apologize and say thank you for being forgiven.

PRAYER

Both pray aloud together: Our Father in heaven, hallowed be Your name. We pray Your kingdom will come and Your will be done in our lives here on earth as it is in heaven. Give us this day all our needs. And forgive all our sins as we have just now forgiven one another. Amen.

What Anger Does

"In your anger do not sin" : *Do not let the sun go down while you are still angry, and do not give the devil a foothold.*
EPHESIANS 4:26–27

*O*ur son diligently practices basketball for an hour and one half to two hours a day. So when he asked if we would spring for the $100 to paint a foul line, "key," and three point line, it sounded like a good investment—a time of joy, a time to celebrate his diligence, a time to reward his self-discipline. As one of his coaches put it, "He really wants it, doesn't he?"

The man we hired to stripe the lines carefully measured the dimensions, then snapped a "blue line" to mark where to paint. He looked quite professional. I left and took my daughter to dinner. When we returned my wife and son were looking at the finished product. Honestly, I don't know why the painter had bothered to measure. It looked as if he had taken a spray gun and waved it wildly in the general direction of the asphalt.

Being the spiritual leader I am, I erupted into a tirade of rage: "How could anybody be so stupid? What an idiot! He has ruined it!" I screamed and went on from there.

After listening to me rampage for two minutes my son shouted, "Stop yelling at Mother! It isn't her fault."

"I'm not yelling at your mother, I'm just yelling!" I yelled. Following this brilliant comment I made several other equally mature observations.

Well, you can imagine what happened. The whole joyful celebration of my son's pursuit of excellence turned into a rather deflated affair.

It's not the big things with which we struggle. Because we *know* they are important matters, we consciously marshal our maturity and handle them well. Knowing this, the devil attacks us in the little things. It's in the little things where we unconsciously let down our guard against immaturity.

We think we are justified in letting off a little steam, but it only ruins everything. And it does so every time. Aristotle said:

A person who is angry on the right grounds, against the right persons, in the right manner, at the right moment, and for the right length of time deserves great praise.

Who among us is worthy of such praise? Instead, in our anger we sin.

P.S. As you might have suspected, the paint job didn't look nearly as bad the next day, but unfortunately, we'd stupidly paid the man in advance, so we are living with it.

DISCUSSION

Husband, answer all questions first, then wife answers: Are you an angry person? Do you quickly lose your temper? If so, why do you think you so easily become angry? How do the little things get your goat versus the big things? If you can't seem to express yourself in this area, what are some ways you could self-examine to learn more about why you are the way you are?

APPLICATION

Ask your spouse to tell you how your anger makes her/him feel and how it affects your relationship. If you are willing, sincerely and earnestly apologize for your sinful anger. Pray together, asking the Lord's forgiveness and healing. Make a pledge to read a book or seek counseling to learn more about yourself and the reasons for your anger. "Don't let the sun go down . . . and do not give the devil a foothold."

PRAYER

Either or both: Lord, I confess that I become too easily angered. My angry outbursts drain the joy out of many a day. Help me to deal with my anger in a constructive way. I pledge to see what steps I can take to make progress. Grant me courage to not let the sun go down on my anger. Amen.

THE NEED TO BE RIGHT

But encourage one another daily, as long as it is called Today, so that none of you may be hardened by sin's deceitfulness.
HEBREWS 3:13

A man told his wife he was going bowling with some friends. Instead they went out drinking. The next morning he woke up with a black eye, unable to remember how he got home. As he looked in the mirror he wondered how he would explain this to his wife.

When he went down to breakfast he told her, "You will never guess what happened. We were coming out of the bowling alley last night and five thugs jumped us. We fought them off but I got this black eye."

"That's interesting," said his wife. "When you came home last night you didn't have it. I gave you that black eye!"

The man thought about it for a moment and then said, "Well, that's my story, and I'm sticking with it!"

One of the greater dynamics in human relationships is the need to be right. This need to be right exists without regard to whether or not we actually are right. The truth is not at issue—the issue is our pride.

One day I was arguing with my wife over some petty matter. I would make my point, then she hers. I kept telling her I couldn't understand her reasoning. Finally, in exasperation she said, "You know what I mean!"

The truth is I knew exactly what she meant. But I was walking in the flesh and pride urged me to twist her words, to pretend I didn't "get it," to play dumb. I wanted to be right, even though I knew I was wrong.

In fact, most people struggle to admit they are wrong. Many of us would rather make our spouse spittin' mad than admit we are wrong. Why are we so argumentative, so immovable? The answer is the deceitfulness of sin. It causes us to insist we are right even when we know we are wrong. Consider what Martin Luther said:

> It is rightly called the deceitfulness of sin because it deceives under the appearance of good. This phrase "deceitfulness of sin" ought to be understood in a much wider sense, so that the term includes even one's own righteousness and wisdom. For more than anything else one's own righteousness and wisdom deceive one and work against faith in Christ, since we love the flesh and the sensations of the flesh and also riches and possessions, but we love

nothing more ardently than our own feelings, judgment, purpose, and will, especially when they seem to be good.[14]

We should gently challenge our spouses when we see the tentacles of sin's deceit wrapped around their clear thinking. A good question to ask, without any rancor, is: "Do you really believe what you are saying is right?"

DISCUSSION

Each answer: Rate your need to be right on a scale of 1 to 10, where 10 represents the need to always be right. Spouse, do you agree with your mate's self-rating? If not, tactfully point out why.

APPLICATION

Make a concerted effort to acknowledge your inclination to insist on being right. The next time you disagree with your mate ask yourself, "Do I really believe that what I am saying is right?"

PRAYER

Either, as applicable: Lord God, I confess that I do love my own feelings, my own judgment, and my own purposes and will. Help me to not be hardened by sin's deceit, but help me to see clearly when I am walking in the flesh. Forgive my pride. Fill me with Your Spirit that I may walk humbly with my mate. Amen.

POWER STRUGGLES

Wives, in the same way be submissive to your husbands so that, if any of them do not believe the word, they may be won over without words by the behavior of their wives. . . . Husbands, in the same way be considerate as you live with your wives, and treat them with respect as the weaker partner and as heirs with you of the gracious gift of life, so that nothing will hinder your prayers.

1 PETER 3:1, 7

*I*t is said that one mule by itself can pull two tons. However, two mules pulling together can pull eight tons.

A husband and wife pulling together can accomplish more by cooperating with each other. When they start pulling against each other, however, things start breaking down.

Why do so many husbands and wives get caught up in power struggles that destroy intimacy, trust, and joint effectiveness? Perhaps this comment from a wife helps explain:

> There is a fine line in today's marriage between the role of the wife and husband. Our society tells women not to be taken for granted. We know God wants us to be helpmates, but society tells us that helpmate means servant, lesser person, maid, etc. We ask our husbands to be our family spiritual leaders, financial leaders, decision makers, and strong fathers; but when they try, we rebel. They come on stronger and we feel like we aren't being respected, so we rebel more strongly. They give up and we tell them they aren't doing their jobs. Or, they come on stronger and the cycle goes on. Many of my friends are caught up in this cycle and neither the husbands nor the wives know how to break out of it.

If we are going to get back to authentic biblical marriage then we are going to have to get back to the Bible. The Bible clearly outlines the authority structure for marriage:

- The wife is a helpmate. "The LORD God said, 'It is not good for the man to be alone. I will make a helper suitable for him'" (Gen. 2:18).
- The husband is appointed to rule over his wife. "Your desire will be for your husband, and he will rule over you" (Gen. 3:16).
- The wife is to be submissive to her husband (see this devotional's first verse).

What does it take to be a submissive wife? To submit is no easy assignment. First, a wife needs to decide on her authority. What is your final court of appeal? Will it be God's Word or the vacant voices of a broken world? Second, a wife must yield her self-will to the will of God. Self-centeredness will put the spotlight on your rights rather than on helping your husband. Third, a wife must respect her husband. This may not be easy—some husbands make the way rough, but you must do your part notwithstanding your husband's response (of course, I'm not referring to abusive situations). (See 1 Peter 3:1–6. See how your submissive spirit, purity, and reverence will win him over, *without talk!*)

How can the husband help? What is his part? First, a husband must be a man worthy of his wife's respect. If she respects you, she can submit to you. (Husband, in your own experience, think how you want to resist the authority of a boss you don't respect.) Second, a husband must treat his wife with consideration and thoughtfulness. We husbands know how to treat our wives right, so let's do it! Third, a husband must also respect his wife as the weaker partner. He must highly value her, esteem her to the highest degree, treat her with dignity, and show her honor.

When husbands and wives are more focused on pleasing each other than on getting their own way, God will free them up to mutually love and respect each other.

DISCUSSION

What issues provoke the power struggles in your marriage? Have you fulfilled the spirit of this devotional's theme verses? Why or why not?

APPLICATION

Write down the things that cause power struggles in your marriage. Be as complete as possible. Husband, yield your right to have your own way. Wife, yield your right to have your own way.

PRAYER

Both: Heavenly Father, we confess there are many things we consider our rights that we have not fully surrendered to You. By faith, we yield all our rights to You. Help us to think of each other as more important than ourselves. Help us to mutually love and respect each other as You have commanded in Your Word. Amen.

FIGHTS AND QUARRELS

What causes fights and quarrels among you? Don't they come from your desires that battle within you? You want something but don't get it. You kill and covet, but you cannot have what you want. You quarrel and fight. You do not have, because you do not ask God. When you ask, you do not receive, because you ask with wrong motives, that you may spend what you get on your pleasures.

JAMES 4:1–3

*T*hey were excited about the year-end bonus. But after twenty minutes of arguing about whether or not to buy a new boat or a new car, she was ready to clobber him.

What types of "desires" would bring a couple nearly to blows? It is hard to picture a couple fully surrendered to the Lord quarreling over their mutual desire to love, serve, and please God.

In truth, we have two kinds of "desires" within. One type is positive. We desire relief from oppressive people. We groan to live in our heavenly dwellings. We long to be with dear friends. We yearn to serve God more faithfully. We strive to provide a good life for our families.

Another type of desire is negative. We desire more stuff. We covet our neighbor's position and status. We crave to control our mates. We lust after the opposite sex. Pride, envy, greed, deceit, arrogance, slander, and malice spring from the sinful desires within (see Mark 7:21–23).

The word "desires" in the second sentence and the word "pleasures" in the last sentence of today's Scripture passage both derive from the same Greek word *hedone*, from which we get "hedonism." Hedonism refers to the belief that the highest value in life is to maximize pleasure and minimize pain.

As the verses note, the "desires that battle within you" result in wanting without getting, killing, coveting, quarrels, fights, a failure to pray, and wrong motives. What is James describing? The flesh warring against the Spirit—with the flesh winning.

Simply put, if a couple continually quarrels and fights, one or both have not yielded themselves to the Holy Spirit. "So I say, live by the Spirit, and you will not gratify the desires of the sinful nature" (Gal. 5:16).

Even the occasional quarrel can be traced to walking in the sinful nature, or flesh, instead of the Spirit. When I agree to speak to a particular group, we ask the sponsor to fill out a form so I can pray and prepare most effectively. Someone once returned a half-completed blank form and wrote on it, "I think this is all you need." I took offense and complained to my wife. She pointed out that the sponsor was a wonderful man and suggested he would never do anything for spite.

I looked over the form more carefully and realized everything I really needed to know was there. But I had already made up my mind. A made-up mind is almost impossible to change. I chose to give in to the negative desires of my flesh rather than the positive influence of the Spirit. So I argued with Patsy. Even though I knew she was right, I would have rather washed windows than admit she was right.

The secret to a peaceable marriage is to deny, with God's help, those negative desires. We must live rightly with the Spirit before we can live rightly with our mate.

DISCUSSION

Are you able to distinguish between the positive and negative desires within you? How would you characterize the amount of quarreling and fighting you do? Do you wound each other with words when you do quarrel?

APPLICATION

The next time you begin to quarrel, stop and analyze why you are becoming upset. See if you can identify the root cause. Then ask the Lord in prayer to remove the temptation and to fill you with the Spirit.

PRAYER

Lord Jesus, we confess that we have wounded each other with our words. We have gone beyond wisdom in our disagreements. We confess that our motives and desires have been born of our selfishness, and not of the Spirit. Forgive us, we pray, and lead us into a full surrender of our lives to Your purposes for us. Amen.

COMFORT ZONE/PRESSURE ZONE

What causes fights and quarrels among you? Don't they come from your desires that battle within you?

JAMES 4:1

*H*e was a deacon, Sunday school teacher, successful businessman, father, friend, and husband. Everything he touched was turning to gold. He became successful beyond his dreams. He relished the passions of business, the money, the "art of the deal." Life was good.

Then for a year and a half he raced out of control, working into all hours of the night and ignoring his family. He went from spending time on daily devotions to independence from God. His wife announced she had reached the end of her rope. All in all he, too, was pretty miserable. He stood on the brink of losing the family he loved so much.

God has created each of us with certain aptitudes, abilities, capacities, and learned skills. These flow together to create an optimum potential for each of us. To strive beyond this level is certain to produce a strain. God intends for us to live in peace with each other, to lead a quiet life, to mind our own business, to be godly husbands and wives, and to rise to our level of competence. In short, God has in mind a *comfort zone* for each of us in which we can love, trust, serve, and obey Him.

But we often become dissatisfied. Desires battle within us to stretch for more. Our flesh fans our appetites into a roaring blaze of greed and ambition. The culture sucks us into its materialistic, valueless vortex. We are ever striving to achieve the next higher rung. The Peter Principle takes effect: We rise to the level of our incompetence.

When this happens, we quickly adjust our spending and lifestyle to the higher income. But we don't have the natural ability and learned skill to support our new rank. We begin to feel the pinch. We begin to feel pressure. What we should do, of course, is ask for our old job back. But our pride persuades us we cannot lower our lifestyle, even though we do not have the horsepower to sustain it. So we begin to borrow money. The only two ways to support our lifestyles are income and debt. Now the debt payments add to the pressure we were already feeling. We have moved from the comfort zone into the *pressure zone*.

The pressure zone stands as a tall barrier to oneness and open communication. When we live in the pressure zone we lose our inner peace, damage our fellowship with God, poison our relationships with others, and risk bringing our marriages crashing down.

How do couples find themselves on the brink of utter ruin? It is because of "the desires that battle within you." We ask God to bless us "with wrong motives, that you may spend what you get on your pleasures" (James 4:3).

The only way out is to stop pretending. We must sit down and calmly, honestly assess our own comfort zone. What would it look like? We must confess our wrong ambition. We must make corrections to fit the level of our lifestyle to the level of our ability. What corrections need to be made? We must reconsider our careers. Have we risen to the level of our incompetence? These hard choices now will save a much harder choice later. The choice now is to move from the pressure zone to the comfort zone. The choice later is, "Who gets custody of the kids?" It happens every day. Don't let it happen to you.

DISCUSSION

Are you living in the comfort zone or the pressure zone? How is it affecting you?

APPLICATION

If applicable and if you are ready, sit down and systematically go through the steps suggested in the last paragraph above on how to get back into the comfort zone.

PRAYER

Either or both, as applicable: O Lord, we have surely played the part of fools. We have been seduced by worldly ways into the pressure zone. Release us, we pray, from this deadly trap. Let us rightly assess our abilities, aptitudes, competencies, capacities, and skills. Grant us the courage to make the hard choices to move back into the comfort zone. Help us to live in peace with each other, to lead a quiet life, to mind our own business, to be godly husbands and wives, and to live at the level of our competence. Amen.

UNREALISTIC EXPECTATIONS

*And if you lend to those from whom you expect repayment, what credit is
that to you? Even "sinners" lend to "sinners," expecting to be repaid in full.*
LUKE 6:34

*R*ecently I saw a cartoon of a bride and groom walking down the aisle
after exchanging vows. She smiled to herself, thinking, *I'll never have to
cook again.* He smiled to himself, thinking, *I'll never have to go out to eat
again.*

Expectations. We all bring them with us, don't we? This illustration may
push the idea to the outer edge, but I believe that, by degrees, this reflects
exactly how we each come into marriage. All of us bring expectations into
marriage—different, often unrealistic expectations. Those expectations are
based on 1) our image of marriage and 2) our unmet needs.

We each have an image of what the ideal marriage looks like in our minds.
We may have gained that image from our parents—what they said and did,
family folklore about our ancestors, a friend's parents, watching television,
reading books, movie stars, or a hero.

We also each have unmet needs. Needs for acceptance, appreciation, and
communion. Needs to alleviate loneliness, a lack of personal fulfillment, and
boredom. We pick our partner because we think he or she will be the white
knight (or knightess) who rescues us.

First, let's relax. It's perfectly normal and okay to have unmet needs. It's
also only logical that we each would have an image of the ideal marriage.
These two factors draw the contours of our expectations. Yet, these two
factors can become real barriers to oneness when they are faulty or corrupted.
When they are, unrealistic expectations result which can destroy a relationship.

Let me give an example from business. I believe the single main reason
that people move from one job to another is that they price themselves out
of the market. In other words, they set unrealistic expectations. Let me
explain. A new employee is needed. She puts her best foot forward and has
a superb interview. She and her employer negotiate a big salary.

As time goes along, however, several things happen. First, the boss's
opinion goes down when flaws are detected. Second, the salary goes up with
annual inflation increases. Third, the employee feels let down by the lack of
support which the boss had promised. Finally, there comes a point in time
when the employee wants more money than the boss feels the employee's

skills are worth. But the boss can't actually come out and say that (though he/she should). So the employee becomes disgruntled, interviews a new employer, puts her best foot forward, and starts the process over.

All of this is based upon unrealistic expectations. The employee prices herself out of the market. The boss can hire another employee whom he/she believes, rightly or wrongly, is better for less money.

In our marriages we often price ourselves out of the market. We increase the price our partner must pay to stay in the game. We set our expectations too high. Or we start out being reasonable, but then raise them as we move along. Marriage is not a business. We must learn to give without expecting anything in return. We must learn to communicate our expectations to our mates, then listen to see if they agree we are being realistic.

DISCUSSION

What was the image of the ideal marriage you brought into your partnership? What were your unmet needs when you married? Looking back, do you think you had realistic expectations? Why or why not?

APPLICATION

Surrender your expectations of your mate to Christ. Commit to love your mate for her/his weaknesses as well as strengths.

PRAYER

Dear Lord, we acknowledge that we have set unrealistic expectations for each other. Forgive us, Father. By faith we now surrender our expectations of each other to You. Help us, by degrees, to focus more on meeting each other's needs than having our own expectations met. Amen.

TACITURN AND LOQUACIOUS

However, each one of you also must love his wife as he loves himself, and the wife must respect her husband.
EPHESIANS 5:33

taciturn *adj.* Uncommunicative: laconic.
loquacious *adj.* Extremely talkative: gabby.

He seems always to be preoccupied. He doesn't have much to say anymore, often answering in grunts. His career has not turned out exactly like he planned. He spends most of his time thinking about how to improve, how to get ahead, how to increase his income.

When they were dating he delighted to share all his hopes and dreams with her. She would sit raptly for hours drinking in his every word and gesture.

When life started to take a different direction than he had hoped, he tried to explain how it made him feel inside. She, too, was disappointed that things were not turning out as expected. When he would begin to share with her she would often speak hastily—sometimes making suggestions which proved neither helpful nor that she fully understood his dilemma. Over time, he slowly stopped initiating conversation and, without fanfare, withdrew into himself.

As he would speak less and less, she would fill the quiet by talking more and more. The more she talked about herself the less he listened. After all, he had huge problems weighing down upon his shoulders—he felt the problems of the whole world. He couldn't care less about who she'd seen at the mall.

The less he listened, the more she ached and felt distant from him. She hid her pain, though, and threw herself wholeheartedly into her own work and volunteer activities. She lived her life her way, and he lived his life his way. But for both it was the wrong way.

A man finds much of his self-esteem in his work. When work goes badly, his self-esteem suffers. He begins to feel like a failure. Yet, it is his wife who can raise him above his circumstances. A wife that respects ("reveres") her husband will give him courage to go on. When, however, she fails to empathize with him, his courage to go on will melt away.

A woman needs to express the details of her life. If her husband ignores her, she feels unappreciated and ends up hurt. A husband who listens attentively to his wife will deeply encourage her. However, if he fails to love her in this way, her spirit shrivels.

140

The Bible tells the husband that he must love his wife. Bible love is *agape* love; it is a moral choice; it is a decision we make as a matter of principle, duty, and propriety. Biblical love is a decision; it is not a feeling. This means you must open up to your wife by choice. You must love her regardless of her response—even if she is too hasty in her advice or does not seem to understand your situation.

The Bible tells the wife that she must respect her husband. Biblical respect is to revere and hold in high esteem. This, too, is a choice; it is a decision we make. Regardless of how the world values your husband's contribution, you have chosen to see the good in this man that others may not now see. But they will, because your respect and support will result in a breakthrough for him. When his work is not giving him self-esteem, you can.

DISCUSSION

Husband, are you taciturn? How did it happen? Wife, are you loquacious? How did it happen? Both: Are you a good listener for your partner? What can you do to restore communication to its proper balance in your marriage?

APPLICATION

Get in touch with whether or not you are really listening to each other. The next time he fumbles for words, just keep listening. The next time she wants to tell you a juicy detail, put down your newspaper and look into her eyes. Set some time aside to talk about each other's work and interests.

PRAYER

Both: Lord, I can see that we have let a wall build up between us. We don't share deeply like we did in the beginning. We have offended each other by being insensitive in the ways we communicate. Help me to be a better listener. And help me to express myself with love and respect. Amen.

A CRITICAL SPIRIT

We who are strong ought to bear with the failings of the weak and not to please ourselves. Each of us should please his neighbor for his good, to build him up.

ROMANS 15:1–2

She first noticed him in their junior year of college. His whole presence appeared effortless. He answered the professor's questions with remarkable confidence. She arranged for a mutual friend to introduce them.

From the beginning she realized that he had an uncanny business sense. Handsome, charming, and smart, he was everything she wanted in a husband. She complimented him for his intelligence and relational skills. She painted the portrait of an incredibly successful career. Her affirmations led to love. They were married the week after graduation.

Soon, though, she perceived some shortcomings in her husband and wanted to "help" him. She became highly involved in managing his career. She helped him select his first job: This one would not have enough potential; that one was beneath him. She picked out all his clothes. She bought him books on time management. She constantly urged him to look for the next position. Over ten years he changed jobs four times, always on leads she had found. She corrected his grammar, critiqued his résumé, and criticized his bosses if they were too slow to recognize his potential.

The constant attention and criticism slowly melted his self-confidence. He never seemed to do anything worthy of praise from his wife. Her habitual tinkering with his career choked off the intimacy they shared briefly in college. He stopped sharing the details of his life with her. He withdrew into a world of sports, television, and the activities of his children. The more he withdrew, the harder she pressed. He felt manipulated.

Certainly this scenario is reversed in many marriages—it's the husband who criticizes the wife. No matter who does it, the defeated spirit that results is the same. To be critical means "to judge harshly and adversely." The spirit of a person is their "essential nature." To have a critical spirit, then, means to have an essential nature that judges harshly and adversely. In how many marriages do one or both partners have a critical spirit? Too many.

How can you know if you have a critical spirit? Ponder these statements: Your mate never measures up to your expectations. No matter how he/she tries to please you, your spouse always comes up just a little bit short. You wish your mate could be more like you—perfect. Well, not perfect, but smart. Really smart.

Are we really that superior? Suppose you can swim five miles, but your mate can swim only one mile. This makes you five times better, right? However, the coast of California is over 6,000 miles from the coast of China. Assume you are standing on California's coast and the China coast represents God's standard. Even if you are five times better than your mate, you are still 5,995 miles from God's standard. Swimming five times farther out to sea only makes you five times as stupid. You will both still drown.

Only by God's unfathomable grace do we get over to the other side. We are all weak people in need of a Savior. We ought to bear each other's weaknesses, not criticize them. "We who are strong ought to bear with the failings of the weak and not to please ourselves. Each of us should please [our mate] for his [or her] good, to build him [or her] up."

When our mates have strengths we should affirm them, but never pressure them to perform. To criticize our mates at the point of their strength is to kill their courage.

Remember, we are all sinners saved by grace. We have each been forgiven much—whether 5,999 or 5,995. We have no basis for a critical spirit. Instead, as ministers of God's grace, we should build each other up.

DISCUSSION

Both answer: To what extent do you think you have a critical spirit? Give an example. How has your mate hurt you with a critical spirit? (Spouse: Listen deeply without giving a quick response.)

APPLICATION

Instead of focusing on our mates—how much is lacking—let's look at ourselves and the size of the debt God has forgiven us. Surely He bears with our failings. Let us commit to bear with each other's failings when we are weak and build each other up.

PRAYER

Either, as appropriate: Heavenly Father, I confess that I have had a critical spirit. I have dragged my mate down. I have extinguished so much that once burned bright. I pray, O God, from the bottom of my heart that I may build my mate up and do nothing to bring him/her down. Help me to bear with my mate's weaknesses, even as he/she bears with mine. Amen.

THE MAKING OF A MISTRESS

An elder must be blameless, the husband of but one wife.
TITUS 1:6

A man finds great delight in his work. It is a source of personal fulfillment for the basic God-given drive within him. He is made to perform, to achieve, to accomplish. Women, of course, delight in their work too, but in this devotional I want to focus on a great problem men face.

Because of the Fall this drive or need must be managed. We do not through a single, once-for-all decision choose to devote just the right amount of time and energy to work, then live happily ever after. Rather, we must each day respond to the unique pressures and opportunities that day brings. We must manage each day in light of our priorities. Do our daily choices reflect the long-term decisions we have already made about the texture and contours we want our lives to display?

Because men often fail to "manage" their inner motivation to attain, they make mistresses.

One man finds his work intoxicating. He feels he is changing the world. He arrives early and leaves late. He takes work home and feels guilty going on vacation. Work has become his mistress.

Another man finds his significance in his community work. His career has become a bore, but his need to achieve still fuels him on. He is out several nights each week. When he is at home he hangs on the phone, touching base with other important people involved in his causes. His organizations have become his mistress.

Another man, his career unfulfilled, throws himself into sports—both as participant and spectator. He would rather play a game of softball than eat. He follows the perpetual parade of television sports spectaculars. He organizes his schedule around the college football bowl games, the NFL football play-offs and Super Bowl, the NCAA Final Four, the NBA play-offs, and the World Series. Sports have become his mistress.

Another man throws himself into the ministry. He serves as an elder or deacon in his church. He volunteers for every church committee that needs an extra hand. If the church doors are unlocked he is there. Religion has become his mistress.

There's no place in a man's life for a mistress. It would be wrong not to enjoy work, community involvement, sports, or ministry. However, whenever any activity or commitment leaves the wife feeling lonely and abandoned, there is the sin of overindulgence. It is giving yourself to something other than the wife who is "bone of your bones." It is spiritual and emotional adultery against your wife.

Early in my career I read somewhere about a man who each day crossed over a bridge that spanned a little stream about five minutes away from his home. Each day on the way home he would think over his day—until he arrived at the bridge. When he crossed over the bridge, in his mind's eye he would take his briefcase and hurl it into the little stream. In this way he did not take work home that would distract from his priority to be a loving husband and father. This gave him five minutes to refocus his thoughts on his wife and children.

When he arrived home he was prepared to greet his wife and each child. He was prepared to enter into their worlds. He was prepared to give attention to those to whom he had made vows and pledges.

As a young husband and father this appealed to me. I, also, crossed a bridge over a small stream on the way home. Following this simple mental cue I was able to each day cut off thinking about my work before I arrived home, preventing my work from becoming my mistress.

No matter how much we love what we do, if it causes loneliness and pain for those with whom we have taken vows and made pledges, we sin against them. A man who cannot manage his desires will soon have a "mistress."

DISCUSSION

Husband, have work and other activities ever been "mistresses" in your life? How are you doing these days? Do you need to make changes? What are they, and will you make them? Wives, do you agree with your husband's assessment? If not, respond to his answers. Husband, listen to her with an open heart.

APPLICATION

Husband, if you have made a mistress of anything, make a plan to correct the situation. If it is work, is there a place you can throw out your briefcase or toolbox on the way home? If it is nonwork-related, decide in advance with your wife how many hours you will devote to your nonwork, nonfamily activities.

PRAYER

Him: Father, I confess that I have made mistresses of _____ (insert answers). I can see how I have erred. Help me to make the adjustments that will let my wife know that I love no other like I love her, that I realize she is worthy of my attention and energy. Amen.

IN SUMMARY

*T*he process can be hard, but it is good to learn the things that pull us apart. Here are some of the important ideas from this section.

Application: Read these thoughts out loud to each other meditatively. One of you read a point and the other make a comment. On the next idea switch roles, and so on, until you have read and commented on each idea. Conclude in prayer.

- Slowly, over the years, he let their love burn down, and one day, feeling cold and isolated, she made her choice, and now nothing will bring her back.
- When we make any person or ambition (except Christ) more important than our spouse, we run the risk of the fire going out.
- In the course of our lives we each, husband and wife alike, will go through several periods of deep, dark frustration. Each of these frustrating times is an opportunity for retreat or advance in our relationship with one another.
- If we take on our problems in the flesh, our urge will be to exclude our partner. If, on the other hand, we deal with our frustrations in the Spirit our desire will be to include our mate in the totality of our pain.
- An almost mystical intimacy develops on the back of shared sorrows.
- Over the course of years the temperature of our romance with each other will slowly, quietly cool off without vigilant effort to keep it heated up.
- The deepest expression of our love comes through our willingness to share in the tedium of each other's daily routines and frustrations.
- Unilaterally deciding to withhold sexual relations from your spouse is banned by the Bible. No permanent abstinence from the act of marriage is ever contemplated in the Scriptures.
- Both husband and wife yearn for a deep love from one another. It is a desire to be one entity, to feel that I am absolutely the most important person or thing in your life—not just because of moral duty, but because you like me, you really do like me.
- At the end of life what counts is not the accomplishments and accolades attained, but the people we have touched and the relationships we have developed.

- It is better for a man to make a small income with dignity than to bluff about his position or resources and lose the respect of his wife. It is good for a wife to bear patiently while her husband struggles through the dark hour of unemployment.
- Bitterness strangles the lifeblood out of a marriage—literally dries up our bones—and makes the words of our mate like fingernails on a chalkboard. Bitterness and intimacy cannot grow in the same heart. The one is poison to the other.
- "For more than anything else one's own righteousness and wisdom deceive one and work against faith in Christ, since we love the flesh and the sensations of the flesh and also riches and possessions, but we love nothing more ardently than our own feelings, judgment, purpose, and will, especially when they seem to be good"—Martin Luther.
- When husband and wife are more focused on pleasing each other than getting their own way, God will free them up to mutually love and respect each other.
- Simply put, if a couple continually quarrels and fights, one or both have not yielded themselves to the Holy Spirit. The secret to a peaceable marriage is to deny ourselves, take up our cross, and follow Jesus. We must walk rightly with the Spirit before we can walk rightly with our mate.
- When we live in the pressure zone we lose our inner peace, damage our fellowship with God, poison our relationships with others, and risk bringing our marriages crashing down.
- We each bring expectations into marriage—different, often unrealistic expectations. Those expectations are based on 1) our image of marriage and 2) our unmet needs.
- Nothing he could do or say ever measured up to her expectations, and she let him know.
- When our mate has strengths we should affirm him or her, but never pressure him or her to perform. To criticize our mates at the point of their strength is to kill their courage.
- If men fail to "manage" their inner motivation to attain, they will make "mistresses."
- No matter how much we love what we do, if it causes loneliness and pain for those to whom we have taken vows and made pledges, we sin against them. A man who cannot manage his desires will soon have a "mistress."

Sharing Those Moments

A man will leave his father and mother and be united to his wife, and they will become one flesh.

GENESIS 2:24

*I*t was about 7:30 A.M. on a hot, muggy June morning. I was working in my study when suddenly I heard and felt a tremendous *whomp*. I hesitated for a second or two before it occurred to me, *that's the noise a hot air balloon makes when the pilot lights the fire.*

I leaped to my feet and raced into the backyard to catch a view. Nothing to the south. Nothing to the west. I bolted around to the side yard where I knew I had clear visibility to the north and could also see into the front yard.

As fate would have it, at that moment the woman across the street was walking to the street in her pajamas to fetch her morning paper. Unfortunately, at the precise instant she turned to go back inside she happened to look across the street and catch my eyes. There I stood, craning my neck over the fence to catch a glimpse of the hot air balloon.

Egads! I ducked behind the fence as quickly as I could and slinked back to my study, knowing I now had a neighbor who thought I was a pervert. I never even got to see the balloon.

We all have embarrassing moments when perceptions and realities collide into a humorous concoction of anecdotes that can be filed away for future use. But these experiences have current value, too, if we will exploit the opportunities.

As soon as Patsy awakened I shared this embarrassing moment with her and we both had a hearty laugh. Instead of spending the day brooding about whether or not my neighbor was going to call the police, I shared the story with my wife and was set free from dwelling on it any longer.

Our spouses are there for us. They are one flesh with us. That mystical fusion of man and woman into a unity forms the backdrop for life's most interesting play. As the saga unfolds she always has a man upon whose shoulder she can cry. He always has a woman in whose bosom he can be comforted. She always has a hero to rescue her from her fears. He always has a heroine who holds the fort together while he hunts for big game.

Our oneness is a unique human relationship. We are not two ships passing in the night. We are not mere roommates sharing the same roof. We are not partners in a business venture. We are one flesh, "A man will . . . be united to his wife, and they will become one flesh."

The Hebrew word for "united" (NIV) or "cleave" (KJV) literally means to be stuck together. One writer described it like two pieces of paper being glued together. You cannot separate them without tearing them both.

Share the extremes of life with one another—the embarrassing moments, the great victories, the dark temptations, the tragic failings, the ecstatic joys. Laugh, cry, sing, and dance. Make beautiful music together. Smell the flowers. Joke around. Lighten up. Be real. You are, after all, stuck with each other.

DISCUSSION

Both respond: Discuss the metaphor for marriage of two pieces of paper glued together. Wife, what is an area of your life in which you are not stuck tightly to your husband? Why have you been holding back? Husband, what is an area of your life in which you are not stuck tightly to your wife? Why have you been holding back?

APPLICATION

Share something right now with your mate that you have been holding back. It may be an embarrassing moment, a failing, a secret joy, or anything else. Be of good courage and do it.

PRAYER

Either or both: Lord, Lord. How we praise and thank You for each other—for the great laughs and the good cries we have shared together; for the comfort we give each other; for the experiences we have been through together. Lord, there is no one with whom I would rather be "stuck." Thank You. Amen.

LOVE IS WHAT LOVE DOES

And now I will show you the most excellent way.
1 CORINTHIANS 12:31

*S*uddenly he became aware of his heavy, labored breathing. A tightness constricted his chest. Adrenaline rushed to his limbs, blood to his heart.

No, it was not a heart attack. Rather, overflowing springs of love gushed forth from his inner man as he considered his wife. His heart, mind, soul, body, and spirit each invested a portion into the flash flood of emotion which overtook him. He had not often "felt" love, but he did this day.

Upon reflection later, he knew his feelings were simply the by-product of his faithfulness to do what biblical love demands. He had invested his creativity, imagination, time, and money to demonstrate love to his wife. Now he was merely reaping what he had sown.

What is love? Love *is* what love *does*. To define love at rest is impossible because love never rests. If love rests it is no longer love, but indifference. Love is always doing. Love is always in motion. To attempt to define what love *is* is a fool's errand. But we can define love by stating over and over again what love does from different angles. In the same way each facet of a diamond yields additional appreciation of its loveliness, so each angle from which we observe love reveals a deeper knowledge of its beauty. Love is the most excellent way.

What is love not? Love is not a feeling. Joyful feelings are a by-product of *doing* love.

How do we *do* love? By demonstrating love sixteen ways. Positively, we demonstrate love eight ways through:

> patience
> kindness
> keeping no record of wrongs
> rejoicing with truth
> always protecting
> always trusting
> always hoping
> always persevering.

We also illustrate love by:

> not envying
> not boasting

> not acting proud
> not acting rude
> not self-seeking
> not angering easily
> not delighting in evil
> and not failing (see 1 Cor. 13:4–8).

It is the most excellent way.

Love is the most important thing. The Bible tells us to love God and love people, the two great commandments. "Keep only these and you will find that you are obeying all the others" (Matt. 22:40 TLB). Jesus commands us to love one another: "My command is this: Love each other as I have loved you" (John 15:12). Love is the only law we need. If we love each other we will fully satisfy all God's requirements. "All ten [commandments] are wrapped up in this one, to love your neighbor as you love yourself. Love does no wrong to anyone. That's why it fully satisfies all of God's requirements. It is the only law you need" (Rom. 13:9–10 TLB).

Love is the glue that holds our marriages together and the oil that keeps us from rubbing each other the wrong way. No bond between a man and a woman can cement us together like love, for a husband and wife will inevitably rub each other the wrong way. Marriage produces friction. Love is also the lubricant that keeps our marriages running smoothly. Love is "the most excellent way."

DISCUSSION

Both answer: Is it necessary to feel love in order to love? How do feelings of love come about? Tell your mate two or three things he/she does that make you feel loved.

APPLICATION

Put a check mark by each of the sixteen characteristics of 1 Corinthians 13 love (see above) which you sense you are doing well. Place an "x" by the characteristics you believe you most need to work on.

PRAYER

Either: Lord Jesus, we know that we only love You because You first loved us. Thank You for giving us love as a fruit of the Holy Spirit within us. Help us to live and walk in the Spirit so that we may actively demonstrate love to each other, thereby creating a faithful witness to the power of Your love to transform lives. In Your name I pray. Amen.

151

LOVE IS PATIENT

Love is patient. . . .

1 CORINTHIANS 13:4

M y wife, Patsy, and her sister flew off to Birmingham for a long weekend to visit the new home of their sister and family who had just moved there. Our children and I decided to surprise Patsy by meeting their returning flight three days later.

As the three of us eagerly peered down the jetway they finally appeared, a sight for sore eyes. They glanced at each other quite surprised. After warm welcoming hugs and kisses we proceeded to the baggage claim area.

Patsy's sister, Marilyn, and I were visiting when I happened to catch a glimpse of my wife out of the corner of my eye. She had knelt down next to a smallish travel cage with a little puppy in it and was affectionately cooing. *How cute,* I thought to myself.

Patsy made a sudden move to open the cage and started to pick up this little puppy. My son ran over and said, "Mom, what are you doing?" While I hyperventilated, Patsy tried to draw our attention to the name on the cage. Finally, we saw that this cute critter was "Katie Morley," an eight-week-old yellow Labrador retriever puppy, soon to weigh sixty pounds.

"What in the world . . ." I said to no one in particular. We had never, *ever* discussed having a dog. In fact, Patsy is allergic to dogs! We'd always had hamsters, and at the time had two rabbits. But a dog! *My lands, this is the kind of thing you usually talk over first. This kind of decision requires prayer!* I thought.

"I tried to call but no one was home," Patsy said. "It was the last female. I had to make the decision on the spot. She's fully registered, though, and comes from good parents."

We must have a *really* good relationship for Patsy to make such a large commitment. Apparently she believed I loved her enough to be patient with her impromptu decision. Truth be known, Katie has become an irreplaceable part of our family.

In marriage we need to know each other so well that we can predict our mate's response. Even if we don't think his/her response will initially be positive, we believe that he/she loves us enough to be patient and kind to us in the wake of our spontaneity. After all, what's life without a little spontaneity? Well, there would be a whole lot less dog food on our grocery bill, for one thing.

DISCUSSION

Both answer: How patient are you with your partner? Would your partner be confident enough in your loving patience to do something impulsive? Are you intimate enough with your mate to predict his or her response if you did something wild and crazy?

APPLICATION

Commit to express a patient, loving response the next time your mate surprises you. Mate, if your partner forgets this commitment, be sure to offer a gentle reminder (remember, love is gentle as well as patient).

PRAYER

Either: Dear God, thank You for the pleasures of life that come from being a little wild and crazy from time to time. Help me to be a little unpredictable, and to accept with gratitude a little unpredictability from my mate. And help us both to remember that love is patient. Amen.

Becoming Best Friends

Let us not give up meeting together, as some are in the habit of doing, but let us encourage one another.

HEBREWS 10:25

*A*s I placed the phone back in the receiver a heavy sadness flooded my emotions. *How could Janie throw in the towel after seventeen years of marriage? I know that she understands believers are not to divorce. Why would she turn her back on her beliefs? Poor John. He sounded so depressed.*

Janie was divorcing John. The mere thought that Christians divorce utterly terrified me. Many of our Christian friends struggled in their marriages. I knew that. But I always thought marriage was forever. I decided that I should begin praying for couples I knew who were having troubles. Without hesitation I was able to list eleven couples. Whew! That scared me even more.

The more I thought about it, the more I sensed that no marriage is invulnerable. As my mind wandered over our own thirteen years of marriage, I realized that I had many interests, ambitions, and priorities, not the least of which was to build a successful business. It dawned on me that Patsy was not my top priority. In fact, to be completely honest, in many ways I viewed her as another human resource to help me achieve my dreams. As a result, I often related to her more like a business partner or treated her like an employee.

It had never occurred to me that she might have her own dreams. I hadn't considered how she might feel about the risks I was taking. Whenever I wanted something I thought she might not like, I would turn on the charm for days, even weeks, before I would make the "big ask." She thought my motives were like those of an eager little boy, but I was taking aim at the big leagues.

I further realized that our relationship was not deep. It wasn't superficial, but that tended to deceive me into thinking it was more meaningful than it really was. But in a moment of pure, clear, candid illumination, the Holy Spirit showed me the truth. I was using Patsy.

I felt dirty, ugly, and ashamed. Before the Lord I repented and asked God to show me what to do. A plan began to take shape. He showed me how to make Patsy my best friend.

Without announcing my intentions, I started hanging around the dinner table after the kids left to do homework or whatever. I didn't have an agenda.

I wasn't trying to do family business, like discussing finances or balancing the checkbook. I just wanted to be with Patsy.

For twenty minutes each day I would ask her about her day, her dreams, her hopes, her fears, her doubts, her concerns. I asked her how she felt the children were turning out and how her spiritual walk was going. I wanted to get to know this woman who had knocked me off my feet over a dozen years earlier. She began to thaw toward me, even warm up. I had forgotten how those big fifty-cent-piece-sized eyes could make my heart go faint.

Within a few weeks we were on the road to becoming best friends. I found that when I chose to respect Patsy, make her my top priority, and treat her with courtesy and appreciation our relationship moved from business to personal. We have continued to spend this special time together. It's not a law that we have to, so sometimes we don't—but not very often. Not long after I changed Patsy gave me a plaque for my desk. It read, "Happiness is being married to your best friend." Thank You, Jesus.

How is your relationship? Is it business or personal? Are you using each other, or are you in this together?

DISCUSSION

Both answer: What do best friends do when they are together? Do you think it would be possible for the two of you to spend a set amount of time together each day?

APPLICATION

If you have not already done so, decide to become best friends. Plan to spend twenty minutes or so together every day. Pick a time that works for you—coffee in the morning, a walk, sitting at the table after dinner, or on the porch before retiring for the day. You have a good start by doing this book together.

PRAYER

Either, as appropriate: Heavenly Father, I confess that I have let many other things get in front of my relationship with my wife/husband. I have let our relationship become too superficial. In fact, I confess that too often I think of it more like a business partnership than a marriage. I even tend to use her/him. My motives are not always pure. Forgive me, Lord. Help us to discover the way for us to become best friends. Amen.

INTENTIONALLY HURTING EACH OTHER

A man of knowledge uses words with restraint,
and a man of understanding is even-tempered.
PROVERBS 17:27

*F*or some time I had been harboring feelings that needed to be expressed. On two occasions I had tried to share these feelings with Patsy, but what I said was painful to her. So I backed away.

Those feelings kept growing and multiplying until one night I felt I would explode unless I could express myself. Sensing she was receptive, a floodgate of feelings, thoughts, and perceptions flowed forth. Somewhere near the middle of my remarks Patsy became very quiet. I could tell that what I was saying was hurting her, yet I felt I could not be whole until it was said. Sometimes pain must be inflicted to bring about healing. Setting a bone is painful, but it necessarily precedes healing.

After our discussion I heard soft, muted sobs coming from behind the closed door of our bathroom. I tried the door, but it was locked. I knocked, but she did not want me to come in. I panicked. *Oh no. What have I done? I have said too much.* I forcibly unlocked the door so I could talk to Patsy and try to comfort her.

As I went in her sobs turned into a long wail and tears were rolling down her cheeks. I was crushed that I had inflicted such pain upon her.

Yet, as painful as that experience was for both of us, we both agreed later that it needed to happen. I had bottled up feelings that needed to be expressed. Sometimes we must intentionally hurt each other in order to make our relationship whole. Some things just need to be said. It may hurt, even to tears, but being completely open and honest with each other is the only possible basis for a genuinely harmonious marriage.

Feelings are not necessarily realities. More often they are perceptions that are irrational and erroneous. Yet, until they are dealt with they pour poison into our brain cells.

What happens when we leave unsaid that which ought to be said? Our relationship cannot attain 100 percent of its full potential. In other words, unspoken secrets create static on the lines of communication between us. If you are irritated by your husband's lack of consideration or your wife's constant worry, no deep, enduring understanding can develop until you express how you really feel. Until you do, your relationship will never reach its full potential.

After some more talk, Patsy felt better but wanted to be alone for a while, so I went to bed. The next morning I awakened with a new spring in my step. I sensed Patsy and I had done something significant the night before. I felt a great release and a deeper sense of intimacy. Patsy didn't immediately share my feelings of liberation. It would take another round of her expressing how *my* feelings made *her* feel and a response from me to put things right.

At the end of this process we both felt closer to each other. Not talking this through had made a wall that blocked us from reaching the full potential of our marriage.

What is that thing you long to tell your spouse but have feared would wound him or her? Until you open up with each other your relationship will never reach 100 percent.

How do you go about saying things that will intentionally hurt your partner? You should have a sense of occasion. Elevate the moment so that your spouse knows you desire to have a non-standard, important conversation. You can create an elevated moment by setting up a time in advance, changing the pattern (like going into a different room than normal for discussions), or writing a letter expressing your need to say some things.

Your approach must be sensitive, prayerful, and loving. To intentionally hurt your partner may sometimes be necessary, but it should never be easy.

DISCUSSION

Both answer: Is there something between you that is keeping your relationship from reaching its full potential?

APPLICATION

Only if you believe this is the "right occasion," share the thing that is keeping your relationship from reaching its full potential, even if you must risk hurting your spouse. Yet, be tender.

PRAYER

Either, as applicable: Dear God, I long for our marriage to reach 100 percent of its full potential. I don't know the full extent of what needs to be said between us. But I do know that I want to make it right—to do the right thing. Forgive where I have been insensitive; illuminate when I have been blind. Show me the way. Help me to express my feelings and hear my mate's feelings. Amen.

TO PRAY FOR ONE ANOTHER

Therefore confess your sins to each other and pray for each other so that you may be healed. The prayer of a righteous man is powerful and effective.
JAMES 5:16

*O*n the night I hurt Patsy intentionally she wanted to be alone for a while, so I went to bed.

As I lay in bed deep sorrow filled my breast for the pain I had inflicted upon my dear wife of twenty years. Her hurt was my hurt. Her pain was my pain. I tossed and turned. At that moment I would have given anything in the entire world if I could somehow have waved a magic wand and made her pain go away. I turned this over and over in my mind, and then it dawned on me.

I can make her pain go away. I can do it through prayer. It is not God's will for this to bring sorrow to our marriage but joy. If I pray anything according to His will He hears me, and what He hears He grants (for comparison see 1 John 5:14–15).

I began to pray earnestly for Patsy. First, I prayed that God would give her the peace that transcends all understanding. Next I prayed that she would know how wide and long and high and deep is the love of Christ for her, that nothing can separate her from the love of Christ. And I prayed that Patsy would know that my love for her is unconditional. With that I drifted off to sleep.

Our words of comfort can only heal our mate's wounds up to a certain point. Beyond words lies the realm of the supernatural healing power of the Lord Jesus Christ. Only He can administer the balm of complete healing. And this comes through prayer.

Your mate's pain may come from a physical affliction, an emotional trauma, a spiritual lacking, or a moral failure. The source may be a broken relationship or an unfulfilled dream. Your spouse may hurt in her/his body or emotions. Her/his spirit may be crushed. She/he may have lost hope. She/he may feel alone and abandoned by friends, children, parents, or even you.

"Pray for each other so that you may be healed." When we get into the custom of praying for the healing of each other, we get out of the silly, "common sense" idea that we are bound by our circumstances. We are not. Jesus can, and will, reach down into the hubbub of human circumstances and do the supernatural—if we ask.

Our problem is that we do not believe in prayer. Oh, we believe in doing it, but we do not believe that God answers it. We think it earns us favor with

God so we pray. We even believe that God hears our prayer. But we do not believe He will really answer us. After all, haven't we all prayed before and not received what we asked for?

Actually, God *always* answers prayer. He gives us exactly what we pray for in *His name*. There is nothing for which we pray that God does not answer. What we must get hold of is that He always answers, but His answers may not always be what we want. It is His will that is being done, not ours. The answer that doesn't come is actually the answer. It is *no*, or it is *not now*, but it is not the lack of an answer.

The secret of prayer is found in praying "in His name." To pray "in His name" means that we are utterly submitted to the purpose of His will. We do not know the secret will of God, nor should we try to know it. Rather, we often need to pray blind. We don't know exactly His will, so we put our requests before Him in the name of Jesus, allowing Him to do what is best.

No matter how afflicted your mate may be, always keep on praying. Your words can provide remedy to a point, but only prayer will bring about a complete healing. In the secret counsel of the Lord God, He is working out all things in conformity to His will and for the good of those who love Him and are called according to His purpose.

God answered my prayer. He did make Patsy's sorrow go away. It took a few days. That was His will. We can always trust the will of God.

DISCUSSION

Both answer: Where are you hurting right now? (You may want to look at paragraph six of this devotional to prompt your thinking.)

APPLICATION

Make a commitment to pray for the hurts of your partner. You may be the only person in the whole world who knows the deep need your partner has to be touched by the healing power of God. If you are comfortable doing so, pray out loud for your mate's hurt right now.

PRAYER

Both, as appropriate: Our most gracious and loving Father, I know that my words can only go so far to heal and comfort my wife's/husband's wounds and pain. And yet I plead with You, O God, to give me just the right words to say. Beyond my words I earnestly pray that You send Your healing balm. I believe You hear me, Lord, and I believe You really answer. I pray this "in His name." Amen.

OVERDRAWN AND UNAWARE

Be kind and compassionate to one another, forgiving each other, just as in Christ God forgave you.

EPHESIANS 4:32

*B*ecause of financial reverses Ellen and John lost the home in which they were raising their four children, ages four through eleven, and had to move. They had moved eleven times in sixteen years. She was used to moving, having grown up a "military brat."

John struggled to provide, Ellen struggled with their financial problems and, as a result, together they struggled to get along—notwithstanding they both had received Jesus Christ. She found their marriage immensely difficult. She may have been accustomed to moving, but she hated it. After losing their home, she despised being forced to move into a rental apartment. He was not particularly overjoyed about it either. Altogether, their circumstances put a great strain on their marriage and took it right up to the cliff's edge of divorce.

She asked him to move out. During five months of separation John didn't see the children once. After much pleading and promising on his part, Ellen finally invited him to move back in. His hopes soared. Three days later, though, she said, "I'm not sure I want this." His soaring hopes were dashed.

After three days' time, John was to leave for a training program with a new company. As they stood in a parking lot saying their farewells, he honestly thought this would be their last goodbye. To his irrepressible joy, Ellen said, "Well, let's give this one more try." They got back together.

That was seven years ago. In spite of her willingness and his ecstasy, their marriage has continued to sputter along.

Recently two marriages of their friends—one a Christian couple—ended in divorce. One partner in each marriage simply walked away.

"I don't get it," Ellen said incredulously. "They had so much more than we do. We don't have anything and we are making it. How can this be?"

Over the next six weeks, John was away from home on business for four of those weeks. At the end of the sixth week he came home to a frazzled, lonely, worn out wife. She was weary from handling the home pressures alone. She said, "That's it. I quit. I'm going on a vacation by myself. I can't take this anymore. I'm going to get some money and spend it on myself. I need a life."

John was utterly terrified. The specter of their prior troubles loomed large. He wisely turned off his pager and spent the rest of the day talking and weeping with Ellen. By taking the time he was able to divert another disaster.

Yet they both could not help but wonder, *What can we do to not be so constantly close to the brink of disaster? How can we manage our marriage in a way that these episodes don't continuously keep occurring?*

What John and Ellen did not know, unfortunately, is that they were not making enough deposits into each other's emotional bank accounts. They constantly lived off borrowed capital. Their accounts were constantly depleted, if not overdrawn.

The question for all of us is similar. "What can we do to make sure our marriage stays on solid ground?" To make a marriage of two-part harmony we must make deposits into the emotional bank account of our spouse. Walls go up when we make too many withdrawals.

DISCUSSION

Both answer: How close have you lived to the brink of marital disaster? What are the deposits you have made that have built up your mate? What are the withdrawals you have made that you suspect have hurt your mate?

APPLICATION

Express your regret to your spouse for the withdrawals you have made and ask for forgiveness. Tell your spouse three ways he/she can make deposits into your emotional bank account.

PRAYER

Both pray: Dear God, I am so sorry for the way I have made so many withdrawals from the emotional bank account of my husband/wife _____ (name). Forgive me, Lord, for my sin. I ask You to direct me into thoughtful ways of making deposits into the life of my mate. Fill me with Your Holy Spirit so that I may walk in the power of the resurrected Christ. Amen.

MAKING DEPOSITS AT THE CHANGE OF LIFE

Husbands, love your wives, just as Christ loved the church and gave himself up for her.

EPHESIANS 5:25

N̲ow where could Annette be? She always meets my plane when I get home from a long trip. I hope nothing has happened to her.

Andy moved quickly to a pay phone and rang the house. One of his daughters answered and told him, "Mother is on the way, but be careful. She's in one of those moods."

For months Andy had ached to know how to help Annette. Her mood swings made her desperately edgy and touchy. He spoke to experts on women and learned that his wife of twenty-five years was going through the change of life. He had tried many creative ways to let her know of his unconditional love and acceptance, but so far nothing had worked. In the minutes he waited for Annette an idea began to take shape.

Andy moved to the curb. When she finally pulled up he greeted Annette with lavish affection, and then took over the driving. As they passed the turn-off to their home she said, "Andy, you're going the wrong way."

"No, I'm not, Annette. We're going to a hotel tonight."

"We can't do that," she protested. "I don't have any clothes or a toothbrush."

"Yes, we can," he replied. "They have toothbrushes at the desk and you can wear my clothes."

"You're out of your mind!"

"Well, I may be, but that's what we're going to do."

After a few increasingly mild protests they arrived at their suite hotel and checked in. After the bellhop disappeared Andy invited his wife to sit next to him on the couch and talk. After a few minutes he nonchalantly put his hand on top of her hand. He could feel her tension. But after a few minutes the tension began to melt away.

Some time later he quietly slipped his arm around her in a nonsexual way. Again, she tensed up, but after a few minutes he could feel her beginning to relax again.

After a while she began to smile again, and they talked far into the night.

At the suite hotel where they stayed you could make your own breakfast. While Annette still slept, Andy quietly slipped downstairs and prepared a smorgasbord and presented her with breakfast in bed.

Next, he phoned the office and said he wouldn't be in until after lunch. They talked through the morning and then he took her to lunch.

That eighteen-hour period of time changed the course of their marriage. Annette survived her change of life. And she never will forget the love, concern, and understanding her husband showed her during that difficult time. He has never stopped acting like a school boy in love after that night either. Andy was willing to "love his wife as Christ loved the church." He was willing to "give himself up for her." The strongest expression of love we can make is to sacrifice ourselves for one another. When we deny ourselves for our mates we prove by our actions that we "get it" about the true meaning of love.

Whether the occasional blues or a full-blown change of life, every wife has times of depressed feelings in which she needs special sympathy and comfort. These times provide an enormous opportunity for the alert husband to make deposits into her emotional bank account.

DISCUSSION

Him: In the past how have you handled a time of depressed feelings by your wife? After reading the story of Andy and Annette, what would you do differently now? Her: Be receptive and thankful for his positive answers.

APPLICATION

Her: Tell your husband three things you would like him to do differently when you are feeling down. Him: Give her your full, undivided attention without interruption. Make a commitment to follow through on her suggestions.

PRAYER

Him: Dear Jesus, I confess that I have not always been sympathetic and comforting when my wife is down. I confess that I have not spent time creatively thinking about how to help her. I confess that I spend more time worrying about how to keep my car running than how to help my wife when she's struggling. O Lord, give me a heart for making deposits into my wife's emotional bank account. Amen.

THE ANATOMY OF A WITHDRAWAL

In this same way, husbands ought to love their wives as their own bodies.
He who loves his wife loves himself.
EPHESIANS 5:28

*I*t had been a perfect vacation—just the right combination of rest and activity. We spent the last several days in the North Carolina Smokies with Patsy's parents in their beautiful, recently acquired mountain home.

Now we were on our way home. Everyone was in a good mood. We were all anxious to get back home to see Katie, our yellow Labrador retriever. I was driving, and we were making good time.

Patsy said, "Don't you think you're going just a little too fast?"

This really bugged me. I never speed . . . unless I'm in a hurry!

I looked down at the speedometer and said, "No, I don't think so. But I will slow down if you want. This is a four-lane road, even though it's not an interstate."

After a few miles I was pushing it again. The trip home took twelve hours driving straight through.

As we pulled into our driveway, Patsy said, "I think I'll call Marilyn tomorrow and tell her it takes thirteen hours to get to Mom and Dad's." Patsy's sister and husband, who live near us, had scheduled a visit to Patsy's parents' the following week.

"Why would you tell her that?" I asked.

"Because we pushed pretty hard driving home from Mom and Dad's, and I think it would have taken thirteen hours if we hadn't been in such a hurry."

"Patsy, I don't think I drove any faster than they would. Besides, it didn't take thirteen hours. It took twelve. If you want to tell them you think it will take *them* thirteen hours, fine. But don't tell them it took us thirteen hours when it only took twelve."

I just couldn't seem to leave this alone. Finally, Patsy capitulated to my demands and didn't respond to my comments any more. A cool tension settled between us. How many withdrawals from Patsy's emotional bank account can you find here?

First, my driving speed scared her. Second, after a brief period I sped back up again (though she never mentioned it again). Third, I debated how fast I drove versus how fast her sister and husband might drive, admittedly a stupid speculation on my part. Fourth, I forced her to tell her sister what I wanted her to say.

There is only one way to describe what I did: Dumb. Would it have made any difference if we arrived home at 9:00 P.M. instead of 8:00 P.M.? Why was the speed I wanted to drive more important than making Patsy feel edgy for all those hours and miles? Why did I press her on what she would tell her sister? Sinful foolishness and pride. Those are the only conceivable answers.

To really love our mate we must deny ourselves. We must put her/his needs before ours. The goal each day of every married person ought to be to make numerous deposits into the emotional bank account of her or his spouse. By the same token, our goal should be to make as few withdrawals as possible.

DISCUSSION

Both answer: In the routine of a typical day what would you estimate your deposit-to-withdrawal ratio to be in your spouse's emotional bank account? For example: 20 deposits and 4 withdrawals would be a 5-to-1 ratio. Two deposits and 10 withdrawals would be a 1-to-5 ratio.

APPLICATION

If your deposit-to-withdrawal ratio shows you are making more deposits than withdrawals, congratulations. Keep up the good work. If your withdrawals exceed your deposits, your marriage is headed for trouble. Make plans to stop making withdrawals and start making deposits.

PRAYER

Either: Heavenly Father, I thank You for the deposits I have made in _____'s (name) life. Forgive me for not being more alert to the withdrawals I unwittingly make. Moreover, grant me, I pray, the tenacity and courage it takes to fill her/his emotional bank account to overflowing. Amen.

MAKING YOUR MATE YOUR TOP PRIORITY

However, each one of you also must love his wife as he loves himself, and the wife must respect her husband.

EPHESIANS 5:33

*P*at Williams always thought he had a great marriage, even ideal. Yes, he and Jill had occasional spats. We all do. But nothing out of the ordinary. At least, not until December 19, 1982.

On that day, as Pat and Jill chronicle in their book *Rekindled*, something snapped. Pat knew he had hurt Jill that morning. Now, after dinner, he wanted to patch things up, to make it right. He followed Jill around the house, pressing her to talk it over. Finally, Jill said, "I just don't care anymore. I hate this marriage. It's boring me to death. I give up."[15]

She went on to enumerate a litany of unanswered complaints from their years together. He looked into her vacant eyes and realized that she was emotionally dead . . . and he had killed her.

How does a couple drift so far apart? The needs of a man and a woman differ so much. Words that describe the needs of men are task, significance, providing, work, money, and meaning. Words that describe the needs of women are relationship, intimacy, nurturing, home, husband, children, and security. Here's the problem: What men are "into" is often not what wives need. When he makes work or some other pursuit his top priority, something inside her withers, then dies. When she makes the children, work, or some other pursuit her top priority, he begins looking for something to numb the pain in his heart. Couples drift apart unless they remain each other's top priority.

By God's grace and Pat's determined effort the Williams rekindled their marriage, but it wasn't easy. Pat led the way by making Jill his top priority.

Have you made each other your top priority? Or is it the children, the business, the home, sports, social work, or even ministry?

Any man who doesn't make his wife his top priority will lose his wife, even if she decides to stay married because she doesn't believe in divorce. Any woman who doesn't make her husband her top priority will lose her husband, even if he decides to stay married because he doesn't believe in divorce. They will lose each other emotionally. The lonely heart will race when the radio plays, "We've lost that loving feeling. Now, it's gone, gone, gone . . ."

The best way to make your spouse your top priority is to begin thinking in terms of her/his emotional bank account. Learn how your mate likes to give and receive deposits. It may be touching, companionship, support, conversation, small kindnesses, or sex. Your spouse has to bank somewhere; it might as well be with you.

No matter where your marriage stands today, making each other top priority will make it better. You may not even know your mate's account number. That's okay. Ask and it will be given to you.

DISCUSSION

Both answer: What has been your top priority? Why? How are you doing emotionally in your marriage? Explain your answer. What changes would you like to make?

APPLICATION

If your mate has been your top priority, congratulations. You are among an elite and small corps of Christians. Thank God. If not, are you prepared to change? If so, pray and ask God for forgiveness for not meeting your mate's needs and commit to making her/him your top priority.

PRAYER

As appropriate: Lord God, I confess that my mate has not been my top priority. I ask You to forgive me for not meeting my mate's emotional needs. I commit to making _____ (name) my top priority after You. Strengthen me for this task. Amen.

DIVORCE

"For this reason a man will leave his father and mother and be united to his wife, and the two will become one flesh." So they are no longer two, but one. Therefore what God has joined together, let man not separate.

MARK 10:7–9

*T*he three of us sat in my office. She spoke at length about how he had not lived up to her expectations. He confirmed that he had really let her down. She wanted to have nice things he would never be able to afford. "Is that so bad?" she asked.

It was clear in my mind that this woman had already decided that she was going to divorce her husband. This saddened me, for they were both friends. Then she asked the loaded question, "Is it a sin to divorce him?"

"Yes, it is," I replied.

Then came the zinger. "But is it the unforgivable sin?"

"No, it is not."

"Then I'm going to do it."

Even a casual reading of the Bible makes clear that God intends for marriage to be permanent. "Therefore what God has joined together, let man not separate." Once we say I do, there is no turning back. Yet, Christians get divorced all the time. Why do they?

Christians who divorce simply don't understand, or choose to ignore, the sanctity, or sacredness, of marriage. They divorce because they don't think they love their partners anymore, notwithstanding God's *command* to love our spouses. The core problem in marriages that end in divorce, I believe, is that one or both partners made a commitment to the *person* they married but not to the God-established *institution* of marriage. Hence, when their partner does not turn out as expected, no higher commitment holds them in check long enough to work it out.

I believe it is more important to be committed to the institution of marriage than it is to the person you marry. Why? If your highest commitment is to your mate, then what do you do during those times you don't like your mate very much, or when you've been let down?

If, on the other hand, you make an unbreakable commitment to the institution of marriage, then you have something to hold on to during stormy times. Unless you are committed to the institution of marriage itself even more than your spouse, you will always hold divorce as an option. As long

168

as you consider divorce an option for you, no matter how remote, you run the risk of someday bailing out.

God never intended for divorce to be an option. It is not part of God's order. God hates divorce. Divorce is alien to the concept of the kingdom of God on earth. "Thy kingdom come, thy will be done, on earth as it is in heaven." Divorce is contrary to the will of God. Divorce means brokenness, while God is in the business of reconciliation. Divorce means someone failed to love another as Jesus loved them.

The Bible does make two provisions for divorce: first, for adultery (Matt. 19:9); second, for desertion (1 Cor. 7:15). Yet, while these two verses allow for the *possibility* of divorce they do not demand the *necessity* of divorce. These provisions are an accommodation to fallen creatures, but God still hates divorce and His order of things is for permanent marriage. "What God has joined together, let man not separate."

DISCUSSION

Both answer: Have you viewed divorce as an option for Christian couples? Based on this devotional's theme verse, how do you think Jesus would answer this question? Which is the greater commitment for you, your partner in marriage or the institution of marriage? Why?

APPLICATION

Make a commitment that divorce is not an option for you. Pray the following prayer to express that commitment.

PRAYER

Either or both: Most Holy Father, Your ways are not our ways. Help us to surrender our own best thinking to the supremacy of Your will, purpose, and plan. Lord, I never want to be divorced. By faith, I commit that I will never consider divorce an option. I make a commitment not only to my mate, but an even higher commitment to the sanctity of marriage itself. No matter what happens I will seek to make our marriage work by Your grace. Amen.

A LACK OF COMMON INTERESTS

[Love] always protects, always trusts, always hopes, always perseveres.
Love never fails.

1 CORINTHIANS 13:7–8

*T*he greatest bond between two people is a common interest. I am best friends with Tom Skinner, the evangelist, because we share interests in tennis, reconciliation, and evangelism.

Couples become friends because they all like bridge. We befriend the parents of other kids on our sons' and daughters' athletic teams, but next season it's a different group of parents. Men become friends with men who share an interest in golf. Women who play tennis bond with women who play tennis. A common interest is like a glue that holds people in relationship.

On the other hand, people who lack a common interest often find themselves alienated from each other. They have no basis upon which to come together, or stay together. Black and white. Rich and poor. Professional and working class. And sometimes male and female.

One of the great tragedies of marriage is to lack a common interest outside of the children. In some homes the children are the glue that makes the marriage bond work. But what happens when the children leave the nest? Sadly, many couples wake up one day only to realize the person sleeping next to them is a virtual stranger. "Who is this person? And what will keep us together?"

As one man jested, "The only thing we have in common is that we were married on the same day."

Patsy and I (and you) have known several couples who didn't make it because they lacked a personal relationship with one another. They had nothing besides children to bond them together. So once the children became independent they simply drifted apart into their own separate interests, often finding someone of the opposite sex in that other interest. They didn't plan for it to happen. But they found pleasure in someone who shared a common interest. Of course, it doesn't have to be that way. What starts wrong doesn't necessarily have to end wrong. Better to make the adjustment now.

The fastest way to a personal bond is to share a common interest. It could be as simple as playing card games, a shared hobby, meeting new people, attending movies, gardening, brisk walking, or a recreational sport. You may enjoy discussing current events, the Bible, theology, or psychology. Perhaps you could jointly perform community service for the local soup line, Meals

On Wheels, or the symphony. Possibly you could render Christian service together on missions trips, stuffing envelopes, or leading a Sunday school class.

No matter how little you have in common, a few bold moves now could completely change your future together.

DISCUSSION

What are the things we have in common besides the children? (Suggestion: Each write down your interests on a separate sheet of paper and compare. Areas to consider: Intellectual, entertainment, travel, the arts, social, sports, professional, ministry, issues, books, friendships.)

APPLICATION

If you have some common interests, what specific steps can you take to share them together, starting this week? If you do not have common interests, review each other's lists to see if your mate has an interest that you would like to explore, and do it. If you find you have no common interests, begin praying, together and separately, for the Lord to grant you the blessing of a shared interest. It will be glue for your marriage.

PRAYER

Both: Dear Lord, I love my mate and desire to grow old together with him/her. Help us to share common interests together that we can both enjoy. Move us toward one another in the days ahead. Never let our love fail. Let it be for always in all ways. Amen.

BALANCING NEEDS FOR SOCIAL INTERACTION

In the Lord, however, woman is not independent of man, nor is man independent of woman.

1 CORINTHIANS 11:11

*W*e each need a different level of social interaction. Balancing our own needs against the needs of our spouse can be a challenge.

For the first twenty years of my career I went daily to a regular office environment. The fast and furious nonstop action intoxicated me. In the routine course of a day I had about as much social interaction as I could take. As a result, I always came home drained. I was up to my eyeballs in social interaction at the office. The last thing I needed was more engagement with people.

Patsy, on the other hand, had been home with the children all day and was ready for some adult conversation. Her need in the evening was greater than my need. Since my social needs had been met at the office, I did not feel a great deal of motivation to interact with her and the children. I did, but it was more out of duty than desire.

I believe this is how most working men and women feel at the end of the day. Yes, there are exceptions—true extroverts who can't get enough of people. But my experience is that most of us can get enough—even too much—of other people. We need times of solitude to refresh our soul, revive our spirit, and renew our faith. These times should come after the needs of our spouse and children have been met.

After twenty years of high-octane office interaction I now have my office in a small building behind our home, while our administrative office and staff are located in an office complex about ten minutes away. The abrupt change from constant social interaction to only occasional social contact has had an interesting effect on my relationship with Patsy.

Before there wasn't enough of me for her. Now the tables have been reversed. There is not enough of her for me. I'm looking for more social contact. So I will "drop in" on her inside the house. Meanwhile, she is very busy, and I often find myself feeling like an interruption.

Funny, I now find myself on the short end of needing conversation with an adult. I can finally appreciate what Patsy was trying to tell me all those years.

The point of all this? Balancing our needs is no easy task. At any point in time our social (and other) needs will likely not be the same as our mates'. This means that marriage partners must make compromises. One will want to talk out of *desire*. The other must be willing to talk out of *duty*. We are not independent from each other.

In the Lord we are not "independent" from one another. The Greek word for independent literally means "at a space," or, in essence, "separate or apart from." We are not that. There should be no space between a husband and wife. We are not separate or apart from each other.

Said differently, we are dependent upon one another. The Living Bible translates this verse beautifully: "But remember that in God's plan men and women need each other." Yes! We *need* each other. But why?

We are interdependent. We depend upon each other to satisfy our deepest needs. When one spouse needs more contact with the other out of desire, the other must respond out of duty. To not meet our mate's needs is an open invitation for someone else to meet them in our place.

DISCUSSION

Both answer: Are your social needs being fully satisfied? How or how not?

APPLICATION

What changes could you make to balance your social needs? If one partner just doesn't feel like he or she has anything left to give, a change must be made. Do something radical. Change jobs. Drop out of the social club or the softball league. Give your mate the first priority over those who will not be there at your funeral, crying.

PRAYER

Either or both: Lord Jesus, thank You that I am married to someone who is willing to meet my needs. I pray that You would give us wisdom over how to balance our needs for interaction with each other against all the other demands upon us. Help us to not expend all our sociability on others, but hold enough in reserve for each other, every day. Amen.

BIG THINGS AND LITTLE THINGS

Whoever can be trusted with very little can also be trusted with much, and whoever is dishonest with very little will also be dishonest with much.
LUKE 16:10

$\mathscr{I}$ have no difficulty handling life's big challenges. I steel myself and face them head-on. No, I never blow it in the big things. Instead, I blow it in the little things—the cumbersome minutiae of the daily grind.

The plaque that has adorned my office for most of my career says, "Anyone can do the big things right . . . but it's the little things that count." It is not in the big things, but in the little things we are often found wanting. Why is that?

We clearly know the big things when they come. We gird ourselves emotionally. We steel ourselves mentally. In short, we prepare to meet them. The big things in life usually come announced. They are high visibility. They command our attention. Starting a business. Buying a home. Starting a family. Sending a child off to college. A threat to our career. A serious automobile accident. The death of a loved one. Financial reverses. An injured child.

We marshal our resources to tackle the big things. Because the big things are so important we fear to fail in them. As a result, "Anyone can do the big things right. . . ."

Often we don't recognize the little things when they come. They slip up on us. They are mundane, ordinary, routine, uninteresting, a nuisance. Maybe it's just a burned dinner. Unmowed lawn. Late to the movie. Run in a stocking. Undone ironing. Bulbs that need changing. Pool that needs cleaning. Two-feet-tall sewing pile.

We don't expect our spouse to react by losing her/his temper over such minors. What's the big deal about a tricycle in the driveway?

Little things left undone—a chance to hug. An opportunity to express appreciation. Saying grace before meals. Not letting a teenager talk back to his mother. Making sure everyone says thank you for dinner. Prompting the children to thank Mom or Dad for working so hard. Little things.

They are low visibility. They often only show up inside the family circle. Other more important matters command our attention. We react instead of act. Because the little things seem so unimportant or routine, we can handle them poorly.

Yet, the repetitious ignoring of the little things important to our mate is like ignoring rising flood waters against a levee. If enough pressure builds, the levee bursts. Little things left undone put pressure on a marriage. That's why "it's the little things that count."

It seems to me that little things I do for Patsy make deposits into her emotional bank account that far exceed their value. In fact, I believe the little things often carry more weight than some of the big things. Why? My wife expects me to handle the big things right. When I do the little things right she is pleasantly surprised.

Many people don't think the little things are all that important. They are wrong. Dead wrong. "It's the little things that count." Small kindnesses. A loving glance. A chore done in secret that is discovered. Consistency. Dependability. Honesty.

Little things make big deposits, while big things often account for only little deposits. On the other hand, every little thing left undone is a withdrawal from the emotional bank account of your spouse.

Remember. Anyone can do the big things right . . . but it's the little things that count. Handle the little things well and you will be given much.

DISCUSSION

Both answer: Do you find it difficult to do the big things right? Why or why not? Do you find it difficult to do the little things right? Why or why not?

APPLICATION

Determine to consistently make many little deposits into the emotional bank account of your partner.

PRAYER

Either: Dear God, thank You that You have given us the strength to tackle the big things in life. Help us, O God, not to fail in the little things. Give us each a greater awareness of and sensitivity to the little things that are important to each other. Help us to meet each other's needs in a way that pleases You. Amen.

MAKING VACATIONS COUNT

This, the first of his miraculous signs, Jesus performed in Cana of Galilee. He thus revealed his glory, and his disciples put their faith in him. After this he went down to Capernaum with his mother and brothers and his disciples. There they stayed for a few days.

JOHN 2:11–12

vacation *n.* A period of suspension of work, study, or other activity, usually used for rest, recreation, or travel.

Because we work so hard we often develop high expectations for our vacations. Actually, vacations produce high levels of stress. Consider this typical scenario.

You both expect the vacation to make right all the times you were not there for each other or the kids during the year. You deplete your savings account to make a big splash.

You get sweaty loading the car. Each person in the car has a different idea of a great vacation. The sun beats down on the car; it is hot; the car is cramped. Your shirt sticks to your back. You arrive tired, with aching muscles.

A problem crops up at check-in. You work it out, then must get used to a small, strange unit. Your vacation villa is not nearly as nice as your own home. There is no microwave. The tub drain doesn't work.

You buy tickets to Disney World. Crowds of others just like you smother each other. You use muscles you haven't flexed in years. Your feet hurt. Your muscles ache. You are tired. Your body clock is off. The food is too rich. But you are having fun.

After several days the close quarters make the family testy. Tempers flare. Sunburns hurt. A draft from the air-conditioning vent blows directly on you. A cold gets passed around.

The next day you take a wrong turn and miss a special tour for which you paid in advance.

Your time together reminds you how different are the interests of every family member. One likes hiking and basketball, another shopping and eating, another reading and napping, another television and video games.

The restaurants are too expensive, but at least the portions are small. Your unit is next to a highway—no view and noisy. Your unit is small. If one person gets up early he wakes everyone else. You can't find a comfortable chair, a good reading light, or any privacy. There are barking dogs and big bugs.

And we wonder why we don't come home rested! We can't understand why our family can't get along with each other on these trips. That which was to pull us together turns out to be a disappointment.

Jesus often withdrew from the crowds. He knew the value of rest and appreciated being alone with loved ones. Even then, the crowds often found Him, which threw His plans awry.

Vacations should and can provide an opportunity to pull the family together. We need a new paradigm for vacations. We ought to leave later and get home earlier. This will provide more preparation and unwinding time. We should adjust our expectations in view of the stress vacations bring. We could spend more time vacationing in or from our own homes. One major activity a day is enough. Build in nap times. Build in time for everyone to do devotions in the morning—people out of fellowship with God will be less patient. Let each family member contribute to the plans. Be sensitive to each other's likes and especially dislikes. Arrange for Mom to have a break from cooking and dishes. Go with the flow. Bend a lot.

Vacations should change the pace. Vacations should recharge, revitalize, and reenergize. Vacations should provide a *complete* break with work. Vacations should refresh our souls, renew our faith, revive our spirits, rekindle our love for God and others, and reignite our passion. Anything less is not a vacation.

DISCUSSION

Both answer: What is your idea of the ideal vacation? How do your vacations usually end up?

APPLICATION

Decide to cut back the planned activities on your next vacation. Build in more "re-creation" time. Talk over how to meet different expectations.

PRAYER

Either: Lord, thank You for the good times of rest and relaxation we have shared together as a family. We pray You will give us the wisdom to be wise in the way we invest our days of vacation. May we not only recover from the daily press, but let us rediscover a fresh intimacy with You and with each other. Put a new bounce in our step. Amen.

SPECIAL INSTRUCTIONS JUST FOR HIM

*G*od gives more instructions to husbands and wives on how to love and relate to each other than for any other human relationship. In this devotion we reproduce each of ten special instructions for husbands in the order in which they appear in the Bible. While these have been examined individually elsewhere in this book, collectively they make quite an impact. More than mere instructions, these pearls of wisdom unlock the secrets of a happy marriage.

APPLICATION

Husband, reflectively read each of these verses out loud. Pause after each one. What strikes you about this verse? Tell your wife how much you hope to meet her needs in each area.

1. *"Leave" your parents and "cleave" to her:* "For this reason a man will leave his father and mother and be united to his wife, and they will become one flesh" (Gen. 2:24).

2. *Accept authority over her:* "To the woman he said . . . 'Your desire will be for your husband, and he will rule over you'" (Gen. 3:16).

3. *Meet her sexual needs:* "The husband should fulfill his marital duty to his wife, and likewise the wife to her husband" (1 Cor. 7:3).

4. *Accept responsibility for her:* "Now I want you to realize that the head of every man is Christ, and the head of the woman is man, and the head of Christ is God" (1 Cor. 11:3).

5. *Acknowledge her as a partner in marriage:* "In the Lord, however, woman is not independent of man, nor is man independent of woman" (1 Cor. 11:11). "Submit to one another out of reverence for Christ" (Eph. 5:21).

6. *Love her:* "Husbands, love your wives, just as Christ loved the church and gave himself up for her. . . . In this same way, husbands ought to love their wives as their own bodies. He who loves his wife loves himself" (Eph. 5:25, 28).

7. *Nourish and cherish her:* "After all, no one ever hated his own body, but he feeds and cares for it, just as Christ does the church" (Eph. 5:29).

8. *Don't be harsh with her or embitter her:* "Husbands, love your wives and do not be harsh with them" (Col. 3:19).

9. *Provide for her:* "If anyone does not provide for his relatives, and especially for his immediate family, he has denied the faith and is worse than an unbeliever" (1 Tim. 5:8).

10. *Treat her with consideration and respect:* "Husbands, in the same way be considerate as you live with your wives, and treat them with respect as the weaker partner and as heirs with you of the gracious gift of life, so that nothing will hinder your prayers" (1 Pet. 3:7).

Plumb the depths of these ten great ideas. Consider how delightful your marriage will be when, by God's grace, you grow into fulfilling each of these instructions. In the next chapter we will probe the Bible's special instructions to wives.

DISCUSSION

Why do you think God decided to give so many instructions to husbands? What major themes emerge from those instructions?

PRAYER

Him: Lord Jesus, I am overwhelmed by the beauty and symmetry of Your instructions to me as a husband. I acknowledge that You know me far better than I know myself. You know perfectly how I need to be instructed. I am humbled by the awesome responsibility You have entrusted to me. As an act of my will, by faith, I pledge myself afresh to meet my responsibilities to the wife You have given me as a precious gift. Amen.

Special Instructions Just for Her

*I*n the last devotional we explored what God says especially to husbands. Today, let's examine God's ten special instructions for wives. While these, too, have been examined elsewhere in this book, collectively they create the portrait of a woman's roles in marriage.

Application

Wife, reflectively read each of these verses out loud. Pause after each one: What strikes you about this verse? Tell your husband how much you hope to meet his needs in each area.

1. *You are his helper:* "The LORD God said, 'It is not good for the man to be alone. I will make a helper suitable for him'" (Gen. 2:18).

2. *"Leave" your parents and "cleave" to him.* "For this reason a man will leave his father and mother and be united to his wife, and they will become one flesh" (Gen. 2:24).

3. *Accept his authority over you:* "To the woman he said, 'I will greatly increase your pains in childbearing; with pain you will give birth to children. Your desire will be for your husband, and he will rule over you'" (Gen. 3:16).

4. *Manage your home:* "She watches over the affairs of her household and does not eat the bread of idleness" (Prov. 31:27).

5. *Meet his sexual needs:* "The husband should fulfill his marital duty to his wife, and likewise the wife to her husband" (1 Cor. 7:3).

6. *Acknowledge him as a partner in marriage:* "In the Lord, however, woman is not independent of man, nor is man independent of woman" (1 Cor. 11:11). "Submit to one another out of reverence for Christ" (Eph. 5:21).

7. *Submit to him:* "Wives, submit to your husbands as to the Lord" (Eph. 5:22). "Wives, in the same way be submissive to your husbands so that, if any of them do not believe the word, they may be won over without words by the behavior of their wives" (1 Pet. 3:1).

8. *Respect him:* "However, each one of you also must love his wife as he loves himself, and the wife must respect her husband" (Eph. 5:33).

9. *Love him.* "Likewise, teach the older women to be reverent in the way they live, not to be slanderers or addicted to much wine, but to teach what is good. Then they can train the younger women to love their husbands and children" (Titus 2:3–4).

10. *Accept your role as the weaker partner.* "Husbands, in the same way be considerate as you live with your wives, and treat them with respect as the weaker partner and as heirs with you of the gracious gift of life, so that nothing will hinder your prayers" (1 Pet. 3:7).

The path to a happy marriage is for both husband and wife to 1) understand, 2) accept, and 3) commit to fulfill this portrait of marriage painted in the last two devotionals.

DISCUSSION

Why do you think God decided to give so many instructions to wives? What major themes emerge from these instructions? Both answer:

- Do you *understand* your marital roles, duties, and responsibilities?
- Do you *accept* your marital roles, duties, and responsibilities?
- Do you *commit* to fulfill your marital roles, duties, and responsibilities?

PRAYER

Her: Lord Jesus, I am overwhelmed by the beauty and symmetry of Your instructions to me as a wife. I acknowledge that You know me far better than I know myself. You know perfectly how I need to be instructed. I am humbled by the awesome responsibility You have entrusted to me. As an act of my will, by faith, I pledge myself afresh to meet my responsibilities to the husband You have given me as a precious gift. Amen.

In Summary

$\mathcal{W}$e stay together because we work at it. In this section we have covered many of the most important ways we can keep the embers glowing. Here are some of the important ideas from this section in review.

APPLICATION

Read these thoughts out loud to each other meditatively. One of you read a point and the other make a comment. On the next idea switch roles, and so on, until you have read and commented on each idea. Conclude in prayer.

- Love is what love does. To define love at rest is impossible because love never rests. If love rests it is no longer love, but indifference. Love is always doing. Love is always in motion.
- Love is the glue that holds our marriages together and the oil that keeps us from rubbing each other the wrong way.
- "I further realized that our relationship was not deep. It was not superficial, and that tended to deceive me into thinking it was more meaningful than it really was. But in a moment of pure, clear, candid illumination, the Holy Spirit showed me the truth. I was using Patsy."
- Sometimes with tenderness we must intentionally hurt each other in order to make our relationship whole. Some things just need to be said. It may hurt, even to tears, but being completely open and honest with each other is the only possible basis for a genuinely harmonious marriage.
- When we get into the custom of praying for the healing of each other, we get out of the silly common-sense idea that we are bound by our circumstances. We are not. Jesus can, and will, reach down into the hubbub of human circumstances and do the supernatural—if we ask.
- Share the extremes of life with one another—the embarrassing moments, the great victories, the dark temptations, the tragic failings, the ecstatic joys. Laugh, cry, sing, and dance. Make beautiful music together. Smell the flowers. Joke around. Lighten up. Be real. You are stuck with each other! Enjoy it.
- To make a marriage of two-part harmony we must make deposits into the emotional bank account of our spouse. Walls go up when we make too many withdrawals.

- The strongest expression of love we can make is to sacrifice ourselves for one another. When we deny ourselves for our mates we prove by our actions that we "get it" about the true meaning of love.
- Unless you are committed to the institution of marriage itself even more than your spouse, then you will always hold divorce as an option. As long as you consider that divorce is an option for you, no matter how remote, you run the risk of someday bailing out.
- Here's the problem: What men are "into" is often not what wives need. When he makes work or some other pursuit his top priority, something inside her withers, then dies. When she makes the children, work, or some other pursuit her top priority, he begins looking for something to numb the pain in his heart. Couples drift apart unless they remain each other's top priority. No matter where your marriage stands today, making each other top priority will make it better.
- Sadly, many couples wake up one day only to realize the person sleeping next to them is a virtual stranger. "Who is this person? And what will keep us together?"
- At any point in time our social (and other) needs will likely not be the same as our mate's. This means that marriage partners must make compromises. One will want to talk out of *desire*. The other must be willing to talk out of *duty*.
- The repetitious ignoring of the little things important to our mate is like ignoring rising flood waters against a levee. If enough pressure builds, the levee bursts. Little things left undone put pressure on a marriage.
- Vacations can be an opportunity to pull the family together. Vacations should provide a complete, total break with work. Vacations should refresh our souls, renew our faith, revive our spirits, rekindle our love for God and others, and reignite our passion. Anything less is not a vacation.

WORTHY OF OUR CHILDREN

Children's children are a crown to the aged,
and parents are the pride of their children.
                                    PROVERBS 17:6

A man told me that when he goes into a room with his six grown children and nine grandchildren, one by one they all get up and leave. There is no overt antagonism displayed. There is no visible acrimony. No one seems to plan it in advance. Yet, there is something in this man's demeanor that sends his children away.

On the other hand, his wife is constantly on the phone with her children and grandchildren. She draws them out and listens attentively. She looks for creative, positive ways to get involved in their lives. She doesn't judge or condemn. She doesn't offer opinionated advice. She simply loves and serves her children. When the family is together her children and grandchildren flock around her.

How is it possible for two people to raise children under the same roof, then end up with completely different relationships with those same children?

Children are people too. In the same way that adults respond to encouragement, attention, genuine interest, and sincere listening, children do, also. Likewise, when children sense no sincere interest in them they take it to mean a lack of love. Children, like adults, know if you are for them or not.

It is not what happened in the room that led this man's children to leave, but what happened through multiplied years of neglect, harsh criticism, overly strict rules, and indifference. We can rule our homes by grace or law, but grace is better. If we rule our homes by law, our children won't be able to wait for the day they can leave.

In today's Scripture passage, the word *pride* figuratively means an "ornament." Through fulfilling our biblical role as parents we become something beautiful in the eyes of our children. They take pride in us. They glory in having us as parents. They see us as brave, caring people worthy of their honor and glory. We become an ornament to grace their lives.

To become the pride, or glory, of our children we must love them deeply. It is a matter of making a choice among the many worthwhile activities that compete for our attention. We must make our children a priority now if we want to have a good relationship with them later. Too many people don't invest time when their children are at home, then wonder why the kids don't want to be around them later in life. You can choose your way, but not the result. Whatever you are sowing now you will reap later.

Marabel Morgan wrote in *The Total Woman* about Donna Robinson, a mom who was having an extremely frustrating vacation with her active two-year-old. To ease the situation her husband stopped for a break. Before going to lunch they took a stretching walk through an adjacent park and cemetery. Glancing at tombstones, one caught Donna's eye: *She was the sunshine of our home.* Donna thought, "If I dropped dead that would be the last thing they would put on my tombstone." She made a commitment to change.

Spend time with your children. Let grace rule your home and not law. Love them deeply. Show them you are for them. Don't be harsh. Let them be who they are. Help them to become all God intends for them. Show them Christ in the privacy of your home. Do these things and one day, many years from now, you will walk into a room filled with your children and grandchildren and they will not leave. You will be their crown and pride.

I've never met a retired person who wants to be near all the wonderful people with whom he or she worked. No, when people retire they want to be near their grandchildren.

DISCUSSION

Both answer: Based on how your parenting is going now, what do you think your relationship will be with your children when they are married and have kids? Would you say your children consider you "their pride"? Why or why not?

APPLICATION

If you want to change your relationship with your children, decide how much you are willing to change. It is good to decide in advance how much you are willing to change. Then make a list of goals you would like to achieve. For example, you may want to include taking children out for special times, developing a new demeanor around the house, reading parenting books, or counseling if needed.

PRAYER

Both, as appropriate: Our Father, help us to make our children our priority now so that we will have a good relationship with them later. Help us both to be the sunshine of our home. Help me to make the changes necessary to prove to my children that I am truly for them. Amen.

THE VALUE OF THE DINNER TABLE

These commandments that I give you today are to be upon your hearts. Impress them on your children. Talk about them when you sit at home and when you walk along the road, when you lie down and when you get up. Tie them as symbols on your hands and bind them on your foreheads. Write them on the doorframes of your houses and on your gates.
                                                    DEUTERONOMY 6:6–9

*S*piritual instruction is not the responsibility of the church but the parents. The church should support the parents in their duty.

We are to "impress" the Word of God on the hearts and minds of our children. This is no periodic endeavor. Rather, we should "talk" about spiritual principles constantly, whether sitting at home commenting on a TV show, walking (or more likely driving) down the road to school or the mall, putting them to bed, eating breakfast, or during family devotions.

Our devotion to Christ should be visible by the actions we take ("symbols on your hands"—what we *do*) and the thoughts we express ("bind them on your foreheads"—what we *think*). We ought to tastefully fill our homes with verses in needlepoint and religious symbols. Bibles ought to adorn our coffee tables and our private desk.

Though we should constantly be communicating spiritual reality and principles to our children, some methods are more effective than others. If that is true, then we as parents ought to give special thought to maximizing those methods. There are two: the dinner table and family devotions.

Almost all education of children, in terms of moral and spiritual values, occurs at the dinner table. Here we have opportunities to discuss every kind of event in the world, community, church, and home. It is in these discussions that our children hear what we really believe and what we really feel.

Needless to say, dinner is more than food. We should do two things at our dinner tables. First, we should guard carefully what we say. How do we talk about people? Is it constructive or destructive? What are we communicating about political values, moral values, and our own temperament?

Second, we should consciously select subjects for the dinner table. What are the values we want to impart to our children? What do we believe that we want them to believe? What do we not believe that we don't want them to believe either?

In addition to these two things we should do *at* the dinner table we should also ensure the sanctity *of* the dinner table. Surveys about our eating habits

186

abound. Filtering them all down, we can draw two basic conclusions. First, about half of families do not eat dinner together (this figure drops further on weekends). Second, of the half that do eat together half of them eat in front of the TV. In simple terms, most families are not together at the place where their children would otherwise be learning spiritual and moral values. So what are they learning? Often what they learn is that *family* is not that important.

Most activities that draw family members away from the dinner table can be adjusted. If a work schedule can't be changed, then change the dinner hour. Tell coaches that you want your kids home for dinner. Take the phone off the hook or put the phone on the answering machine and turn off the sound. We won't change the way the world eats dinner, but we sure ought to change the way we eat it.

In the next devotional we will take up the subject of family devotions, the second method of communicating spiritual reality and principles to our children.

DISCUSSION

Both answer: Have you squarely taken the responsibility for the spiritual instruction of your children? If you have, how? Is your dinner table a high priority in your family? Why or why not? What does your dinner table communicate to your children, and how could you improve it? What other opportunities do you have to give your children spiritual instruction?

APPLICATION

If you have been neglecting your dinner table as a place of spiritual instruction, resolve together to make it a high priority. Discuss ways to do this: First, make it a "required appearance" for every family member; and second, determine how you will speak and act and what special subjects you want to be sure to discuss. (If dinner is not feasible because of work or other commitments, try a different family mealtime.)

PRAYER

Either or both: Heavenly Father, we recognize that the spiritual instruction of our children is our responsibility, not the responsibility of the church. Help us to make our dinner table important so that our children can be grounded in spiritual life for all their days. Amen.

FAMILY DEVOTIONS

Train a child in the way he should go,
and when he is old he will not turn from it.
PROVERBS 22:6

*A*s my personal ministry, I teach a large Bible study on Friday mornings. No small commitment, I usually spend fifteen hours a week on this ministry, most of which is preparing the message.

One day it fell on me like a heavy boulder. *You are giving your very best thinking to these men, most of whom will not be in your life more than a few years. Meanwhile, you are doing nothing for your very own children—the ones you love the most and who most need you.*

I reasoned that if I was going to share biblical truths with others that I should also share them with my family. So several years ago, when our kids were thirteen and nine, we began holding a fifteen-minute family devotion just before the kids leave for school.

We do not even attempt to do this every day. I have a standing Friday morning commitment, and the kids from time to time need to leave early or are running especially late (I say "especially" because they are always at least a little late!). So we usually make it three or four mornings a week.

We only have devotions during the school year. During the summer we take a break. It's good for kids (and dads) to have a break. Besides, they get up at different times during the summer.

On a typical morning when we all come together the kids are in various stages of preparation to leave. It doesn't matter. We put the dog in her pen and don't answer the phone. We start at 7:00 A.M. and end at 7:15 A.M.

From the start I try to set an upbeat, enthusiastic tone, although sometimes I don't feel that way myself. I try to hook them with a story, quote, or question that relates to their world and interests. Some are better than others. Next, I relate the point of the opening hook to the Bible. Next, I point out the spiritual principle and how it can apply to us today. Finally, I close off with a question or see if they have a comment. I allow about ten minutes for all of this. It would be just as effective to simply read from a youth devotional like *Youth Walk* (check with a Christian bookstore).

After the Bible portion of the devotion we close in prayer. They are worried about running late (first period teachers give detentions if they are tardy for school) so I tell them exactly what time it is before we begin prayer. In the early days it became clear that the prayers were shallow and self-centered:

"Lord, let us have a good day and bless our family." So we now pray for one needy or hurting person each day in addition to personal and family needs. This may be someone suggested by the kids, Patsy, or me. The person may be a youth, an adult, or a family. The problems are usually related to health, finance, or broken relationships. It is not necessary that everyone in the family knows the person we pray for personally.

From time to time our daughter, who is older, has read something that touched her and asks if she can do the devotion. Usually this is at the last minute after I have already prepared something, but I always eagerly say yes to her initiative.

Most mornings they don't start out looking very interested. This is hard to get used to. If the hook is moving or especially relevant they get into it, but not always. Many mornings their eyes look glazed over and I wonder if it's worth all the effort.

My daughter attends a small discipleship group of teenaged girls led by a woman in our church. She told my wife one day, "I don't know what you do in those family devotions, but often when I ask a question Jen says, 'Well, my dad says this,' or 'My dad says that.' She makes great contributions to our group. That must be a special time!"

After hearing that report I guess I don't *really* wonder if it is worth all the effort. Why not give it a try?

DISCUSSION

Both discuss: If you do not have family devotions, is this something that you would like to try? Why or why not? If you are already doing family devotions, how can you tweak them to be even more effective?

APPLICATION

Try having family devotions for a month and evaluate their contribution to your family life.

PRAYER

Lord, we know that nothing we can do for our children exceeds giving them a heart for You. Help us to set aside a regular, consistent time for family devotions. Help us to do it for them, as well as for You. Amen.

WOODY ALLEN PARENTING

Turn the hearts of the fathers to their children, and the hearts of the children to their fathers; or else I will come and strike the land with a curse.
MALACHI 4:6

No child custody fight has ever been more scandalous than the bitter battle between Mia Farrow and Woody Allen. Mr. Allen sought custody of the three children, ages five, seven, and seventeen, who are part of their complicated lives.

Woody lost his case when the judge found him to be an inadequate, irresponsible, and self-absorbed father. The judge noted that Allen lacked familiarity with the most basic details of the children's lives, such as the names of their doctors, teachers, friends, or even their pets.

It is true that Woody Allen represents a counterview to the entire Christian ethic. Yet if we think it over, he is not too different from most fathers in three respects.

First, Woody Allen must really love his children. No man would endure the public abuse and ridicule he had to endure unless he truly believed in his cause. Second, like most fathers, his other interests absorbed most of his time and attention. Third, Mr. Allen, like most of us, obviously received no training about how to be a responsible father to his children.

Personally, I have never met a father who didn't love his children. Yet, most men I know are far too consumed with trying to win the rat race. And I have met few fathers who have received adequate training for the task.

We can imagine that there are many fathers—Christian fathers—who lack familiarity with the most basic details of their children's lives. Father, do you know the names of your children's doctors? How about their teachers? Their friends?

Husbands, let's be frank. We love our children. We want only the best for them. But we have come to believe a devil's lie that what they need is the best schools, the best camps, the best clothing labels their friends are wearing, and that they don't really want to spend time with us. What they actually need more than anything in the world is us.

A young boy was moping around day camp until a youth worker asked, "What's wrong?"

"Oh, nothin'."

"Well, something's wrong. You can tell me."

"Naw. It's nothin'."

"Come on now, tell me."

"Well, I guess so. It's my dad. I ain't got no dad. Can't do nothin' without a dad."

When we turn our hearts to our work instead of our children we invite a curse on our families. Let us become wise to worldly ways and let us "turn the hearts of the fathers to their children."

There is no step to "turn your heart toward your children" that is more practical than to take a parenting class or to read a book on how to be an effective dad. Check it out.

DISCUSSION

Husband, name your children's doctors, teachers, and friends. What do your answers tell you? Wife, how do you feel about the job your husband has been doing as a father (be gentle but honest)?

APPLICATION

Husband, if you need to "turn your heart toward your children," locate a good book on fathering at a Christian bookstore or, if you prefer, check out a good parenting seminar through your church. Wife, if this devotional applies to you, take similar steps.

PRAYER

Either, as appropriate: Lord Jesus, I confess that I am guilty of "Woody Allen parenting." I really do love my children, but I have let other interests absorb my time and attention. I need to be trained. Help me to take the necessary steps to give my children more of what they need: me. Amen.

SHOWING SELF-CONTROL WITH OUR KIDS

Fathers, do not embitter your children, or they will become discouraged.
COLOSSIANS 3:21

My teenaged daughter and I crossed swords and exchanged words. I can't remember exactly what it was over. Anyway, I went to my office, which is located behind our house, to pout.

I knew she would be coming to make some copies for a school project in a few minutes. Sure enough, about ten minutes later my daughter came into the office.

As she walked in I said, "What are you doing? You're not welcome here."

She stopped dead in her tracks, the first wave of the emotion of rejection sweeping over her. I could see that I had driven a stake through her heart. Stunned, she turned and walked quickly away.

I could not believe my own ears. I have hurt my daughter on many occasions and in many ways, but this was the very first time I had ever hurt her intentionally. Something inside of me died. My mind reeled: *How could you sit here and premeditate words designed to hurt your very own daughter? In sixteen years you have never said anything to hurt her on purpose. You have gone too far.*

The deepest sense of regret I have ever experienced came upon me. Suddenly I was lost, a piece of debris floating aimlessly in a wild storm. I could not think clearly; I could not get my bearings. I shook my head to clear it, but I had pushed things too far.

In sheer panic I went to my wife and explained what I had done. She told me Jennifer was back in her bedroom crying. After a few moments of advice from Patsy, I went back to see Jen. I began by apologizing. I told her straight up exactly how I felt—exactly how I had hurt her on purpose. I told her how dirty it made me feel. I made promises. I asked her forgiveness. We patched things up. Thankfully, she is very mature for her age.

By taking quick steps a major change in the course of our family life was averted. Had I let my pride rule we would surely have never been quite the same as a family ever again. It was a watershed moment. It was a supreme test. The devil may have won a skirmish, but he lost the war. Ultimately, the flesh was overcome by the Spirit.

I have never since hurt my son or daughter on purpose, but it would be a bald-faced lie to say I have not hurt them at all. The closeness of family life produces friction. We rub each other the wrong way. We're sinners who sin. The job of the adult is to be mature and set the tempo. We are to act our age. We are to be above the petty outbursts of selfish behavior that our children will surely display in the course of growing up.

If we do not control ourselves, our children are sure to become embittered against us. There is a profound difference between rightful anger and how we often respond. We are too severe. If our son deserves to be sent to his room for fifteen minutes, we send him for thirty minutes. Why? Because we overreact. We are not just. We are immature. We lose control.

We need to look to the Holy Spirit to give us the fruit of self-control. "Better a patient man than a warrior, a man who controls his temper than one who takes a city" (Prov. 16:32). We can overwhelm our children with sorrows if we do not look after our temper. We must control ourselves. Patience is a virtue, especially so when we relate to the young people in our lives.

DISCUSSION

Both answer: Do you tend to hurt your children intentionally? Do you think you have embittered your children? Are you quick or slow to apologize when you are in the wrong? What can you do to exhibit more self-control in the future?

APPLICATION

Both: Write down the times you can remember when your anger or discipline has been too severe—times you have intentionally said things to hurt your children. Go to your children and ask their forgiveness. Make a new pledge of self-control. Pray and ask God to forgive you and to empower you by His Spirit to live in peace with your children.

PRAYER

Either: Lord God, we have not been above losing our self-control with our kids. We do not want to embitter our children in any way. Help us to act with maturity toward our kids. Give us Your Spirit so that we may display the fruit of self-control. Amen.

PROVIDING STRUCTURE

His father had never interfered with him by asking, "Why do you behave as you do?"

1 KINGS 1:6

*D*avid. The mere mention of his name opens a floodgate of emotion. David the giant killer. David the friend of Jonathan. David the author of Psalms. King David. David, a man after God's own heart.

David ushered in a golden age for Israel. Under his skillful leadership the nation achieved its most prosperity, its greatest military strength, its best culture, tremendous religious reform, and became a major world power.

His professional achievements were extraordinary. Sadly, though David succeeded at the office, he failed at home. History records that one son, Amnon, raped his half-sister, Tamar. Another son, Absalom, then killed Amnon in revenge. Absalom conspired against his father and was later assassinated. Later, another son, Adonijah, also conspired to ascend his father's throne. He died at the hands of yet another son, Solomon.

One daughter raped. One son a rapist. One son a murderer. Two conspirators. Three dead sons. Where did David go wrong? The Scriptures give us the answer. When Adonijah conspired to be king, the Bible says, "His father had never interfered with him by asking, 'Why do you behave as you do?'"

Parenting is the task of giving children structure, boundaries, and limits. It is the business of guiding, directing, and encouraging. It is the work of supervising and controlling. It is the responsibility to instill values, morals, and ethics. In short, it is positive "interfering."

In a national survey of high school juniors and seniors commissioned by Sylvan Learning Centers and the National Association of Secondary School Principals, teenagers said that parents didn't give them enough structure. A lot of students wished their parents would say "No." Teenagers wanted their parents to get involved (to "interfere," if you please) in their schools, to take interest in homework, and to clamp down on how they spend their free time.[16] Remarkable? Not really. Our children long for structure, interest, and guidance. Our children crave our interference!

One day my daughter asked me if she could go to the beach with some friends, then added, "Dad, please tell me I can't go." She was really tired and wanted a day of rest, but couldn't bring herself to turn down her friends.

One reason for the sorry moral state of America is that a whole generation of parents did not hold their children accountable: "Why do you behave as you do?" The 1960s produced permissive parenting, which has yielded to today's laissez-faire, "don't interfere" parenting style.

Too often we neither guide nor question our children's behavior. We are tired, we've been through this before, we get frustrated repeating ourselves, the message doesn't seem to be getting through, and so on. Even when our children rail against the discipline we provide, however, in their heart of hearts it is exactly what they want. Children want structure.

It will be a hollow victory if we succeed at work but fail at home. We each need to evaluate the amount of structure and accountability we provide our kids. Do you put the question to your children, "Why do you behave as you do?" Interfere with their lives—that's what they want.

DISCUSSION

Each answer: How are you doing with the kids? Do you provide enough structure and guidance? Are you holding your children accountable to your values and biblical principles?

APPLICATION

Decide together what is best for your kids: Should you 1) provide more or less structure, 2) provide more or less guidance on how they spend free time, and 3) be more or less involved with their schools and school work? Take action as appropriate—you are still the parent.

PRAYER

Either: Heavenly Father, thank You for the precious children You have entrusted to us. Help us not to succeed in our careers but fail at home. Grant us discernment to know how much structure to give our kids. Help us to "interfere" with their follies. Help us to maintain steady interest in them and have the courage to ask, "Why do you behave as you do?" Amen.

PRAYING FOR OUR CHILDREN

The prayer of a righteous man is powerful and effective.
JAMES 5:16

*R*ick and his wife have four beautiful children. Everyone in the family is walking with the Lord. Rick has been a genuine spiritual leader in his home. Recently he explained how it all started.

When Rick was a youngster, his mother and three other ladies would meet once each month to pray for the salvation of their children. Between them they had nine kids. Today all nine children know Christ and live for Him.

Here's the interesting thing. These godly women never prayed out loud. In other words, they assembled each month for silent prayer. It is not how we pray for our children that's important, but that we pray.

In *The Man in the Mirror,* I included my own daily prayer list for my children. Since then I've added some additional items. Here is the revised list. You may find that by adding and subtracting a few subjects you can tailor-make your own list:

- That there will never be a time they don't walk with You
- A saving faith (thanksgiving if already Christian)
- A growing faith
- An independent faith (as they grow up)
- Persevering faith
- To be strong and healthy in mind, body, and spirit
- A sense of destiny (purpose)
- A desire for integrity
- A call to excellence
- To understand their spiritual gifts
- To understand the ministry God has for them
- Values and beliefs, a Christian worldview
- To tithe and save 10 percent of all earnings
- To set and work toward realistic goals as revealed by the Lord
- That I will set aside time to spend with them
- To acquire wisdom
- Protection from drugs, alcohol, tobacco, premarital sex, rape, violence, and AIDS
- The mate God has for them (alive somewhere, needing prayer)
- To do daily devotions

- Forgiveness and be filled with the Holy Spirit
- Glorify the Lord in everything
- Any personal requests or matters they've discussed with their mother.

Can you think of anything that has more potential to produce godly character and a successful, fulfilling life for your children? The prayers of righteous parents are both powerful and effective.

Think about it. You are probably the only two people in the entire world who would be willing to pray for each of your children on a daily basis. Will you?

DISCUSSION

Each answer: How often do you currently pray for your children? What do you pray? Are your prayers strategic or haphazard?

APPLICATION

Make a copy of the prayer list in this chapter, modify it for your own situation, and put it in a daily location, such as your Bible. Begin praying each day for your children as the Lord directs you.

PRAYER

Either: Lord Jesus, You have blessed us with priceless treasures in our children. Help us to be faithful in raising them to walk after Your ways. May there never be a time they don't walk with You. We pledge to pray for them on a regular basis, knowing we may be the only ones so willing. Help us to be faithful. Amen.

LEADING OUR CHILDREN TO FAITH

Consequently, faith comes from hearing the message, and the message is heard through the word of Christ.

ROMANS 10:17

*M*att was back in his bedroom doing homework for the one-on-one discipleship program he was going through with another man. He had trusted Christ for only a few months.

His eleven-year-old son, Brett, saw him sitting at his desk and asked what he was doing. "I'm preparing for the first lesson of a discipleship meeting, 'What It Means to Be a Christian.'"

Brett, a bright kid, asked if he could do the homework with his dad. Elated, Matt said, "Of course!"

Matt would read a paragraph out loud, then his son would read the next one. They took turns looking up the verses in the new Bible Matt recently purchased. They enjoyed doing this together immensely.

When they came to page six, Matt read the Sinner's Prayer printed in the material. He asked Brett if he would like to pray the prayer and give his life to Jesus. Brett answered, "Dad, I don't think I'm ready yet."

Matt said, "That's fine," and they finished the lesson.

At that point Brett said, "Dad, could we go back to page six. I think I'm ready now. I would like to give my life to Christ."

Matt went back to the Sinner's Prayer, repeated it out loud a phrase at a time, and Brett repeated out loud after his father:

Lord Jesus, I need You. Thank You for dying on the cross for my sins, which I acknowledge and confess. I open the door of my life and invite You to come in. By faith, I believe and receive You as my Savior and Lord. Thank You for forgiving my sins and for giving me eternal life. Take control of my life and make me into the kind of person You want me to be. Amen.

Remarkable. In a mere matter of months, God smashed to smithereens the old pattern of secularism that had for generations kept this entire family bloodline mired in the quagmire of sin's deceit.

Thankfully, God's Word does not return void. "My word that goes out from my mouth: It will not return to me empty, but will accomplish what I desire and achieve the purpose for which I sent it" (Isa. 55:11).

When we faithfully share Christ with our children we release the power of God for their salvation. Surely, each child must choose, and not every child does, but unless we tell them how will they hear? "Faith comes from hearing the message, and the message is heard through the word of Christ."

The single most significant contribution we can make to our children is to give them a heart for God. We cannot force them to believe and be saved, but we can create the most promising environment possible.

DISCUSSION

Which of your children have received Christ? Which ones have not? Which ones are you unsure of? Both of you offer thoughts on the statement, "The single most significant contribution we can make to our children is to give them a heart for God."

APPLICATION

Determine the spiritual condition of each of your children. For those who don't know Christ or those you are unsure about, purchase children's evangelistic materials from your local Christian bookstore and review them with your kids.

PRAYER

Either: Dear Lord, our children are the greatest gift You have ever given to us. Thank You for our child(ren) who have received Christ. Help us to do everything possible to create an environment conducive for the one(s) who have not also received Jesus Christ. We ask You to work in their hearts for salvation. We pledge to faithfully share the message through the Word of Christ. Amen.

SPENDING TIME WITH OUR KIDS

Fathers, do not exasperate your children; instead, bring them up in the training and instruction of the Lord.
EPHESIANS 6:4

Fathers, do not embitter your children, or they will become discouraged.
COLOSSIANS 3:21

*I*t is not insignificant that the only two New Testament instructions given specifically to fathers about their children deal with exasperating, embittering, provoking, angering, and discouraging our kids. The King James Version translates Colossians 3:21, "Fathers, provoke not your children to anger, lest they be discouraged."

We all know dads can become too angry, or angry too often. Notice, however, that the dad's anger is not the point of today's verses, it is the *children's* anger. It is not about children who provoke their fathers, but about fathers who provoke their children. How do dads embitter their children? Consider how one father discouraged his daughter.

THE TROUBLE WITH DAD

Have you ever heard of a father who won't talk to his daughter? My father doesn't seem to know I'm alive. In my whole life he has never said he loves me or given me a goodnight kiss unless I asked him to.

I think the reason he ignores me is because I'm so boring. I look at my friends and think, "If I were funny like Jill or a superbrain like Sandy or even outrageous and punk like Natasha, he would put down his paper and be fascinated."

I play the recorder, and for the past three years, I've been a soloist in the fall concert at school. Mom comes to the concerts, but Dad never does. This year I'm a senior, so it's his last chance. I'd give anything to look out into the audience and see him there. But who am I kidding? It will never happen."[17]

Dr. Paul Warren of the Minirth-Meier Clinic reports that kids often sit in his office literally angry to tears because their dads always have something more important to do than be with them.[18]

Simply said, relationships create responsibilities. When we say "I do" or bring children into the world we create responsibilities.

Time is everything to a relationship. We exasperate and provoke our children to anger when we do not give them enough time. A lack of time, both quality and quantity, will embitter and discourage our children.

The solution? Give time to whom time is due.

DISCUSSION

Her: Today 56 percent of women work outside the home, roughly equally divided between working moms and empty nesters.[19] Do you think wives need to also give heed to this admonition given to dads? Why or why not? Him: Why do you think men have a predisposition to not give their kids enough time? Both: How has this issue affected your marriage and family?

APPLICATION

Relationships create responsibilities. Time is everything to a relationship. Give time to whom time is due. Why not make a commitment to excel in this area of giving time to whom time is due? Start your week by putting each of your kids' activities on your calendar. Treat them as top priorities to the fullest extent possible.

PRAYER

Husband: Lord, I've always thought of these Scripture verses in terms of my anger. Now I see that this is the anger I create in my children through neglect. Lord, help me to give time to whom time is due. Guide me to make the most of the few brief years my kids will live in our home. Amen.

Encouraging Daily Devotions

Train a child in the way he should go,
and when he is old he will not turn from it.
PROVERBS 22:6

Nothing weighs more heavily on my mind than giving our children a rich spiritual heritage that will follow them like a shadow all their days.

Nothing determines our own spiritual passion and vitality more than keeping a daily time of private devotions during which we pray, meditate, and study God's Word. In fact, this daily habit, even if only a few minutes, sets the tenor for the entire day. To begin each day in humble surrender sets the whole course for our lives.

What, then, could be more helpful to our children than instilling in them the habit of a daily devotion?

Patsy and I offered our children a deal. "If you will do a daily devotion for at least twenty-five days each month, we'll buy you a tape or compact disc."

"That's nice, Dad."

"That's not all. In addition, if you do your devotions at least twenty-five days each month for ten out of twelve months we'll pay you $250. You can miss any two months and still get paid." Their eyes popped open.

"Wow, Dad! Are you kidding?"

"No, we're not kidding. But that's not all. If you will do your devotions all twelve months in a row, we'll double the amount and pay you $500. And you still only have to do twenty-five days a month."

By this time the children had become quite interested! They asked questions, and a great discussion ensued. We agreed they could use any youth devotional materials they wanted; our goal was to form the habit more than anything. We suggested they spend about five minutes a day; we didn't want them to think of time spent with the Lord as a burden. If they missed a day they could make it up; we wanted to communicate grace, not law. We suggested they keep track by marking off on a calendar; we proposed an honor system to demonstrate we trusted them.

At the end of the first year both children not only received the full bonus, but both had a perfect record of 365 days. They are well on their way to establishing a spiritual discipline which can keep them close to their Lord all their days. Some might call it bribery. I like to think of it as giving our children what they *need* in the context of what they *want*. They need a daily walk with Christ. They want opportunities to make money. We are using every opportunity to train them in the way they should go, trusting God they will not turn from it when they are older.

The greatest gift we can give our children is a heart that thirsts for God. We cannot force our children to love God, but we can create the most probable environment in which they will.

DISCUSSION

What are you currently doing to give your children a heart that thirsts for God? Are you satisfied that you are doing your part in training your children in the way they should go? Why or why not?

APPLICATION

Adapt the idea of instilling the habit of daily devotions to your own situation and implement it. The amount of money or some other reward is not important, except that it communicates that you are serious.

PRAYER

Either: Heavenly Father, our children are the greatest gift You have ever given to us. We want to be faithful to do our part to give them hearts that thirst after You. Help us to implement a habit of daily devotions for them that will follow them all their days. And we know that this idea will work best if we ourselves are faithful to spend time with You each day. Amen.

On Dragging Children to Church

Let us not give up meeting together, as some are in the habit of doing. . . .
HEBREWS 10:25

*M*any parents wonder, "Should we force our children to go to church if they don't want to go?" This can best be answered by another question, "Should we force our children to go to school if they don't want to go?"

The idea that our children's faith will somehow be damaged if we force them to church is preposterous. The best way to damage their faith is to not take them to church! Would we expect our child to become an accomplished pianist if he never went to piano lessons?

Why are we afraid to drag our kids to church when they complain? I think the gravity of their faith is one reason. We fear we may somehow turn them off. The question, "Will my kids stay true to the Christian faith?" is the number one concern of Christian parents according to a survey by *The Banner*, a Christian Reformed Church publication.[20]

Why is church so important? Youth is a time of idealism and zeal. Young people are searching for a cause, a mountain to climb, a challenge, a mission in life, something worth making a sacrifice for, a world to change and conquer. They are searching for the meaning and purpose of life. Most important of all, youth is the time of selecting ideas that will shape the rest of their lives. If we don't direct them, who will? Do you want the education system to be the primary supplier of your child's life view? This alone should make us focus sharply on the spiritual instruction of our kids through our own efforts and church.

If your kids don't like church, maybe you need to consider another church. Is the gospel being preached? Is Jesus held in high regard? According to the Barna Research Group, more than two out of three people who become Christians do so by the age of eighteen.[21] Is there a definite commitment on the part of the pastoral staff to win young people?

A recent survey on apostasy among college students revealed that children raised in consistently Christian homes are more likely to keep the faith. The more regular their church attendance and the later in life doubts about their faith came, the more persistent they remained in their beliefs. Those students who had abandoned their early religion cited hypocrisy, racism, dishonesty, and parents who only attended church on special occasions and holidays.[22]

204

The risk is not that we drag our children to church, but that we do not live a consistent life of faith before them. For example, dropping kids off at the church door and then leaving is hypocrisy. Keeping a private life different from your public life is a turn-off. To not insist that children attend church sends a mixed signal about the priority of faith.

The objective of taking our children to church is for them to become followers of Jesus Christ. You cannot follow someone you don't know much about. Train them. This is your best hope that later they will not turn away.

There are many stories of college students who wandered away from their faith only to return because their parents had not given up the habit of meeting together in church.

DISCUSSION

Both answer: What is your policy on children attending church? How faithful are you in your own church attendance? What effect do you think your consistency is having on your children? Are you in agreement about the importance of church attendance?

APPLICATION

Make the commitment once and for all that you and your children will attend church and Sunday school regularly. The instruction and consistency will serve them well all their days.

PRAYER

Either or both: Dear Father, we pledge ourselves to bring up our children in the fear and admonition of the Lord. We will, by Your grace, make sure our children are in church regularly. We pledge to train them in the habit of church attendance, and place our trust in You that when they are old they will not give up their faith. Amen.

CHILDREN NEED SOMETHING THEY CAN DO WELL

Do you see a man skilled in his work?
He will serve before kings;
he will not serve before obscure men.
                                    PROVERBS 22:29

*W*hen their daughter turned six they enrolled her in piano lessons. She couldn't concentrate. When she turned seven they drafted her for baseball. She never did actually get a hit. When she turned eight they signed her up for singing lessons. She couldn't carry a tune.

When she turned nine they enrolled her in art class. But she couldn't draw. When she turned ten they took her to ballet school. She didn't like ballet. Acting classes at eleven. Nope. Chess lessons at twelve. Sorry. Swimming. She almost drowned. Soccer? Didn't like to run. Basketball? Too much sweat.

However, she started reading Nancy Drew mysteries when she was nine. By the time she entered seventh grade she was an avid reader. Her vocabulary was immense. She devoured two and three books a week. In the ninth grade she won the spelling bee. In the tenth grade she joined the debate team. In her junior year she won every debate. All in all, she felt pretty good about herself. She discovered something she could do well because her parents persevered in helping her uncover her natural talents, abilities, and interests.

It is unfortunate. Researchers tell us that the single most critical factor in self-esteem for children is physical appearance. Should it surprise us that in a culture obsessed with beauty, sex, money, and clothes that our kids would be concerned about appearance? Fortunately, children can also gain a measure of self-esteem by developing artistic, athletic, and academic abilities.[23]

Parents have a wonderful opportunity to make sure each of their children learns to do something well. The opinion they gain of themselves is crucial to their overall success in life. By helping them discover latent abilities and aptitudes we can help them build a confident mental image of themselves.

A skill—whether ballet, basketball, or biology—develops when an attempted activity reveals natural aptitude and is nourished through practice. By helping our children develop skills we give them the gift of self-esteem.

Kids don't know yet, of course, that in the real world it is more important to have skill than good looks.

Three cautions, however. First, don't make your support conditional on how well they do. Don't communicate by your actions that your child must perform well at something for you to approve of and accept them. Make it fun for them. Don't get into the performance trap.

Second, differentiate between doing something well and being the best. The cost of being the best is high, and few can attain it. Parents who push their children to be the best set them up for huge disappointments. By all means, we should teach our children to be diligent and to give their personal best, but without putting them under the burden of being "number one."

Third, don't deny your children their desire to look as attractive as possible. We all judge others by their appearance. This may not be right, but it is a fact of life. Clothes, shoes, and hairstyles carry great weight with their peers. With modesty and within budget, help your children by letting them enhance their physical appearance to the maximum.

Kids will naturally gravitate to things they do well. Be sure to give them every opportunity. One of the most important parenting tasks we can undertake is to help our children find something they can do well.

DISCUSSION

Both answer: When you were growing up did you have a positive or negative self-image? Why? Did your parents help you to do something well? If yes, how did it help you? If no, what was the impact?

APPLICATION

From your answers to the discussion questions, you can see how important it is for each of your children to do something well. Make a prioritized list of all the activities each child now does and could possibly do. Which of these current activities do they do well? Make a plan to expose each child to a wide variety of opportunities. Be on the lookout for things they seem interested in and are naturally suited to do well.

PRAYER

Either: Dear God, You have blessed us with wonderful children. We know that their future depends in no small measure upon our faithfulness to help them discover who they are and what they can do. Help us to expose each child to enough opportunities so that she/he can find something to do well. Amen.

In Summary

*T*his concludes the section concerning our children. Surely nothing is more precious to us. Here are some of the central ideas presented.

APPLICATION

As you review this summary, take time to thank God for all the ways He has blessed you through your children. Read these thoughts out loud to each other meditatively. Conclude in prayer.

- We must make our children a priority now if we want to have a good relationship with them later. Too many people don't invest time when their children are at home, then wonder why the kids don't want to be around them later in life.
- Personally, I have never met a father who didn't love his children. Yet most men I know are far too consumed with trying to win the rat race. And I have met few fathers who have received adequate training for the task.
- Husbands, let's be frank. We love our children. We want only the best for them. But we have come to believe a devil's lie that what they need is the best schools, the best camps, the best clothing labels their friends are wearing, and that they don't really want to spend time with us. What they actually need more than anything in the world is us.
- The closeness of family life produces friction. We rub each other the wrong way. The job of the adult is to be mature and set the tempo. We are to act our age. We are to be above the petty outbursts of selfish behavior that our children will surely display in the course of growing up.
- We often are too severe. If our son deserves to be sent to his room for fifteen minutes, we send him for thirty minutes. Why? Because we overreact. We are not just. We are immature. We lose control.
- We need to look to the Holy Spirit to give us the fruit of self-control. We can overwhelm our children with sorrows if we do not look after our tempers. We must control ourselves. Patience is a virtue, especially so with the young people in our lives.

- Parenting is the task of giving children structure, boundaries, and limits. It is the business of guiding, directing, and encouraging. It is the work of supervising and controlling. It is the responsibility to instill values, morals, and ethics. In short, it is positive "interfering."
- It will be a hollow victory if we succeed at work but fail at home. We each need to evaluate the amount of structure and accountability we provide our kids. Do you put the question to your children, "Why do you behave as you do?" Interfere with their lives—that's what they want.
- You are probably the only two people in the entire world who would be willing to pray for each of your children on a daily basis.
- When we faithfully share Christ with our children we release the power of God for their salvation. Surely, each child must choose, and not every child does, but unless we tell them how will they hear?
- The single most significant contribution we can make to our children is to give them a heart for God. We cannot force them to believe and be saved, but we can create the most promising environment possible.
- Simply said, relationships create responsibilities. When we say "I do" or bring children into the world we create responsibilities. Time is everything to a relationship. We exasperate and provoke our children to anger when we do not give them enough time. A lack of time, both quality and quantity, will embitter and discourage our children. The solution? Give time to whom time is due.
- Nothing determines our own spiritual passion and vitality more than keeping a daily time of private devotions during which we pray, meditate, and study God's Word. What, then, could be more helpful to our children than instilling in them the habit of a daily devotion?
- The objective of taking our children to church is for them to become followers of Jesus Christ. You cannot follow Someone you don't know much about. There are many stories of college students who wandered away from their faith, only to return because their parents had not given up the habit of meeting together in church.
- Parents have a wonderful opportunity to make sure each of their children learns to do something well. The opinion they gain of themselves is crucial to their overall success in life. By helping them discover latent abilities and aptitudes we can help them build a confident mental image of themselves.

LOVE IS NOT SELFISH

[Love] . . . is not self-seeking.

1 CORINTHIANS 13:5

*A*fter six years of driving the same car I decided to make a change. I bought a brand-new car that I felt reflected the image I wanted to project. The car I chose happened to come with a driver's-side air safety bag.

The air safety bag had not been a criterion of my purchase, but I quickly came to appreciate its value. In fact, you might say I talked as if buying a car with this feature had been my idea all along.

Six months later Patsy's car died. Well, it didn't completely die. Actually, it was worse than death. If it had died, at least it would have stopped costing so much money for repairs. Instead it teetered on death's doorstep and ran up the repair bills. This sorry car of hers was sending us into the poor house. We finally decided to trade it in for something new.

After careful research I picked the car that I hoped to persuade Patsy to fall in love with. It was one size smaller than mine, but it was brand new. It didn't have a driver's side air safety bag, but the price was a considerable savings over the car I had purchased just months earlier.

After carefully explaining the features, the benefits, the safety ratings from *Consumer Reports*, and the attractive economics, I was ready to "let" Patsy choose this car for herself. We drove to the dealer and looked at the car from all the appropriate angles; I dutifully kicked the tires (what is that for, anyway?), then we sat in the car. I inhaled deeply to enjoy that exhilarating new car aroma, hoping Patsy would take the hint and follow suit.

Without much fanfare Patsy said the car looked fine. I thought, *Fine? Is that all you can say—fine? After all the work I did researching this thing out.* "Okay, well, let's pray about it and see what the Lord wants us to do," I offered. We prayed and went home.

After dinner that evening Patsy looked me in the eyes and said, "Let me see if I understand this car situation correctly. Your car has a driver's-side air safety bag, right?"

"Right."

"And the car you want me to buy does not have a driver's-side air safety bag, right?"

"Correct."

"Does this mean, then, that my safety is not as important as your safety?"

Pow! Honestly, I had never thought it through. I was so concerned about saving some money that the thought never ran through my selfish mind. I had bought the safest possible vehicle for myself but was quite willing to relegate Patsy to a less safe car.

I knew the arguments. I needed to have a nicer car because of business reasons. My car would be the main family car, so we don't need *two* main cars. She could always take my car when she needed more room. We'll take my car when we go on vacations. And so on. (Never mind that she drives many more miles than I do.)

These were, of course, merely rationalizations so that I could justify driving the car I wanted while putting her into something more economical. What I said by my actions was that I thought my safety was more important than hers. The height of selfishness.

The inclination of our flesh is only evil all the time. In the flesh we are self-seeking, self-centered, self-deceiving, selfish sinners. "The heart is deceitful above all things and beyond cure. Who can understand it?" (Jer. 17:9)

The next day we bought Patsy the same model car I had purchased.

DISCUSSION

Both answer: What are the ways the husband has been selfish lately? What are the ways the wife has been selfish lately? Ask each other if you have done something or continue to do something that is particularly troublesome to your mate. What are the reasons for your selfishness?

APPLICATION

Ask your mate to forgive you for your selfishness. Pray together and ask the Lord to forgive you.

PRAYER

Either, as applicable: Lord Jesus, I can see that I tend to think of my own needs first. I confess that I have not been looking out for the best interests of my mate as I should. I have been self-seeking, and I am sorry. Please forgive me and show me how to correct my ways. Amen.

SHOWING MUTUAL RESPECT

Husbands, in the same way be considerate as you live with your wives, and treat them with respect as the weaker partner.
                    1 PETER 3:7

And the wife must respect her husband.
                    EPHESIANS 5:33

A man told me recently that he rarely cusses. When he does cuss, it is only in front of his wife.

A woman speaks with courteous hospitality to her boss when he calls her at home. When she hangs up, however, a fusillade of angry criticisms pours forth for the extra work he wants done.

In marriage we can find the most relaxed relationship on earth. We feel a comfortableness with our spouse like no other—an altogether wonderful state. Unless we guard ourselves, though, we can wound the spirit of our mate. As the saying goes, "familiarity breeds contempt." We must strive to show each other respect.

There are two problems for the man who cusses around his wife but no one else. First, the quality of our character is most revealed in little things, not big things. Christianity finds its truest test in traffic, when the car breaks down, when an appointment suddenly cancels at the last moment, and in the confines of marriage. Our spouses will decide if Christianity is true *for us* based upon how we live when we think they don't notice.

We may think of ourselves as altogether righteous. We think, *If I can't let off a little steam with my mate, where can I?* The problem is the report the spouse would have to give. How we are behind the tightly drawn curtains of our own private castle is how we really are. By taking his wife for granted, the "cussing husband" has shown a lack of respect for his wife and damaged his Christian testimony with the very person for whom he has the most responsibility.

The second problem for this husband is that there must be nothing in his behavior to make the wife stumble in her faith. Another example will further illustrate. A friend was to play in a golf tournament for his company. The sponsor, however, had hired the scantily clad waitresses from a local bar to act as hostesses. His wife was deeply disturbed and did not want him to play. This man cannot simply ignore her concerns and tell her, "I have to play. It's business." He must treat her with consideration and respect as the partner God has given him. In this case, they had a wonderful opportunity to study the Scriptures together to determine their mutual responsibilities and, also, to build more trust into the relationship. To do less is to take each other for granted and fail to show mutual respect. Incidentally, he decided not to play after all.

The wife who is angry at her boss is a problem too. The wife (or husband) who expresses such anger about a superior or coworker must remember what her husband sees. If all he ever hears is her bitter complaining about the extra work load forced upon her, then he will perceive that is 100 percent of her relationship with her boss. In reality, 90 percent of the relationship works quite well and only 10 percent presents a problem. The *presumption* is that the husband knows this. The *perception* is that the wife is bitterly unhappy in her job. Don't take for granted that your spouse knows everything you know. Show some respect.

Husband and wife are to respect each other, not take each other for granted. The respect she renders is like awe or reverence (not, of course, in the same sense as she would revere God). The respect he renders is esteem of the highest degree, dignity, and honor.

Marriage magnifies imperfections. In the intimate space of marriage we must be alert to represent our Lord to each other. Marriage is the most important place to live for Christ. We must do nothing to make each other stumble. We must not assume our spouses understand where we are coming from when others raise our ire. Don't take each other for granted.

DISCUSSION

Both answer: Do you "lose your Christianity" around your spouse? In what ways? Why do you think it happens?

APPLICATION

Talk out the areas in which you take each other for granted. Commit to be more self-aware and to live like Christ before your mate, not just your acquaintances.

PRAYER

Either or both, as applicable: Lord Jesus, I confess that I have lived an overly casual life before my mate. I have mistakenly thought that behaving in a Christ-like manner was not as important in my marriage as in other places. I can see that I was wrong. Help me to live with integrity before my mate. Amen.

LIVING BY PRIORITIES

"Love the Lord your God with all your heart and with all your soul and with all your strength and with all your mind"; and, "Love your neighbor as yourself."

LUKE 10:27

priority *n.* Something we give precedence by assigning a degree of urgency or importance.

Priorities act as a grid through which we filter our moment by moment decisions. Priorities are actually *pre*decisions. When we decide in advance what's important to us, then we have a pattern to follow when the heat of the moment confronts us in the nitty gritty details. The principle is this: Decide what to do on the basis of your priorities, not your pressures.

Priorities are different from goals. Goals are specific things we want to accomplish. Priorities precede goals. Priorities guide us into which goals to set or not set. Priorities are the important strands that run through our lives.

In every marriage each partner has priorities. Invariably, these don't exactly match the priorities of the mate. Worse, many times we really don't even know the priorities of our life mates.

Every couple should live by priorities, set priorities together, and work toward common priorities to the greatest extent possible. Priorities should be determined while spending much time alone with the Lord, then with each other. An inquiring spirit of self-examination, self-denial, and surrender will lead to godly priorities.

Here are the three top biblical priorities for married couples.

1. *Love God.* The first commandment is to love God with all of our heart, soul, mind, and strength—the totality of our being. Many of us succumb to having passion for the work of God, but not God. We must draw a distinction between our work for God and our walk with God. Besides doing good works, the other great competition for our first affection is money. To love God is to be the first priority of every believer.

2. *Love each other.* The second greatest commandment is to love one another. Every wife and husband should make each other her/his top priority, second only to God. We must put our mates above every other earthly concern, even children. Yet we must never make our spouses more important to us than our personal relationship with Christ. The unique "one flesh" nature of marriage elevates it above every other human relationship. We "leave" our parents and "cleave" to our mate.

3. *Love your children.* The most important thing a husband or wife can do for their children is to love each other. Loving our children closely follows

loving our mate. We must learn to actively love our children ahead of people who only want us for what we can do for them. The principle is to prioritize by asking, "Who's going to be crying at my funeral?" When a friend heard this idea it revolutionized the way he made decisions. For example, a man asked him if he could do a radio interview. My friend, who would ordinarily leap at such an opportunity, saw his son had a baseball game scheduled at that time. He said, "I'm sorry. I can't do it. Maybe some other time. Thanks for asking." As it turned out, the radio interview was rescheduled so he could do both.

Priorities act as filters through which we can filter our day-to-day decisions because we have decided *in advance* what is most important.

A husband and wife will have other priorities, like work, rest, recreation, and ministry. However, loving God, loving each other, and loving our children form the indispensable core of a happy marriage. Notice the common denominator of love.

DISCUSSION

What is a priority? Have you lived by setting priorities? Why or why not? Compare your priorities to the three discussed—how do you match up?

APPLICATION

Make a commitment to live by biblical priorities. First, love God with all your heart. Second, love your mate as yourself. Third, love your children who are a reward from God (see Psa. 127:3).

PRAYER

Either: Lord Jesus, help us to make these three relationships into our top priorities. Above all, help us to love You. Give us a passion not only for our work for You, but especially for our walk with You. Help us to make each other our top human priority. Give us the wisdom to assign an urgency to demonstrating our love to our children. Amen.

FINANCIAL PRESSURE

Better one handful with tranquillity than two handfuls with toil and chasing after the wind.

ECCLESIASTES 4:6

*A*fter building and selling a successful business, Steve found himself the steward of substantial funds. He could easily retire or pursue low-risk business interests, never again to worry about being a "servant to the lender."

Steve set a debt policy for himself that he would never borrow more than he could write a check to pay off from liquid cash. I agreed to hold Steve accountable for his debt structure.

Within six months Steve was right back in the middle of building a whole new business. It's truly a unique gift he has. Somewhere in the middle of all the building, however, Steve violated his own debt policy. He felt the intense pressure of debt tighten around his chest.

We met one morning to go over his finances. "I can't believe I put myself in this situation," he said. "And for what? If I ever get out of this in one piece, that's the last time."

In over twenty years of ministering among men, the greatest pressure I have ever observed men struggling with is financial pressure—more so even than health or marriage problems. Financial pressure comes from three directions: 1) supporting a lifestyle, 2) servicing debt, and/or 3) catastrophic loss of income due to unemployment, investment loss, or both. All create cash flow problems.

Men and women under financial pressure show all the symptoms of toil and chasing after the wind: stressed feelings, irritability, a short fuse, working long hours, feeling guilty taking a vacation, irregular sleep, poor eating habits, and lack of exercise.

These direct symptoms create a second tier of problems in the marriage: Communication dries up, often one partner tries to shield the other from the financial problems, time with each other decreases, hasty words are spoken, and resentments build. It's a vicious downward spiral.

The root problem of financial pressure (except catastrophic loss of income) is a spiritual disease called *lack of contentment*. The Bible says, "Better one handful with tranquillity than two handfuls with toil and chasing after the wind."

Simply put, the level of the lifestyle determines the level of financial pressure. It takes more energy to earn a living and service debt than to simply earn a living. It's a choice between tranquillity and toil. "But godliness with contentment is great gain" (1 Tim. 6:6).

Today's verse is a *principle*, not a *command*. A command is a direction or order we *must* follow as *duty*. A principle, on the other hand, is a basic truth or standard as a general rule we *should* follow as *wisdom*. We are not required to follow the principle in today's verse, it is not duty; but we ought to because it is wise.

A lack of contentment will yield to a higher lifestyle which will bring debts which will produce all the symptoms of financial pressure which will lead to a difficult marriage. Is it worth it? Have you chosen tranquillity or toil?

DISCUSSION

Both complete these sentences:

The financial pressure in our marriage is caused by _____.
The symptoms of financial pressure on me personally are _____.
The second-tier problems these financial pressures have caused in our
     marriage are _____.

APPLICATION

Consider together the lifestyle level that you can realistically afford based upon the way God has equipped and called you. Would this represent tranquillity for you? How about contentment? Would it be worth it to establish a new, lower baseline of pressure?

PRAYER

Either: Lord God, we have let ourselves be seduced by a debt laden culture into believing contentment and tranquillity come from having more things. It is a devil's lie. All we have gained is toil, debts, and financial pressure. The stress of it all makes our marriage like stale bread. Lord, we pledge to seek a new lifestyle that will allow us tranquillity. Help us to make the needed adjustments. Help us to be content. Amen.

DEBT IS DUMB

My son, if you have put up security for your neighbor,
if you have struck hands in pledge for another,
if you have been trapped by what you said,
ensnared by the words of your mouth,
then do this, my son, to free yourself,
since you have fallen into your neighbor's hands:
Go and humble yourself;
press your plea with your neighbor!
Allow no sleep to your eyes,
no slumber to your eyelids.
Free yourself, like a gazelle from the hand of the hunter,
like a bird from the snare of the fowler.

PROVERBS 6:1–5

*I*n the late 1980s I was the personal guarantor on a huge number of real estate construction and permanent loans totaling a sum that stretched into the stratosphere. What's odd about this is that we had no personal debt, yet I was willing to risk all our personal assets to guarantee these loans.

One day, today's verses hit me between the eyes like an elephant gun. Frankly, when business was good I winked at these verses (and a host of others). They just didn't register. As Demosthenes said, "Nothing is easier than self-deceit, for what each man wishes that he also believes to be true." However, when business went bad I found myself pouring over the Scriptures looking for guidance. It is interesting how guidance can't be found unless you are looking for it. Sometimes we are not ready to receive the truth.

On that day, amidst tears of confession and repentance for living by my own ideas, I pledged to follow the advice of Proverbs 6:1–5 to the letter. I made getting out of personal debt my overarching business goal. From that day forward my consuming passion was to get completely out of all personal liabilities. It is simply not fair to risk the security of our families to satisfy our greed or misguided need to build an empire.

But getting out of debt is no easy process. It took nearly seven painfully long years to put things right. Finally, though, I could say, "I owe no man anything except the debt of love!" (see Rom. 13:8). Know what my only regret is? The torture I put Patsy through.

We live in an era in which the culture makes you feel like an ill-informed, dense-minded, baboon-brained hayseed if you are not living life to the fullest, maximizing your debt potential.

Because business has done such a superior job with its ethic of "sell," the average family has done a superior job adopting the value of "consume." Values like self-denial, saving, and deferring until we can pay cash for our wants are considered old-fashioned—hopelessly out of date.

The Bible isn't specific. The Bible does not prohibit debt, neither does it give clear guidance on how much debt one can take on or for what purpose.

Hence, Christian advisors come to different positions on whether a believer should take on debt. A few say no debt under any circumstances. A few advise debt only for appreciating assets. A few apply the principle of wisdom. Most suggest never borrowing to pay for current expenses. Regardless of the exact position, the thrust of counselors inevitably conveys at least prudence and usually caution.

While the Scriptures don't prohibit debt, they constantly deal with the negative impact of debt. Nehemiah's people borrowed money to buy food and pay taxes. They ended up in slavery. Proverbs 22:26–27 cautions us not to put up security for debts, lest our beds be snatched. Today's verses clamor for immediate attention! All of this leads to a single overarching conclusion which I call Morley's Money Maxim: Debt is dumb! . . . Well, isn't it?

DISCUSSION

Both answer: What is your attitude toward debt? Have you taken on a load of debt with personal liabilities? How have your debts affected your relationship with your spouse?

APPLICATION

If you are in debt consider making getting out of debt your overarching financial goal. Visit a Christian financial planner or a friend who is financially wise to devise a realistic plan. There is no pressure like debt pressure.

PRAYER

Dear God, we have let ourselves get caught up in the values of this world. We have taken on too much debt, and it hurts. We pledge to free ourselves in any ethical way possible from "our neighbor's hands." Grant us, we ask, a whole new biblical attitude toward debt. Amen.

MAKING MAJOR DECISIONS:
A PERSPECTIVE

The lot is cast into the lap, but its every decision is from the LORD.
PROVERBS 16:33

*W*e've—okay, okay . . . *I've*—made more than a few dumb decisions in twenty years of marriage. When I was younger I didn't give much thought to the risks associated with major decisions. I figured I always had more than enough time to make it up if I was wrong. Things change.

Here are some considerations to help make better decisions:

1. *Know that many major decisions do turn out wrong.* A man became restless after twenty-one years with the same company. He could not isolate the source of his feelings, but decided he needed a change. Since that time he has bounced around from job to job, never keeping the same position more than three years.

A couple decided to move to a "better" neighborhood. There was nothing wrong with their present neighborhood. In fact, they loved their neighbors, the location was convenient, crime was low, the mortgage payment was a pittance, and they couldn't really find anything wrong with their existing home. Their new house required much more upkeep than they had figured. The higher payments created a great deal of tension between them. Soon they began pointing fingers at each other, blaming one another for deciding to leave the old neighborhood.

If you are not content with yourself where you are, you will not be content where you are going. It is an error to think that changing our circumstances alone will make us happy or content. Often we cling to some selfish ambition that is at odds with leading a surrendered life.

2. *Count the cost of making the wrong decision.* Perhaps the greatest lesson I've learned about making major decisions is determining the cost of making the wrong decision. When decisions turn out right, "I" am brilliant. When they turn out wrong, "you" really blew it! Think about this next statement: The greatest time waster in our lives is the time we spend undoing that which ought not to have been done in the first place. Do you agree?

Usually we can recover if we make a bad choice. Sometimes, however, we can't. Never make a major decision that bets the entire ranch on being right.

220

3. *Most decisions are obvious given enough information and time.* When do we make poor decisions? When we don't have our facts straight and when we are hasty. Keep collecting data. Write it down so you don't forget it. The mind by itself may blow one small fact all out of proportion. Writing it down puts things in perspective. Talk to wise counselors; get other people's perspective. Talk to experts who have skill—better to operate from fact than feeling.

Ours is an impatient world, a hasty world, an impulsive world. If my computer takes three seconds to sort 20,000,000 bytes of data instead of one second I get frustrated. Let's get real! It takes time to make a wise, major decision. The mind may know quickly what to do, but it takes time for our emotions to catch up. We have built up opinions on most subjects which only time can change. We must wait for that gut feeling, which is nothing other than our subconscious mind informing our conscious mind of the results of its thorough and complete analysis.

DISCUSSION

Each answer: What is *the* major decision you are facing right now or in the near future?

APPLICATION

Sift your major decision through the following questions:

- What is causing you to consider a change? What is your motivation? Are you discontent with your circumstances or yourself?
- What is the cost if your decision turns out wrong? How much time will it take to undo the decision if it turns out badly? Can you, in fact, recover if you are wrong?
- Have you gathered enough information? Do you have all the facts? Have you allowed enough time to assimilate the data? Are you being impatient?

PRAYER

Lord Jesus, we are facing a major decision, and we don't know what to do. By faith, we will apply the principles in this devotion. Help us, we pray, to make the right choice. Amen.

DISCERNING GOD'S WILL

The world and its desires pass away, but the man who does the will of God lives forever.

1 JOHN 2:17

*T*he major decisions we make in marriage will come more easily if we abide in Christ daily, beginning each dawn in humble surrender to God, seeking to please Him in all our ways. Today let's briefly explore each of seven different means God has given us to help discern His will.

1. *The Bible.* The single most important question to ask is, "Has God already spoken on this matter?" The Bible is chock full of commands (which are duty to obey) and principles (which are wise to follow). We don't have to wonder whether reporting $1,800 of incidental income to the IRS is God's will. We know it is. Obedience is the trademark of a biblical Christian. Talk over the Scriptures together.

2. *Prayer.* Jesus said, "Until now you have not asked for anything in my name. Ask and you will receive, and your joy will be complete" (John 16:24). Over and over and over again we are invited to present our requests to God. Prayer is the currency of our personal relationship with Christ. Spend it liberally. Pray together over major (why not all?) decisions.

3. *The Holy Spirit.* God lives in us in the person of the Holy Spirit. He is our counselor, convicter, comforter, converter, and encourager. Consciously depend upon Him and He will both guide you and intercede for you. "The Spirit intercedes for the saints in accordance with God's will" (Rom. 8:27). The Holy Spirit is the one who "clothes" us with power from on high. The Holy Spirit will never lead in contradiction to His written Word.

4. *Conscience.* In seeking God's will we must live by the pledge of a good conscience toward God and other people. "Dear friends, if our hearts do not condemn us, we have confidence before God" (1 John 3:21). Keep in mind that while a guilty conscience provides clear evidence you are not in God's will, a clear conscience may not guarantee you have correctly discerned God's will. Conscience is more effective as a red light than a green light. To go against conscience is neither wise nor safe.

5. *Circumstances.* Some people are born short, some tall. Some black, some white. Some in America, some in Argentina. Some to poor parents, some to rich. God's will is often revealed clearly by the circumstances in which we live. "He determined the times set for them and the exact places where they should live" (Acts 17:26). If you want to purchase a house which

will require a $100,000 mortgage and you can only qualify for $75,000, then circumstances have told you God's will.

6. *Counsel.* "Plans fail for lack of counsel, but with many advisers they succeed" (Prov. 15:22). Often we need nothing more than a good listener to help us crystallize our thoughts into coherent words. Other times, we need the advice of a trusted friend. Seek out each other's counsel.

7. *Fasting.* Fasting is a lost spiritual discipline today. Fasting slows down the physical functions so that the mind can be more in tune with Christ. Fasting is another way to demonstrate a seriousness about your concern to the Lord.

Use these means for finding the will of God. Do them only occasionally and it will amount to nothing more than priming a rusty pump. Do them regularly and the will of God will gush forth like deep well springs.

DISCUSSION

Each answer: Which of these seven ways to discern God's will do you regularly use? Which ways have you neglected that you would like to give more attention? Do you generally seek God's will individually or as a couple?

APPLICATION

Pick the areas in which you would like to improve. What is one thing you could do this week to help you along?

PRAYER

Either: Lord God, thank You for the abundant provision You have made for us to find Your will. Help us to be faithful to employ all of these means. We are having difficulty discerning Your will for the decision before us (name it specifically). Grant us the grace to fully utilize all the gifts You have given us to know Your will. Amen.

MAKING MAJOR DECISIONS:
A PROCESS

Do not conform any longer to the pattern of this world, but be transformed by the renewing of your mind. Then you will be able to test and approve what God's will is—his good, pleasing and perfect will.
ROMANS 12:2

ost of the major decisions we make in life are not dictated by Scripture: whether or not to change jobs, which job to take, whether or not to move to another city or across town, how many children to have, which church to attend, what kind of personal ministry to undertake, what kind of car to drive, and so on. Yet, choices like these comprise some of the most important and difficult decisions we make.

Here is a useful, practical process for finding the will of God. Keep in mind this is not a process for getting our own way. We must be certain that we truly want what God wants. Otherwise we will twist things to our own way. Each step builds on itself, and you may find the answer becomes obvious at any point along the way. If it doesn't make itself clear, keep moving through the steps until it does. As suggested by today's Scripture, this process focuses on "renewing the mind"—using our God-given intelligence and wisdom to make good choices that are not dictated by our emotions or sinful desires.

1. *Write down the decision in exact terms.* Nothing clarifies our thinking more quickly than paper and pencil. It's said that half the solution is knowing the problem. Precisely what is the decision you need to make? What are the choices?

2. *Write out a "purpose statement" that precisely explains why you are considering this decision.* It is helpful not only to know *what* you are trying to decide, but *why. Why* are you trying to decide *what* you are trying to decide? What is the context? For example, if you're considering a different home, do you *have* to move? Is it a need or a want? Are you unhappy?

3. *Submit your "purpose statement" to a series of questions.* Here are some suggestions:

- What are you trying to accomplish, and why?
- What is your objective or desired end result?
- What are your expectations, and why?

- How does this decision fit with your calling as a Christian?
- Are you considering this decision from a sense of calling or duty?
- What would Jesus do if He were you?
- What is the "next" right step to take?

4. *If your answer still hasn't become obvious, list each option on a separate sheet of paper.* On the left side list the advantages of that option; on the right side list the disadvantages. As Louis Agassiz said, "A pencil is one of the best of eyes." Usually, one option will prove itself clearly desirable—or undesirable—at this point.

5. *If the answer still hasn't come, wait.* You can never predict what God is doing in your life. God is committed to working for your good, not your harm. Commit to let God set the agenda. Never push God. If the answer isn't obvious, trust Him to make it clear in His timing. You can rush ahead if you must, but you do so at your own peril. Better to wait upon the Lord. Give Him the time He wants to work some things into and out of your character.

Remember: God is not the author of confusion. Satan is. If you are still confused, wait. Peace is the umpire.

6. *At all times, employ the seven steps of guidance to discern God's will covered in the previous devotional.* Whatever major decision you face, you can find God's will if you patiently apply a wise process.

DISCUSSION

Both answer: What is the major decision you face right now? What process have you applied to discern God's will? How can the process outlined above help you find His will?

APPLICATION

Submit your major decisions to the steps listed in this devotional. Take one decision you face right now and go through this process together.

PRAYER

Either: Heavenly Father, we desire to bring You glory through the decision we must make. We long to know Your good, pleasing, and perfect will. We submit ourselves to be transformed by the renewing of our minds. Help us to discern what we should do through this process of finding Your will. Amen.

BUILDING MARRIAGE AROUND THE BIBLE

Your word is truth.

JOHN 17:17

*E*ach marriage selects, knowingly or not, a moral centerpiece around which it builds. The Bible is the most sensible, practical, and promising centerpiece around which to build a romantic, fulfilling marriage. There are three reasons to base your marriage upon the Bible.

First, the Bible is true. In a lecture I attended, Edith Schaeffer said her husband, Dr. Francis Schaeffer, often said, "There is only one reason to become a Christian and not two—it is true." At the end of the day, if the Bible is not true then we were a pack of fools. But the record of history shows that great thinkers through the ages have believed in God and believed that the Bible is true. Daniel Webster said, "If there is anything in my style to commend, credit it to an early love of Scriptures."

What has become of some of those who criticized the Bible? Tom Paine said, "In five years from now there will not be a Bible in America. I have gone through the Bible with an ax and cut down all the trees."[24] He died in 1809. In a typical year over ten million Bibles are purchased in Christian bookstores in America alone. So long, Tom.

The Bible reveals to us a knowledge of God, a knowledge of self, a knowledge of how salvation is found, and a knowledge of how God intended marriage to be. Because it is true, it is a reliable, moral compass for us.

Second, the Bible is practical. Whatever need you have, the Bible has the answer. Often the answers are pointed and specific; other times the guidance is more general. However, I personally have never had a problem upon which the Bible was silent.

When ethical and practical issues come up in marriage, it is good to have settled on your final court of appeal. If you build your marriage around the Bible, then God becomes the tiebreaker. Whether you need more insight, guidance, comfort, encouragement, or hope, the Bible contains practical advice for living up close with your mate.

Third, the Bible changes lives. Exercising to get yourself in shape will change your life. A diet that sheds twenty pounds will change your life. A college education will change your life. Sending your last child away to college will change your life. But nothing will change your life like the Bible.

For example, once you have read that the husband "must love his wife as he loves himself, and the wife must respect her husband," you can never think the same again. You begin to be convicted and drawn to work it out in daily living. "My word that goes out from my mouth: It will not return to me empty, but will accomplish what I desire and achieve the purpose for which I sent it" (Isa. 55:11).

Because the Bible is true, it has authority and power. It accomplishes its intended purpose. Personally, I have never known anyone whose life has changed in any significant way apart from the regular study of God's Word. The greatest potential for meaningful change in our marriages is to submit to the authority of God's Word and regular study. When once our souls begin to fill up with the beauty of God's own words, we come into possession of life transforming power.

The Bible is true, practical, and it changes lives. What better basis upon which to build an intimate, loving, open, honest marriage? Wise is the couple that builds their marriage on the Bible.

DISCUSSION

Each answer: What percentage of your life view is based on the Bible and what percentage have you picked up from the culture? How has that affected the way you address problems and opportunities in your marriage? (For example, your views toward career, lifestyle, debt, saving, child discipline.)

APPLICATION

Settle the issue of the moral authority over your life. Make a pledge to accept the Bible as the inerrant Word of God by faith. Study the Bible. Let it become your final court of appeal.

PRAYER

Dear God, by faith we accept the Bible as Your inerrant Word. We believe it is true. We surrender our own best thinking to the moral authority of Your Word. We commit ourselves to regularly study the Bible. Let Your Word accomplish in our lives whatever You desire—"the purpose for which You sent it." Amen.

CONNECTED TO THE CHURCH

Let us not give up meeting together, as some are in the habit of doing, but let us encourage one another—and all the more as you see the Day approaching.

HEBREWS 10:25

After Hurricane Andrew, the devastating 1992 storm that ravaged South Florida, many people began rebuilding their church buildings even before their own homes and businesses. Why would they do that?

Consider how the church meets the needs of our families: weddings, baptisms, confirmations, funerals, fellowship dinners, evangelistic outreaches, worship services, preaching, ministry opportunities, accountability, the Lord's supper, Sunday school classes, special classes, conferences, women's groups, men's groups, nursery, Mother's Day Out, and hospital visits. No institution supports marriage and family like the church.

Consider for a moment what America would look like without the church. Where would be the great hospitals, schools, and universities? Where would be the soup lines, the coalitions for the homeless, the rescue missions? Would anyone be doing inner city youth work or providing homes for unwed mothers? Where would be the voices calling out for abstinence from premarital sex or the right to life? Who would be the voice of justice and the hands of mercy? Who would be the feet of the gospel of salvation? Who would be the light in the darkness, the salt seeking to preserve society and culture? As someone said, "The church has many critics, but no rivals."

There are five reasons every married couple should attend a vibrant Christ-centered church together. Let's consider each of them:

1. *Worship: Experience with God.* The ultimate, overarching purpose of church is to worship God. Most important of all, church gives us a special place to stoop down and render religious homage, respect, awe, and reverence to the God who is. The Greek word for worship literally means "to kiss, like a dog licking its master's hand." I've heard it said that the only thing that has more germs than a public telephone is a dog's tongue. How gracious of our God to let such sinners as us "lick His hand"! Worship is an *experience with God.*

2. *Fellowship: Encouragement from God.* Times come when we need spiritual, emotional, social, and prayer support that can only come from a group committed to caring for and loving others. We cannot love people unless we are connected to them in some way. The church gives us a larger

228

family of which we can be a part. Who besides the church? God uses other believers to encourage each other. Fellowship is *encouragement from God*.

3. *Growth: Knowledge of God.* The church is a place to learn about God—to be disciplined. The preaching and teaching of God's Word—what it says, its meaning, its message, and how it applies—are critical elements in the life of a Christian. Growth is acquiring a *knowledge of God*.

4. *Service: Work for God.* Every Christian is called to serve God through personal ministry, or service (see Eph. 2:10). The church is the principal outlet for discerning your spiritual gifts, becoming equipped to serve, and finding an outlet to serve the body of Christ and to reach out to the broken, hurting world all around us. Service is doing *work for God*.

5. *Accountability: Persevere in God.* No Christian ever led a vibrant, obedient life on his/her own. Without the help of a few friends to keep us on track we, too, like sheep will go astray. A major purpose of the church is to provide a framework for accountability. Besides formal church discipline, successful churches link people together in smaller groups where there is increased visibility. Visibility increases accountability. Accountability is to *persevere in God.* [25]

DISCUSSION

Both answer: Which of the five reasons for attending church have you not considered? Consider the second and third paragraphs at the beginning of today's devotional again. Have you fully appreciated the church for its contributions to your family and our society?

APPLICATION

If you are not regular church attenders, plan to begin this week. If you are regular attenders, express your appreciation to the pastor(s) and staff for the benefits your family has received.

PRAYER

Either, as appropriate: Dear Lord, we confess that we have not recently considered all the ways the church provides for our needs. We confess that we have also taken for granted the many ways the church has benefited our society and culture. We pledge afresh to be active, participating members of a local church body. Amen.

FINDING A CHRIST-CENTERED CHURCH

And he is the head of the body, the church; he is the beginning and the firstborn from among the dead, so that in everything he might have the supremacy.

COLOSSIANS 1:18

*J*esus Christ is the head of the church. We attend church because He wants us to attend. To attend church means to gather with other believers to worship the Lord—to give Him the supremacy. The church is the people, not the place—though we certainly need a place to meet.

There are two principal considerations in selecting a church: *beliefs* and *worship style.* Let's look at both.

BELIEFS

What does the church believe? What does the pastor believe? Some of the most basic beliefs you should consider include:

1. Are Jesus and the cross central to the life of the church?
2. Are the Scriptures viewed as the authoritative, inerrant Word of God?
3. How does the church believe people are saved?
4. Does the church believe all people are sinners in need of a Savior?
5. Is the church evangelistic?
6. Does the church administer discipline, and how?
7. Is the Word of God preached?

WORSHIP STYLE

Churches vary widely in style of worship. None of these styles is more right than another. The important issue is to find a church that helps you worship God in a way that honors Him and is comfortable for you.

Gordon MacDonald has identified six "leading instincts of the soul" which lead people to prefer worshiping God along six different lines.[26] You will likely be most inclined toward two or three of these.

1. *Majesty: The Aesthetic Instinct.* The person with the aesthetic instinct seeks to be overwhelmed by the majesty of God. This person is happiest when the worship environment includes beauty, order, tradition, and artistic integrity.

2. *Joy: The Experiential Instinct.* Almost opposite from number one is the experientialist, who wants to "feel" the presence of God and respond with a full range of emotions, including clapping, singing, prayer, weeping, laughing, and more.

3. *Achievement: The Activist Instinct.* The activist sees everything through the lens of service. The world needs to be changed, and this person feels closest to God when making a contribution to the work of the kingdom.

4. *Listening: The Contemplative Instinct.* The contemplative is profoundly concerned about the inner life, about opening up to God in the quiet of his or her own soul, about sensing God's presence. This person's prayer is a two-way conversation.

5. *Truth: The Student Instinct.* The student loves truth. The study of the Bible forms the core of this person's worship style. Happiness is found in a church that emphasizes the preaching and teaching of the Word.

6. *Love: The Relational Instinct.* The relationist finds God most present when people are bonded together in fellowship, worship, or mutual support. This person is torn when there is conflict, lifted high when the walls come down.

Which of the six instincts make you feel closest to God—like you are worshiping Him?

DISCUSSION

Both answer: Why is it important to know what your church believes? Which of the six instincts makes you feel closest to God?

APPLICATION

Take a moment right now and order the six instincts by putting a "1" in the margin by the instinct you most identify with and so on through number "6." If you don't have a church presently, plan to start attending the church of your choice regularly. When you visit a church rank it on each of these six styles, then compare with your own ranking. Answer the questions about beliefs. These exercises will help you make a more sensible, reasoned selection.

PRAYER

Lord Jesus, thank You for giving us the church. May we see it as You intended, a place to gather with fellow believers for mutual worship, support, and encouragement from You and from each other. May we serve You with renewed gladness in our hearts through the church. Amen.

PLANNING FOR PREMATURE DEATH

If anyone does not provide for his relatives, and especially for his immediate family, he has denied the faith and is worse than an unbeliever.
1 TIMOTHY 5:8

*S*he seems cheerful enough, but in a sad sort of way. What is she doing here? Why would a woman her age be waitressing at a breakfast diner? She must have been somebody's wife once upon a time. Why didn't he take better care of her? She seems worth more than this. These thoughts ran through my mind as I watched our waitress interact with her other customers.

According to the American Association of Retired Persons (AARP) the median income for older persons (65 or older) in 1991 was $14,357 for males and $8,189 for females.[27] In other words—not enough. As one man put it, "The problem with retiring is that you get used to a certain lifestyle. It's just not that easy to cut back. You can never have too much income in retirement."

In fact, after adjusting for inflation, "real" income decreased from the prior year by 2 percent for women and 3 percent for men. The major source of retired income is Social Security (37 percent of income), and one of every eight older people still work. One of every five older people (20 percent) are classified as poor or near poor.[28] According to financial expert Ron Blue, 11 out of 12 women will become widows, and the average age of all widows in America is 52.[29]

I'm not making these figures up! And I sure don't mean to scare you, but it should. These sobering statistics make two things crystal clear. First, retirement is a financial mine field for most retirees. Second, it is a burden most men dump into the laps of their widows through their earlier death.

Is it right for a husband to spend so much on a lifestyle today that his wife will be forced to abandon it when he is gone? Should a wife spend too much money today to her own eventual harm? Is it not appropriate to provide enough for the future (through insurance, savings, and investments) so that whatever lifestyle you have together, the survivor can keep it once left alone? Should not a couple live by a lifestyle today that will allow them to retire in comfort whether together or widowed? These are not questions that can be lightly passed by.

Husband, nothing will testify more to how you loved your wife when you were alive than how she is able to live when you are dead. "In the house of the wise are stores of choice food and oil, but a foolish man devours all he has" (Prov. 21:20).

Husband, this may be difficult, but I want you to imagine your wife after you are gone. What adjustments will she have to make? Will she have to go to work, or have you provided enough insurance to take care of her needs? Will she ever end up waitressing in a diner somewhere? Picture her slaving away all day, then coming home to an empty one-room apartment. Have you provided for your immediate family?

DISCUSSION

Earnings go to one of four places: 1) *current expenses* (including stewardship giving), 2) *debt payments* for past expenses and acquisitions (e.g., vacations, cars, furniture), 3) *savings plans* for anticipated future expenses and acquisitions (e.g., college, car), or 4) *retirement plans*. Where is your money going by percentage? Where would you like it to go?

Example*		*You—Current*	*You—Desired*
Current Expenses	70%	____%	____%
Debt Payments	26%	____%	____%
Savings Plans	2%	____%	____%
Retirement Plans	2%	____%	____%

*The percentages in this example are not intended to represent norms.

What do your percentages tell you about your lifestyle? What do they tell you about your retirement years?

APPLICATION

Based upon your answers to the questions in today's narrative and the Discussion questions, commit to take whatever steps are necessary to ensure your retirement will be financially independent. Then if one of you should die prematurely you will have made provision. If this is over your head, see a Christian financial planner.

PRAYER

Lord, thank You that You have given us a spirit of power, love, and a sound mind. Help us, we pray, not to devour all we have, but to put away stores of "choice food and oil." May we not live for today at the expense of tomorrow. Help us to provide adequately for our retirement. Amen.

PROVIDING FOR RETIREMENT

Turn to me and be gracious to me,
for I am lonely and afflicted.

PSALM 25:16

God sets the lonely in families.

PSALM 68:6

Once I was invited to preach the Father's Day sermon at a particular church. When I arrived I was taken back by how few men appeared to be of fathering age.

I asked the youth pastor, "What percentage of the congregation would you estimate to be elderly (over sixty-five)?"

"Seventy percent," he immediately responded.

"And of those, what percentage would you say are lonely?" I further inquired.

"All of them."

* * * * *

Recently a retired man told me, "The notion that when you retire your financial needs will go down is a myth. The trouble is that you build yourself into a certain lifestyle. It's not that easy to just up and change everything."

"How much money is enough, then, to retire?" I asked.

"You can never have too much retirement income," came his reply.

There are two great problems in retirement: *loneliness* and *money*. Let's briefly address today the problem of loneliness.

As a general rule, the quality of our relationships in retirement will mirror the quality of our relationships today. Loneliness is a choice, one that we make years before we retire—a decision we are making right now. True, some people won't be lonely even if they retire to the North Pole and talk to penguins all day. For most of us, though, the decisions we make right now determine whether we will be lonely in retirement.

We can avoid loneliness in retirement by sound planning and making some investments in other people's lives. The Bible proclaims that we reap what we sow. Here are several ideas. Take them to heart:

- Retire *to* something instead of *from* something. Plan for the future, don't merely escape from the past. Identify activities you want to undertake.
- Give your children *now* the time you hope they will give you *then*, no strings attached. Run your home on grace, not law. Make it a refuge they want to retreat to, not flee from. Nothing will make you happier than spending time with your grandchildren. Do you think the way you are relating to your children now will make them eager to have their children spend time with you when they have kids of their own?
- Contentment comes from making investments in people and relationships, not from accumulating money and possessions. Plan your finances, but don't count on them to make you happy in old age.
- Develop a few close friendships with other couples around common interests (i.e., bridge, golf, ministry). Try to form most of these from your church family.
- Develop a common interest together now, apart from kids, friends, and business (i.e., walking, collecting, travel, tennis).

There are two ways to be lonely: One is to be alone; the other is to have nothing in common with your mate. No married person ought ever to be lonely.

DISCUSSION

Both answer: Do you find it surprising that a pastor would say that all of the elderly people in his church were lonely? Why or why not? Do you think you will struggle with loneliness if you stay on your present course? Explain your answer.

APPLICATION

Discuss the five ideas mentioned above and write down a few goals as they come to mind.

PRAYER

Lord God, we earnestly pray that neither of us would be lonely in retirement. We ask you to give us something to retire to, not from. Help us to be a blessing to our children. Grant us a few close friends, and help us to have interests in common. We ask this in Jesus' name. Amen.

Providing for Retirement— Part 2

In the house of the wise are stores of choice food and oil, but a foolish man devours all he has.

PROVERBS 21:20

The second great problem in retirement is money—a lack of adequate financial resources. There are two reasons couples come up short of money in retirement: poor planning and catastrophic illness, which wipes out savings. (This is a chapter on retirement, not medical catastrophe, but let me say parenthetically that you must insure yourselves against catastrophic illness.)

However you spend today inexorably determines how you will retire later. There are four lifestyle/spending approaches couples follow:

1. *To live "above" your means.* This spendthrift couple teeters perpetually on the brink of financial disaster. From the outside looking in they appear rich. The pursuit of self and pleasure motivates them. Big cars, fancy clothes, luxurious home, big vacations. Yet every bit of it is financed to the gills. Behind closed doors there are many fights and quarrels. They live up to limits of their income and beyond. They are constantly refinancing and borrowing more. Eventually, this house of cards will come tumbling down.

2. *To live "at" your means.* This couple wants more of the good life. They are not so foolish as to borrow for experiences or depreciating assets, but neither are they so wise to think about a rainy day. They are stretched to the max. They are thinking about moving to a bigger home, though they cannot find peace about it. They are like ones who hear God's Word, but the worries of this life and the deceitfulness of wealth choke it and make it unfruitful (see Matt. 13:22). They feel a great strain in their relationship over money. Sooner or later, this couple must make a choice. Do they start borrowing to relieve the pressure, or do they downsize their standard of living?

3. *To live "within" your means.* This submissive couple recognizes that the Bible calls us to be stewards of what God has entrusted to us. Everything we have belongs to God, who entrusts resources to us for a season. They think about and plan for the future. Not only do they save for a rainy day, they have a well thought out retirement plan as well. They tithe joyfully. They, too, are tempted by the pleasures ballyhooed by the Madison Avenue

236

pinstripers, but they examine themselves regularly lest they should be hasty and abandon their stewardship.

4. *To live "below" your means.* This unusually disciplined couple has decided to live a lifestyle lower than they could easily afford. They do this for the sake of their children and the sake of God's kingdom. They want their children to walk with God and not become materialistic. They do not want to be distracted by the worries, riches, and pleasures of this world (see Luke 8:14). Though they use the things of this world, they have not become engrossed in them (see 1 Cor. 7:30–31). They recognize that the world and its desires pass away, but the one who does the will of God lives forever (see 1 John 2:17). They have the gift of giving, and would rather make eternal investments than spend up to the limits of their income.

Only couples in the third and fourth categories can reasonably expect to become financially independent in retirement. Which category do you live in?

DISCUSSION

Both answer: Which of these four approaches to lifestyle and spending have you been using? Is it by design or default?

APPLICATION

Determine which category you should be in. What changes do you need to make, if any? Commit to a specific plan to make the changes you agree upon. Consider asking another couple to hold you accountable and meet with you quarterly to review your progress.

PRAYER

As appropriate: Heavenly Father, we have erred in our finances. Unless we make changes now our retirement will not turn out well. Help us, O Lord, to have the self-discipline to live within (or below) our means and plan for our retirement. Amen.

ONE PERSON WHO REALLY CARES

You have stolen my heart, my sister, my bride;
you have stolen my heart with one glance of your eyes.
SONG OF SONGS 4:9

*D*eep down within the most quiet place in our hearts, she whispers softly. Not often do we hear her. The daily din of a thousand pressing pleas drowns out her voice.

Yet, every now and then, when we sit still beside a stream, into our conscious thoughts her quiet voice protrudes. Like a muted hum just below the line that separates the conscious from unconscious, she begins. The sound is distant, vaguely familiar, and we strain to hear. We know she is there, calling, but just beyond our grasp.

Because God is kind, one by one, that cacophony of other voices sleep. Suddenly, in a single, white-hot moment, her voice explodes within our breast with a thousand prickly points. Moisture collects in the corners of our eyes. Though we have climbed the tallest mountains, tamed the wildest beasts, and conquered the greatest foes, in a singular moment of lucid clarity she jars us to remember that what we long for most of all is for one person, just one, to really care.

"All I want in life is for one person, just one person, to really care about me," she whispers. "I don't merely mean someone to care when I have a problem or when I'm down—though that, too; but someone who would care deeply about me every moment of every day.

"Oh, how I wish for just one person who would daydream about me, about what I am doing, about how he can show his love for me in a hundred little ways. Someone to accept me just as I am, no strings attached.

"My heart aches for someone to squeeze me close and tell me that he cares. I waste away waiting for someone who would listen—really listen—to the longings of my heart. I had a dream once. It died when no one listened. Pick me a wildflower, won't you? Put a note under my pillow, please. Tell me that you are the one, the one God gave to really care about me."

The most intense need of every man and woman though many push it down deep and deny it, is to be in relationship with one other person who really cares. It is an intense craving to be loved by another. God has made us for love—to love and to be loved. Our greatest joy is to sense we are the top human priority of another person. Likewise, the loneliest person in the whole wide world is the spouse who doesn't feel like anyone really cares.

The less you care for your mate the less you will recognize your own need to have one person who really cares. The less you care the harder you are to care for. The busier you are the harder it is to hear that quiet voice. Though we fill our lives with a thousand good things, what does it matter if no one really cares?

Soon the guests will have all gone home. The crepe paper will droop. The lights will be dim. In rocking chairs you will sit side by side, alone. The question remains, "Does anyone really care?"

Go sit together, still, beside a stream.

DISCUSSION

Each answer: Do you feel like you are really cared for? How has your feeling changed since you began doing this book together?

APPLICATION

Decide that you will be that one person for your mate who really cares, that you will always be there. Look each other in the eyes and express your undying commitment to be the one who really cares, no matter what.

PRAYER

Either or both: Lord Jesus, because You cared we, too, can care. Soon we will be old, and all alone. Help us, O God, to invest in each other every moment of every day. We are the only two people who are really in this together. I want to be the one who really cares. Amen.

IN SUMMARY

*O*ur future together holds the wonderful prospect of great joy. This joy will be in direct proportion to the wisdom we employ, the quality of the decisions we make, and our devotion to each other now. Let's review some of the key ideas from this section.

APPLICATION

Read these aloud and offer a comment about each one.

- How we are behind the tightly drawn curtains of our own private castle is how we really are.
- There must be nothing in the behavior of the husband to make the wife stumble in her faith, and vice versa.
- Marriage magnifies imperfections. In the intimate space of marriage we must be alert to represent our Lord to each other.
- A husband and wife will have other priorities, like work, rest, recreation, and ministry. However, loving God, loving each other, and loving our children form the indispensable core of a happy marriage.
- Financial pressure comes from three directions: 1) supporting a lifestyle, 2) servicing debt, and/or 3) unemployment. All create cash flow problems.
- We live in an era in which the culture makes you feel like an ill-informed, dense-minded, baboon-brained hayseed if you are not living life to the fullest, maximizing your debt potential.
- Because business has done such a superior job with its ethic of "sell," the average family has done a superior job adopting the value of "consume."
- While the Scriptures don't prohibit debt, they constantly deal with its negative impact.
- If you are not content with yourself where you are, you will not be content where you are going.
- 1) Know that many major decisions do turn out wrong. 2) Count the cost of making the wrong decision. 3) Most decisions are obvious given enough information and time.

240

- The greatest time-waster in our lives is the time we spend undoing that which ought not to have been done in the first place.
- We must be certain that we truly want what God wants. Otherwise we will twist things to our own way.
- The major decisions we make in marriage will come most easily if we abide in Christ daily, beginning each dawn in humble surrender to God, seeking to please Him in all our ways.
- The Bible reveals to us a knowledge of God, a knowledge of self, a knowledge of how salvation is found, and a knowledge of how God intended marriage. Because it is true, it is a reliable, moral compass for us.
- Personally, I have never known anyone whose life has changed in any significant way apart from the regular study of God's Word.
- The Bible is true and practical, and it changes lives. What better basis upon which to build an intimate, loving, open, honest marriage? Wise is the couple that builds their marriage on the Bible.
- Consider how the church meets the needs of our families. No institution supports marriage and family like the church.
- Is it right for a husband to spend so much on a lifestyle today that his wife will be forced to abandon it when he is gone? Should a husband allow his wife to spend too much money today to her own eventual harm? Is it not appropriate to provide enough for the future (through insurance, savings, and investments) so that whatever lifestyle you have together, the survivor can keep it once left alone? Should not a couple live by a lifestyle today that will allow them to retire in comfort whether together or widowed? These are not questions that can be lightly passed by.
- There are two ways to be lonely: One is to be alone; the other is to have nothing in common with your mate. No married person ought ever to be lonely.
- Husband, nothing will testify more to how you loved your wife when you were alive than how she is able to live when you are dead. "In the house of the wise are stores of choice food and oil, but a foolish man devours all he has" (Prov. 21:20).
- However you spend today inexorably determines how you will retire later.
- The most intense need we each have, though many push it down deep and deny it, is the need to be in relationship with one other person who really cares.

Notes

1. Oswald Chambers, *My Utmost for His Highest* (Westwood: Barbour and Company, Inc., 1963), 112.
2. Gary Smalley and John Trent, *The Gift of the Blessing* (Nashville: Thomas Nelson Publishers, 1993).
3. Paul Tournier, *To Understand Each Other* (Atlanta: John Knox Press, 1962), 13.
4. Ibid., 19.
5. Ibid., 22.
6. Ibid., 24.
7. Ibid., 25.
8. Claudia Arp, *Almost 13* (Nashville: Thomas Nelson Publishers, 1986), 91.
9. David A. Seamands, *Healing for Damaged Emotions* (Wheaton: Victor Books, 1981), 107.
10. James B. Simpson, compiler, *Simpson's Contemporary Quotations* (Boston: Houghton Mifflin Company, 1988), 170.
11. Magazine quotation.
12. Willard F. Harley, Jr., *His Needs, Her Needs* (Grand Rapids: Fleming H. Revell Company, 1986).
13. Ed Wheat, *Love Life for Every Married Couple* (Grand Rapids: Zondervan Publishing House, 1980), 67.
14. Philip Hughes, *A Commentary of the Epistle to the Hebrews* (Grand Rapids: William B. Eerdmans Publishing Company, 1977), 149.
15. Pat and Jill Williams, *Rekindled* (Tarrytown: Fleming H. Revell Company, 1985).
16. Associated Press, "Students: We Want Parents to Push Us," *The Orlando Sentinel*, Tuesday, May 12, 1992.

17. Abigail Wood, "The Trouble With Dad," *Seventeen*, October 1985, p. 38 as it appears in *Missing From Action: Vanishing Manhood in America* by Weldon M. Hardenbrook (Nashville: Thomas Nelson Publishers, 1987).
18. Paul Warren, et al., *The Father Book* (Nashville: Thomas Nelson Publishers, 1992).
19. George Barna, *The Frog in the Kettle* (Ventura: Regal Books, 1990), 98.
20. "How Faith Becomes Their Own," *Parents and Teenagers*, October/November 1989, 11.
21. *Born Again: A Look at Christians in America* (Glendale: The Barna Research Group, 1990), 17.
22. "Children raised . . .," *National and International Religion Report*, May 31, 1993, 3.
23. Lawrence Kutner, "Children's self-esteem colors their world," *The Orlando Sentinel*, February 2, 1993.
24. Walter B. Knight, *Knight's Treasury of Illustrations* (Grand Rapids: William B. Eerdmans Publishing Company, 1963), 9.
25. Patrick Morley, *The Man in the Mirror Discipleship Series* (copyright 1992, Patrick Morley, all rights reserved).
26. Gordon MacDonald, *Christ Followers in the Real World* (Nashville: Oliver-Nelson Books, a division of Thomas Nelson, 1989), 69–89.
27. "A Profile of Older Americans: 1992," prepared by the Program Resources Department, American Association of Retired Persons and the Administration on Aging, U.S. Department of Health and Human Services.
28. Ibid.

About the Author

Patrick Morley, best known as an author and speaker, began his career as a businessman. He founded Morley Properties which, during the 1980's, was one of Florida's 100 largest privately held companies. He has been the President or Managing Partner of 59 companies and partnerships.

Morley's vision is to help bring about a spiritual awakening in America. Through his ministry Morley speaks at outreach events and city-wide evangelistic missions throughout the U.S. and abroad.

He graduated with honors from the University of Central Florida, which selected him as its Outstanding Alumnus in 1984. Morley is a graduate of the Harvard Business School Owner/President Management Program and holds a One Year Certificate in Theology from Reformed Theological Seminary. He also serves on the Board of Directors of Campus Crusade for Christ and teaches a weekly Bible study to 125 businessmen.

Morley's previous books include *The Man in the Mirror*, *Getting to Know the Man in the Mirror*, *Walking with Christ in the Details of Life*, and *The Rest of Your Life*. He resides with his family in Orlando, Florida.

PATRICK MORLEY Ministries

Would you like to learn more about the ministry of Patrick Morley?

The vision of Patrick Morley Ministries is to help bring about a spiritual awakening in America in this generation. Ministries include:

- city-wide missions
- evangelistic speaking
- publishing
- teaching
- men's ministry

If you would like to receive information and be placed on our mailing list, please cut this from the book, complete and mail.

Name _____

Street _____

City_____ State _____ ZIP _____

Tel (_____) _____ Fax (_____) _____

Patrick Morley Ministries
P.O. Box 574222, Orlando, FL 32857-9936   (407) 331-0095